International Communication
and Globalization

International Communication and Globalization

A Critical Introduction

edited by
Ali Mohammadi

SAGE Publications
London • Thousand Oaks • New Delhi

SAGE Publications Ltd
6 Bonhill Street
London EC2A 4PU

SAGE Publications Inc.
2455 Teller Road
Thousand Oaks, California 91320

SAGE Publications India Pvt Ltd
32, M-Block Market
Greater Kailash – I
New Delhi 110 048

British Library Cataloguing in Publication data

A catalogue record for this book is available
from the British Library.

ISBN 0 7619 5553 4
ISBN 0 7619 5554 2 (pbk)

Library of Congress catalog card number 97–067416

P96
.I5
I68
1997x

Typeset by Mayhew Typesetting, Rhayader, Powys
Printed in Great Britain by Redwood Books, Trowbridge, Wiltshire

Contents

Contents

Notes on the contributors

Oliver Boyd-Barrett is Director, Distance Learning, at the Centre for Mass Communication Research, University of Leicester. He has written extensively on the international news agencies, news flow, and media education. Recent books include *The Globalization of News* (with Terhi Rantanen, eds, Sage, forthcoming); and *Approaches to Media* (with Chris Newbold, eds, 1995).

James Halloran is currently Research and Emeritus Professor at the University of Leicester. He was Director of the Centre for Mass Communication Research from when he founded it in 1996 to 1991, and was President of the International Association for Mass Communication Research (of which he is now Honorary Life President) from 1972 to 1990. He has acted as consultant to UNESCO, the Council of Europe, and to many media and educational institutions, and he is the author of numerous books and articles on the media and the various aspects of the communication process.

Cees Hamelink is Professor of International Communication at the University of Amsterdam, The Netherlands. He was President of the International Association for Mass Communication Research from 1990–94. His publications include *Global Communications and Cultural Autonomy* (1983), *Finance and Information* (1983), *Transnational Data in the Information Age* (1984), *The Technology Gamble* (1988), and *Trends in World Communication* (1994).

Richard Maxwell is the author of *The Spectacle of Democracy: Spanish Television, Nationalism, and Political Transition* (University of Minnesota Press, 1995) and numerous articles and chapters on international communication and political economy of media and culture.

Ali Mohammadi is Reader in International Communication and Cultural Studies at Nottingham Trent University. He has co-authored, with A. Sreberny Mohammadi, *Small Media, Big Revolution: Communication and Culture, and the Iranian Revolution* (1994) and co-edited *Questioning the Media* (1995).

Ralph Negrine is Senior Lecturer at the Centre for Mass Communication Research, University of Leicester. He has edited books on the 'new' media and written on many aspects of communications policy. His most recent book is *The Communication of Politics* (1996) also published by Sage.

Majid Tehranian is Professor of International Communication at the University of Hawaii at Manoa, and Director of the Toda Institute for Global Peace and Policy Research. His most recent books include *Technologies of Power: Information Machines and Democratic Prospects* (1990) and *Restructuring for World Peace: On the Threshold of the 21st Century* (1992).

Katharine Kia Tehranian is Assistant Professor of American Studies at the University of Hawaii at Manoa. Her latest publications are *Restructuring for World Peace: On the Threshold of the 21st Century* (1992) and *Modernity, Space, and Power: The American City in Discourse and Practice* (1995).

John Tomlinson is Principal Lecturer and Head of the Centre for Research in International Communication and Culture at Nottingham Trent University. He has contributed to several journals on social theory, cultural imperialism, and globalization. His most recent book is *Cultural Imperialism: A Critical Introduction* (1991).

Acknowledgements

I would like to thank Dr Robert Bennett at Coventry University for his sincere editorial comments and support, and Professor Richard Johnson at the Centre for Research in International Communication and Culture for reading each individual chapter and providing valuable insights. Thanks also to Frances Banks, the secretary of the English and Media Studies Department for her kind and usual help. I would also like to thank Dr John Tomlinson, the head of CRICC, for his encouragement and useful discussion.

I would like to dedicate this volume to the memory of Dr Ali Assadi-Nik, the first generation of Western-educated Communication Researcher in Iran.

Introduction

International Communication and Globalization offers the opportunity to read critically in the field of communication studies: to read with awareness and to consider key international issues. It is the first reader of its kind. It offers basic chapters and summaries of research, new approaches to studying international communication, and an understanding of how this communication operates in relation to the process of globalization in a postmodern world. At the end of each chapter you will find a list of questions to help you in your studying and revision.

In this introduction we look at some of the key terms of our title and outline the order of topics in the book.

International communication

International communication is a complex and fast-growing sub-field within the major field of communication and media studies. It encompasses the issues of culture and cultural commodification (the turning of cultural products into commodities), the diffusion of information and news broadcasting by media empires around the world, and the challenges faced by the developing world in the light of these processes. Within the context of such a New World Information Order, it considers questions of power and the process of technology, censorship and human rights. Within the context of a concern with technology, it studies television satellite broadcasting and the roles of the nation state, freedom of information and of technology itself. It explores the new means of transnational communication. It offers an overview of international organizations such as UNESCO, other UN agencies and non-governmental organizations (NGOs).

After the Second World War it became quite obvious that certain types of information were very powerful for the maintenance of peace and tranquillity in the international system. In order to have a balance in culture and information affairs among the nations, the United Nations Educational, Scientific and Cultural Organization (UNESCO) was established. UNESCO's purpose was not only to encourage all member states to co-operate in the field of education, science, culture and communication, but also to provide a platform for member states to discuss peacefully how to maintain a reasonable view on cultural and intellectual rights, flows of news and information, and freedom of expression.

The first article of UNESCO is supposed to foster collaboration among the nations through education, science and culture, justice, human rights and, most importantly, freedoms for the whole people of the world. Today's evidence shows that Hollywood films, the bulk of magazines, a great variety of videos, most television programmes as well as news and information about the world we are living in, are produced in the West. It is here that the economic power and the control of technology lies. UNESCO and other UN agencies became a conduit for those nations which have the technologies and the power to use international communication for legitimizing their position and their policies. This imposition is not only a matter of news values and agenda setting, imbalances of this kind also create two worlds – 'the haves and the have nots' – in communications and in other terms. A 1994 Human Development Report shows the incredible income gaps between rich and poor sections of the populations in the developing world are close to bringing chaos and uncertainty for the future. As Schiller (1996) notes, the gap between rich and poor nations is widening. Even in a rich nation like the United States the growth of the economy lies with 40% of the population who hold 68% of the nation's income, while 60% of the population remains in the margin – similar to the people of the Third World. Schiller also raises a very important question about the rapidly rising poverty across the globe:

> Will the creation of privately financed and owned high-speed, multi-capability circuits carrying broad streams of messages and images, lessen the gaps in living conditions that presently exist across the globe? Time-Warner, AT&T, Microsoft, and their rivals cannot be preoccupied with social inequality. Their focus is on revenue. (Schiller, 1996: 97)

Decolonization in itself has not made the world more just and peaceful. The evidence shows more news and images come from the Western world and the access to non-Western culture in terms of information, knowledge, entertainment and images becomes more scarce. UNESCO and many other NGOs may have been able to establish the recognition of a multicultural world but they have not been very successful in maintaining it.

In its relation to other approaches – for example, sociology and cultural studies – the study of international communication explores the ways in which terms like globalization and postmodernism are themselves conceptualized and the ways in which questions of culture and power intersect with issues around social identity and the production of wishes and desires. For further discussion of the issues of culture and identity see Chapters 7 and 8 of this volume.

Pocket-sized video cameras, video-cassette recorders, laptop satellite signal receivers and transmitters, fiber optics, microwave relays and laptop personal computers and fax machines, mobile telephones and the Internet have expanded international communications almost beyond the human imagination. Radio and, more importantly, television bring listeners and viewers live coverage of the landing on the moon, the winter and summer Olympics, the pomp and ritual accompanying the meetings of heads of states, World Cup football and rugby. All of these play a role in the way people in the postmodern world are living.

Globalization

Some communication scholars believe it is important to examine the global development of international communications (Frederick, 1993; Hamelink, 1994a; Stevenson, 1993; Schiller, 1996). By 'globalization', scholars refer to the way in which, under contemporary conditions especially, relations of power and communication are stretched across the globe, involving compressions of time and space and a recomposition of social relationships. Schiller (1989, 1996) and Hills (1986) have drawn our attention to rapid market changes as one consequence of deregulation and, furthermore, the emergence of not only new mega corporations, but also a new class of merchants of cultural commodities, entertainments and information technology. This class Bagdikian usefully names 'Lords of the Global Village' (Bagdikian, 1989). All of the chapters in this volume use the notion of globalization to understand contemporary developments in international communication – more or less critically. For a fuller discussion of the debates surrounding this term, see chapters 4, 6 and 7.

Other scholars believe that by globalizing the world through the electronic highway it is impossible 'to govern' the world (Schiller, 1996). The rapid development of satellite communications is crucial here if the rest of even the Western world is to keep up with the United States. By removing distance, satellite communication is a major factor in the globalization of the market. Similarly, computerization is a precondition of the information economy. Schiller suggests that one of the reasons why the United States wanted to capture the control of international communication circuits from British cable interests was to build satellites 'to bypass the British Empire's monopoly in international communication' (Schiller, 1996: 93).

Today, one of the most significant functions of globalization is the so-called 'free flow of information'. If we consider CNN a global corporation, its major function is news and information, but this news service is constructed from a mainly US perspective. In a similar way, US cultural industries and media entertainment based on the doctrine of the free flow of information have had influence all over the whole world.

The present plan of constructing an information highway in the West means better access for US global firms to global markets. They are already in a dominating position. The information highway will be at the service of those countries that can afford to pay for the information. Building and owning the electronic information highway will be especially beneficial to those firms that are mainly US-based. As history since the Second World War has shown, US companies always lead the global market. Schiller indicates that 37,000 companies 'currently occupy the command posts of the world commercial order, the largest 100 transnational companies, in 1990, had about $3.2 trillion in global assets, of which $1.2 trillion were outside of their own home countries' (Schiller, 1996: 94).

We should also note that Time-Warner, Bell Atlantic, AT&T, IBM and COMCAST are the largest players in cultural commodities, communication and information technology in the world today. In the face of the gigantic power of transnational corporations, it is not clear what will happen to the role of nation states. Many critics predict 'the end of the nation state'. Jean-Marie Guehenno (1995), for example, asks a very important question: without the nation, can democracy survive? It is hard to imagine a world which, in the twenty-first century, may be dominated by a few transnational companies. Will nations and states become manipulated and powerless?

The rapid growth of domestic markets is occurring in developing countries as well as in Western societies. The important dimension of the global market is a lack of equal competition. The US-based mega corporations will eventually fill the cultural space of the world market, in a situation in which there is a shortage of actual programmes for international television.

International communication also affects the cultural balances and boundaries of the world. Kenworthy (1996) divides the world into eight large cultural blocs: the Latin, Anglo-Saxon, Germanic-Scandinavian, Slavic, Muslim, African, Indian and Sinitic cultures. The Anglo-Saxon culture covers Britain, North America, Australia, New Zealand and South Africa. Since the Second World War the cultural influence of these regions has been growing very fast. Most of the mega cultural firms are based on the commodification of Anglophone culture. Most cultural traffic flows out of the Anglophone regions. Whether one agrees with Kenworthy's categories or not, it is critical to look at the globalization process in relation to cultural production and the shifting zones of cultural influence.

International communication: traditions of research

In order to understand the impact of international communication in a self-aware and critical way, we need to appreciate the different trends of research that have emerged since the 1960s. From the outset different schools of thought have been in contention over their understanding of international communication. The first part of this book contributes to an answer by introducing the key research tendencies, which we call 'orthodox' and 'critical' communication research. The nature of the research in the field of international communication and globalization is explained in the introduction to Part I.

Part II of this book examines the rapid development of international communication as a consequence of changes in communication technology (such as the fax machine, satellite broadcasting television, etc.). The contributors of this section are also especially concerned with the impact of market relations, financial institutions and new technologies on the countries of the Third World, and on the inequalities between the 'haves' and 'have nots'. Also in the frame is the emergence of corporate media systems as an aspect of globalization.

Part III discusses the relation between the processes of privatization, deregulation and the imposition of market relations characteristic of this phase of globalization and the questions of morality, ethics and alternative paradigms. Are there alternatives to the 'morality' of the market and 'the free flow of information'? What are the likely prospects of this current phase of modernization, given the previous developments of the system?

The contributions in Part IV look more closely at some cultural aspects of the processes of contemporary globalization. It is also in these cultural debates that the postmodern concept emerges. Part IV, therefore, engages in a fuller debate about postmodernism and also discusses those disciplines – sociology and cultural studies especially – where the debate about cultural globalization has figured most strongly.

The postmodern world

We are moving towards the twenty-first century with uncertainty. Globalization, as a kind of myth of our times, is hard to grasp. How can we comprehend change when the progress in communication technology is so rapid? If weapons of mass destruction are more under control, tolerance of ethnic difference and self-expression seem to have been reduced to levels of incomprehending barbarism. The Chechniya, Afghan and Balkan wars are cases in point. In the race for globalization, unqualified competitiveness has been projected as the key to success. Tense mergers and hostile take-overs are the economic games we live by.

There is a well-established debate today about whether the late twentieth century (or some earlier period) has seen the emergence of conditions which are beyond modernity, or, in the best-known version of the argument, are 'postmodern'. Some argue that the postmodern world will see the end of inequality and ignorance (Drucker, 1957). Others, like Daniel Bell (1973), see the postmodern world as a manifestation of new action and social relations. Bell's visionary perceptions are very similar to Toynbee's (1963) thesis of the development of the sameness everywhere in the world.

One feature of postmodernity, as the name implies, is a radical break from previous periods. This includes disbelief in the old narratives of human progress (now seen as flawed), not least because they excluded the experience of most (non-European) peoples in the world. Theories of 'modernization' which flourished in the decades after the Second World War were one late example of this kind of Western-centred or Northern-centred framework. As such confidence erodes, the problems and confusions of the contemporary world are uppermost, confusions especially around competing identities, cultural fragmentation and the different modes of experience in terms of time and space (e.g., Best and Kellner, 1991). In these circumstances, centring on media questions in his final speech at the Edinburgh Television Festival in 1993, the playwright Dennis Potter urged us to be aware that 'our television has been ripped apart and falteringly re-assembled by politicians who believed that value is a monetary term only, and that a cost-accountant is thereby the most suitable adjudicator of what we can and cannot see on our screens'. He also warned against the threat to democracy from the mega corporations, urging us to watch carefully the implementation of the laws against what he called 'cross-ownership'.

Potter's warning, and his emphasis on ethical and political issues, was timely on several counts. The take-over of public space by advertising merchants and the powerful flow of US television programmes, films, music, news, entertainment culture, theme parks and shopping malls now set the cultural standard from Brazil to Dubai. We suffer, at the same time, the culture of commercial primacy and chronic economic uncertainty, especially in the poorer parts of the world. We are living in a world where, it seems, no power can challenge capitalism. Yet what modernity and modernization in this sense have signally failed to do is to close the gap between rich and poor in an unjust world. It is arguable that this is the main political and ethical challenge in the world today. Will postmodern theorists find a way to challenge the new forms of knowledge, information and economy whose only concern appears to be profit? Will virtual reality for a small group of nations in the North be at the expense of an increasing actual poverty for people in the South?

Part I

RESEARCH IN INTERNATIONAL COMMUNICATION AND GLOBALIZATION: CONTRADICTIONS AND DIRECTIONS

As we noted in the introduction, Part I is concerned with contradictions and directions of research in international communication and globalization. What are the major perspectives in international communication and globalization research?

It is worth noting first, however, that the study of *international* communication is a relatively recent phenomenon. Until recently, especially in Europe, communication research has been restricted by national geographical boundaries and based on local needs and community interests. Communication research has been fragmented and often neglected. But as McQuail (1994) suggests, the geopolitics of Europe, with rapid movements towards unification, the integration of European economies, the internationalization of communication – all examples of transnationalization – have stimulated a rapid growth of communication studies in Europe. As the study of international communication has been stronger in the United States, though, the view of the world in US communication studies has often been decidedly 'American'. It is arguable that a truly global study of communication, which takes account of the experiences of more peripheral societies and economies, is really very recent indeed.

Today it is useful to distinguish between two main traditions. The first is strongest in Europe, though there are well-known practitioners in the United States too. This 'critical' tradition has been marked by qualitative and theoretical research and has been closely associated with a broader study of 'culture' in the sense of forms of consciousness and ways of life. The dominant tradition of communication research in the United States, by comparison, has been mainly quantitative, with aspirations to 'science' and often closely related to the policies of mainstream institutions and government establishments. Because the debate between these traditions is still sometimes fierce, it seems important to start this volume by exploring the directions and contradictions.

In the United States the history of research in international communication goes back to the First World War and was concerned with psychological warfare and propaganda as a project of the War Department. The field of communication study concerning international communication was not established in the universities until the 1950s. In 1926, however, Harold

Lasswell undertook a systematic and pioneering study of the psychological warfare and propaganda techniques of the First World War and then, with Walter Lippmann, the chief leaflet writer and the editor of the US propaganda unit, for the first time investigated the impact of communication technology on the Western world. Lippmann, as an experienced propagandist of the First World War, with his two very important books, *Public Opinion* (1922) and *The Phantom of Public* (1925), promoted communication as part of the study of social science in US universities (Simpson, 1994).

During the 1930s Lippmann and Lasswell both articulated communication studies as an instrumental process for imposing one doctrine on others. Lasswell established a formula for research in communication: 'Who says what to whom with what effect', and both Lasswell and Lippmann suggested that the articulation of communication technology as a form of domination became the foundation of research in communication studies in the United States. The positivist method of research into communication and social science as a whole was also being applied for the first time in leading academic institutions such as Columbia and Chicago universities (Simpson, 1994). In the 1950s the Lasswell formula and its derivatives became the slogan of commercialization and advertisement in the United States. Now, the tradition for research in communication is mainly promoting consumerism, and criticizing and abhoring communism with the application of the quantitative and qualitative methods.

The first two chapters of this volume illustrate the traditions of international communication in Western Europe and the United States. By examining the experiences of two cultures and traditions we see that they have different histories and outlooks in the field of communication studies.

In the United States the study of communications started seriously after the Second World War but in Europe communication research was not regarded as an important field of study until more recently. However, it is important to remember that psychological warfare and propaganda techniques began in Germany before the Second World War with Goebbels's intellectual journal *Das Reich* published through the University of Berlin although these were not areas studied among academics (Simpson, 1994).

In the following chapters, the points of view of well-established scholars, who argue forcibly for the virtues of each direction, will be discussed. It is worth adding that neither the Boyd-Barrett nor Halloran chapters represent state-of-the-art research in international communication studies. Rather, they were asked to contribute to this volume because their work has been central to the development and the defence of the different research traditions and because they have both engaged in strong arguments over the general directions of work in the field. Neither can be taken as entirely representative figures: Halloran, for example, is more interested in questions of policy than much European research has been, and is more hostile to cultural studies than most current researchers in the media; Boyd-Barrett, though very critical of the directions of research, clearly believes he can learn something from it. We invite you to read their contributions, however, as a kind of dialogue, framed by our own editorial comments. The dialogue tells us a lot, we think, about the political and other investigations that have been involved in differences of opinion among scholars in this field.

If Halloran is a supporter and practitioner of critical research, Boyd-Barrett questions its role and status in the period after the demise of the Soviet Union. He suggests that critical analysis needs to liberate itself from its present mould and to focus on the real world problems which will dominate the twenty-first century, especially the weakening of nation states, the destruction of natural environments (land masses, oceans, Space), cultural conflicts, and the re-emergence of cultural cleansing in Europe. He argues that alternative modes of development have failed to sustain themselves and evidence shows that many governments in the South are not fit to govern themselves. Boyd-Barrett also criticizes Third World communication research scholars. They have spent too much time criticizing the Western models without providing a coherent communication structure in keeping with their own development needs. Consequently, it is very hard to stop Western cultural penetration, especially as most of the technological innovation and information comes from the West.

Boyd-Barrett argues that Western capitalism is still on the way to further progress and dynamism but we do not know what will happen to the existing level of inequality in the world. The information highway stems from the demand for the expansion of market and technological accessibility in the West. It is not clear in the developing world who can afford to pay for technical availability if this trend continues.

Nonetheless, there is a positive potential for critical analysis by the year 2000. The accessibility of technology with its wide angle can reflect some problems; among these is the resurgence of tribalism and cultural conflict. These are creations of a global culture which was built on the modern communication system. Western-driven private enterprise, and the challenge to indigenous cultures, brings to a global audience the triumphs and horrors of human civilization.

Whatever the impact on culture, Boyd-Barrett believes that the globalization process, driven by technological advances, will expand much further. Today, it is not clear to us what will be the impact of digital culture on people, while the globalization of Western culture in all dimensions is proceeding.

James Halloran, in his chapter, looks at trends in communication research with a focus on the international dimension. Based on his own experience in this field, going back to the early 1960s, he draws our attention to three major areas:

- A brief overview of general trends in communication research, focusing on the proposal for an international programme of critical communication research put forward in relation to the UNESCO manifesto of the early 1970s.

- A critique of the prevailing thematic structure of US communication research which, Golding argues, offers no challenge to the international status quo and serves the vested interests of the established powers. Communication research in the United States is mainly concerned with mass society, mass culture and the modernization process as the only way forward for social change. The US style communication research is preoccupied with such questions as the creation of media events, the manipulation of public opinion and the invention of persuasive topics for election campaigns.
- An identification of the foundations of this paradigm of research – new at the time in the early 1960s – in the work of Wilbur Schramm (*Mass Media and National Development*) and Daniel Lerner (*The Passing of Traditional Society*) and, later, in the establishment of the Institute for Communication Studies at Stanford University, soon the leading university in this field.

Halloran draws on his own personal experience as he considers these areas of research. Himself a key critic of US-style communication research and a leading British researcher, he starts with the highlights of the Montreal conference of 1969 and criticizes the unquestioning faith in the benefits of technological progress. By looking at the different levels of the impacts and the flows of global cultures, he brings us to the present which is more concerned with the process of globalization and the emergence of nationalism. Globalization in the 1990s is seen as the end result of a decade of deterioration and greed.

Halloran would like to see a much sharper research focus on the economic power structures of the world as they impact on international communication, the process of globalization and media development. The major requirement of the globalization process, from this point of view, is the globalization of moral responsibility, in a world where the rich pay only 4% interest on debt compared with the 17% paid by poor nations. The gap between the 'haves' and 'have nots' widens daily. Why isn't more international communication research concerned with this fact? How can citizenship be a goal in the absence of information and communication systems? Halloran believes that the North must help the South, or the present order of international communication, economic and information orders will not be sustainable.

1

International Communication and Globalization: Contradictions and Directions

Oliver Boyd-Barrett

In this chapter, Boyd-Barrett surveys the various concepts of globalization across many different disciplines and discourses. He relates this concept to the development of international communication research through its various phases across the twentieth century. From the pigeon to the advent of satellite communication technology this chapter explores the many tensions about the research directions and contradictions in this contested field. Of great significance here was the growing discontent in the liberated ex-colonial countries, based on the realization that formal political freedom was not accompanied by freedom from the global system of capitalism.

In this chapter you will find a brief discussion of dependency discourse and globalization discourse, and to study of media in general. Analysis of the globalization ranges across three major camps: the positivist tradition; neo-Marxist political economy and its critique of media institutions; and the cultural studies camp, which focuses on the study of popular and mass culture, their role in the reproduction of social hegemony and inequality, and on how media texts work to create meaning. (For further information, see Johnson, 1986.)

The concept 'globalization' is open to many meanings. Authors vary considerably in how wide a range of things they intend it to include, whether they think it is good or bad, and in which explanatory theory or model of the world they locate it. Most authors will allow that it has to do at least in part with the increasingly global reach of transnational corporations, and with the transnational character and interrelatedness of local economies. Some focus on evidence of growing cultural convergence, whose clearest manifestation is the software and hardware of transnational media products across telecommunications, computing, film, video, television, magazines, or compact disk, and the physical presence within given localities of shops, commodities (including cars, tobacco, perfume, do-it-yourself hardware, among others) and other businesses, banks or advertising agencies that are clearly recognizable as part of giant transnational if not global corporations.

Others again are more interested in 'culture' in a sense close to that used by Raymond Williams (1961) – the day-to-day expression of shared human experience – and they look for evidence of convergence in the things that people think about, the ways in which they think and in which things are expressed through everyday social practices. What they find is not so much a homogenized global culture, as a world in which, increasingly, every locality is typified by cultural hybridity and heterogeneity, subject to transnational and global forces.

The English city of Leicester, in which I write this chapter, is the home of large populations of first, second and third generation Asians, who have come to Leicester for many different reasons that relate to the entwined histories of Britain and Asia and to a range of economic and political forces which have propelled or stimulated geographical mobility. The Asian communities represent a medley of different languages, religions and histories; many Asians now purchase videos, subscribe to satellite stations, listen to radio channels, read newspapers and magazines which address one or another aspect of their identities as Asians. Some children attend ethnically distinct schools. Yet they share between them and with the white English communities a significant measure of common experience of English language, English (and global) media, awareness of political history and agendas, educational curricula, occupational aspirations and, not least, the day-to-day physicality of the city, its houses, shops, offices, factories, garages, trees and parks, roads and cars, dust, sun and rain, and knowledge of the ways in which this physicality changes from one area of the city to another, from one season to another. For the whites this presence in very large numbers of Asians represents a partly incorporated otherness which subverts what was once perceived to be a clear-cut separation of England from Asia and which intrudes on older simplicities about the separateness of Christian, Muslim, Hindu, and Sikh. The cultural mix of the City, therefore, is more complex than it once was; cultural complexity is rep-resented among other things in gender relations, language, dress, food, commodities, and other differences which are informed and transformed by the things that are held in common. These cut across older divisions of social class. This, then, is an aspect of globalization: cultural hybridity arising from the play of global forces through British imperialism, post-war decolonization, ethnic conflict within Asia, employment opportunities, global trade.

Different emphases among scholars who write about globalization reflect allegiances to different theoretical perspectives. Lying not far behind the concern for global media products and their implications for local cultures, for instance, is a political-economy perspective whose attention is attracted, for very good reason, by the staggering concentration of economic power which is now represented by the media and mixed media/non-media corporations which produce and distribute media hardware and software globally, concentrations which are either directly interlinked with or which parallel similar but more locally specific concentrations. Even if this perspective is now less likely to assume that global media products have a direct, pernicious implication for local culture (a view which, rightly or wrongly, tends to ascribe to local culture a purity, essentiality, indivisibility and goodness, which very often is impossible to substantiate), there is a concern that the content of global media products is determined by the dynamics of global marketing, and that economies of scale enjoyed by the 'global popular' undermine the markets for local cultural production in very many countries. The interest in cultural hybridity, on the other hand, is often fed by a cultural-studies perspective which in recent years has taken a key interest not simply in the different meanings which different members of audiences can take from media texts, but in the range of different social and cultural practices within which media are situated and consumed.

In essence, we may say that the 'globalization' concept is at the confluence of many different disciplines and discourses, variously linked, as Tomlinson illustrates (Chapter 7), to theories about mediatization, information age, Americanization, Westernization, capitalism, and postmodernity, to name but a few; these discourses, in turn, are associated with different ways of seeing and of presenting arguments, different criteria for truth-claims and different ideas as to what constitutes useful and relevant evidence. There are further practical difficulties to do with differences between specialist areas of academic work in the extent to which current literature has caught up with the demand for globalization themes, and how far relevant data have been collated.

With specific reference to the field of 'international communication', most authors are willing to acknowledge that issues of media and communication are important, if not central, to discussions of globalization, while they are equally anxious to avoid charges of 'media-centricity' (e.g. equating globalization with media exports) for the quite proper reason that media-centric analysis frequently exaggerates the role of media, marginalizes other features or dimensions of transnational and transcultural influence, and, worse yet, fails to take adequate account of the social, political, economic and cultural forces that work on and shape the media. Not least of these, of course, are the large public relations and marketing machineries of political parties and business corporations (which Maxwell, in Chapter 8, illustrates with reference to marketing technique) whose pace of growth is quickened by global processes of democratization and privatization and whose subtle and less than subtle interventions in media representations must increasingly question the model of media as autonomous agenda-setters.

While recognizing the dangers of media-centricity, there is a need for a strong though not exclusive interest in media in particular, as well as in international communication more generally. The significance of communications media has to be established with reference to their whole context: political, regulatory, economic and cultural; in addition, media activities are subject to investigation from a number of different academic disciplines. None of this diminishes the necessity, in my view, for a focused examination on media themselves – multi-disciplinary and contextualized as any such study must be – sufficiently single-minded to engage in the world-wide data gathering, essential for an understanding of this highly complex, global, industrial and cultural nexus. Others will want to draw on such research as a resource for exploration of yet broader and more speculative dimensions of global theory and society, but who will have neither knowledge nor familiarity enough to permit passage beyond the 'black box' model of media which, through ignorance, is unable or unwilling to recognize the dynamics of industrial practice itself as a fertile source of explanations for many aspects of globalization.

Interest in the role of media as vehicles of globalization evolves out of a tradition in mass communication research which acknowledges that media practice is suffused with the transnational. Early studies of media had typically framed them as national or sub-national (local) institutions, and devoted disproportionate attention to the functions of elite national media in prestigious realms of activity such as political reporting. Yet studies of major news agencies (institutions which gather and distribute news on a global basis for the benefit of both 'retail' media and corporate non-media clients including government ministries, banks and brokerage houses) reveal that they were among the very first modern transnational corporations, sophisticated players in nineteenth-century news, telegraphic and cable communications on a global scale, subverting nation states and national media to achieve their own business goals and to protect the security of their own cartel practices (Boyd-Barrett, 1980). The cartel sliced up the global market, including Asia, Africa, the Americas, Australasia, the Middle East and Europe among its members. This one example already yields us vital clues: that transnational activity was established long before the post-Second World War boom in the development of transnational corporations; that it was spear-headed, among others, by media organizations; that these activities were intimately related to state, capital and civil society; that their activities, by definition, transcended local cultures and practices.

The development of transnational communications infrastructures, from pigeons, through telegraphic Morse to telephone and radio is a key feature of nineteenth-century history of the great industrial powers, as is the development of still and moving-image technology, and of print technology for markets of millions of readers of diverse religious, gender, ethnic and social class groups. Studies of European newspapers reveal the influence of nineteenth-century awareness of North American technology and North American reporting and media entertainment practices on European thinking (Lee, 1976). In the early twentieth century, while governments exploited the transnational potential of media for propaganda purposes, business interests aligned themselves behind the export value of media, most spectacularly of Hollywood film from the 1920s and 1930s onwards, but also of radio, syndicated press features, distribution and exhibition facilities, and advertising (Tunstall, 1977). Media scholarship itself has contributed to processes of transnationalization. The development of mass communication research from its inception was closely linked with overt and covert US government activities against the spread of communism. Lasswell's famous dictum 'who says what to whom with what effect', is the essence of propaganda research (Simpson, 1994).

Despite such evidence, much of the early research on media in the developed countries underestimated such transnational features, and retained the nation state as a basic unit of analysis. In their very focus on national media, scholars sometimes have played an unwitting part in helping construct a myth of nationhood, confirming on selective media their authority to speak for and on behalf of a 'nation' which the media themselves helped construct – alongside the paraphernalia of icons of 'national' power and influence such as national flags, anthems, monarchies, state architecture of government buildings. The media are themselves such icons: 'national' radio and television stations and newspapers, and lionized 'popular' media celebrities and programmes, including news and newsreel genre, radio and television shows (including historical drama celebrating a 'common heritage', sit-coms that cue affectionate laughter at the linguistic, social-class and regional variations that stitch together the fabric of the 'national family', and 'national' sports events).

Against this background the concept of 'international' communications is a 'marked' concept, denoting that communication described as 'international' is something exceptional, out of the ordinary, worthy of specialist attention. The concept of 'globalization' subverts the notion of 'international' as out-of-the-ordinary; 'globalization' asserts the global-in-the-local, that is to say that the local is suffused and pervaded by a global which simultaneously extracts and selectively disseminates the local. News media bring to the consciousness of almost all citizens instant information about events, personalities and processes from throughout the globe, and this information is a permanent cognitive backdrop against which they make meaning of their lives; simultaneously, the news media selectively identify and construct news stories in particular localities which are then projected to wider and sometimes global audiences. In my office in Leicester I am surrounded by information technology gadgets which have been manufactured and assembled in various parts of America, Asia and Europe; I use these gadgets to communicate about university matters with colleagues, and also to fashion academic articles and teaching materials which, because I direct a distance learning programme, are disseminated to over thirty different countries throughout the world. Students in these countries sometimes communicate with me about the teaching materials by e-mail, and their comments and reflections may influence discussions which I have with my colleagues and influence what I write in future.

As though recognizing the limitations of what (during 1995) has been called the 'global popular' (e.g. the blockbuster cinematic releases for immediate global consumption whose icons, codes and conventions can easily be decoded across linguistic and cultural boundaries), the global communications industries also study ways of customizing or innovating product that is suitable for mass marketing within geo-cultural, geo-linguistic or geo-political regions, while at the local level media producers increasingly draw on the codes and conventions, if not the actual imported product, of the global popular to stamp their own product, channel, distribution network as 'professional', 'competitive' and attractive to audiences and, more importantly, advertisers (typically selling transnational products via North American and West European advertising agencies – so that even if programme schedules, as in India, generally 'look' Indian, they are being paid for, essentially, by transnational corporations mainly originating from the major and mainly Western economies) (Pendakur, 1991).

Past journeys

Tension between the concepts of 'international communication' and 'globalization' is resolvable if we keep in mind the theoretical movements of media scholarship as these have developed dialectically over the past five or more decades. I will say a little about each of the major phases of development in this area, and then with reference to later chapters, I will try to assess where I think the field now is, and where it may be going.

We can say that this branch of scholarship is an additive process of successive hegemonic discourses starting with a discourse of *propaganda* during and after the First World War, exemplified in the work of Lippmann on 'public opinion' (1922) and Lasswell on war-time propaganda (1926) and which related primarily to the competitive military and trade objectives of the great powers. This yielded after the Second World War to a discourse of *free flow of information*. This is a sub-species of the liberal free market discourse; in essence, it championed the rights of media proprietors to sell wherever and whatever they wish (Nordenstreng, 1995). As most of the world's media resources and concentrations of media-related capital, both then and still now, were concentrated in the developed countries, then it was the media proprietors in these countries, their governments and national business communities that had most to gain. The concept of 'free flow' therefore served both an economic and political purpose. Media organizations of the media-rich countries could hope to dissuade others from erecting trade barriers to their products or from making it difficult to gather news or make programmes on their territories. Their argument drew on premises of democracy, freedom of expression, the media's role as 'public watchdog' and their assumed global relevance. For their compatriot businessmen, 'free flow' assisted them in their advertising and marketing of goods and services in foreign markets, through media vehicles whose information and entertainment products championed the Western way of life and its values of capitalism and individualism. For governments, 'free flow' helped to ensure the continuing and unreciprocated influence of Western media on global markets, strengthening the West in its ideological battle with the Soviet Union, and in generally subtle rather than direct ways providing vehicles for the communication of government points of view to international audiences.

Like other liberal free market discourses before it, this one was succeeded, for a time, by a political-economy revisionism, in this case the discourse of *dependency*, a contra-discourse that attacks the processes of monopolization or concentration, towards which unfettered 'free' markets inevitably lead. This was linked to growing discontent in the recently liberated ex-colonial countries upon realization that formal political freedom was not accompanied by freedom from the global system of capitalism, a system that was largely controlled by the interests of the ex-imperial powers, in part through international regulatory organizations such as the World Bank, International Monetary Fund and now the World Trade Organization. What was true of the economic realm seemed also to be true of the ideational realm at the levels of language, culture, education and, of course, the media, all of which were seen still to be dependent on the practices of former imperialist powers. Such practices often commanded greater support when confronted by rival but local claims to prestige from indigenous populations or groups.

Discourses of free flow and dependency took physical form within the forums of international diplomacy, most notably the United Nations and its various agencies, particularly that of UNESCO, but also among the nations of the Non-Aligned Movement (NAM). It is through this period that the terms 'cultural imperialism', 'media imperialism', and 'New World Information and Communication Order' (NWICO) emerge. These models did not necessarily equate nation with cultural homogeneity. They recognized the significance of the co-option of national elites into the global economy through the bargaining and recruitment practices of transnational corporations in local markets, and they were intrigued by, if pessimistic in their evaluation of, local centres of media production and export, such as the Indian film industries, Egyptian soap opera, Brazilian 'telenovelas', etc. But they did tend to assume that nation states were the most significant units of analysis in international communication.

The dependency discourse gave way, in turn, to another but different free market discourse. This took form in the Reagan–Thatcher 'new world order' revolution which re-invigorated the principles of capitalistic free enterprise, contributed to the fall of the Soviet Union and its satellites, and brought in its wake the processes of media 'deregulation' and privatization that were deeply to score the following twenty-year period. They also energized processes of market expansion and concentration of transnational corporations and demonstrated with growing clarity through the final years of the twentieth century how far the significance of political divisions of the world had been matched or even superseded by rival but giant transnational corporations. By the mid-1990s, for example, the personal wealth of the two founding directors of Microsoft (Keegan, 1996) was greater than that of several developing countries put together. The media market, capitalizing in particular on the reach of modern satellite technology, was a prime example of nearly all the trends that are referred to within the discourse of 'globalization'.

The influence of social science (in particular, psychology, social psychology, sociology, politics) in mass communication studies in this period was increasingly intermixed with that of scholars from literature and the humanities in a broad-based and powerful 'cultural studies' movement. This started out as an exploration of how mass media texts worked to secure the voluntary compliance of the masses to their own subordination to the ideas and interests of elites, and of how, in the process, the masses simultaneously relinquished allegiance to their own, authentic class cultures in favour of mass culture. This focus was transformed over time to a very different interest in the diversity of actual media audiences and audience 'readings' of texts. We can call this the *'autonomous audience'* discourse. It was anchored in ethnographic observation of the real-life complexity and rich texture of the contexts within which media are used and consumed. Supported by the application of social anthropology to the study of speech, literacy and meaning-making, this movement had some similarity with the empiricist–positivist phase of 'limited effects' research in post-war North America. In both instances the underlying political implication appeared to be that it is people, not media, who make meaning. This undermined naïve versions of cultural imperialism – but only for so long as it was supposed that cultural imperialism was primarily about individual rather than broad systemic 'effects'. The newer discourse of the autonomous audience drew freely on the insights of postmodernism, looking at how intertextuality of both texts and the mental schemas of audiences contributed to meaning.

From this period we find the study of media (in general, and with relevance for the analysis of globalization) split across three broad camps. One is the continually thriving but largely unremarked positivist tradition, often working at the service of what Lazarsfeld (1941) and Halloran (1981) had long identified as 'administrative' or 'conventional' research. In the field of campaign research, for example, we find a vibrant continuation of this tradition, and a surprising robustness and assertiveness in its yield of usable findings for campaign managers (Atkin, 1996) – essential reading for any scholar otherwise inclined to dismiss positivism or to assume that its findings have either no consequence or are too uncertain. This tradition does not have a strong input into international communication theory, but does have a place in studies of the relationship of media growth to 'development' and 'modernization' as measured in terms of crude indicators such as sales of hardware and gross national product, etc., and is also informed by techniques of global promotion and marketing (Maxwell, Chapter 8).

Another camp is the neo-Marxist political economy and its critique of media institutions, linking these to other major centres of political, economic and social power in society. There has been a robust literature in the area, for example charting the processes of deregulation, privatization, vertical and horizontal integration of television industries in different parts of the globe, the response of older public service broadcasters (Negrine, Chapter 3) and tendencies towards convergence (e.g. bringing together print, broadcasting, telephony, computing, music, electronic networking) or even, as some have argued, reconvergence. Important as such studies indubitably are in an industry which has recently witnessed concentrations and amalgamations of unprecedented proportions, there is still a relative dearth of studies of professional practice, especially as this affects the transnational activities of media (see recent work by Johnston, 1995 and Negus, 1992). This is unfortunate not only because it threatens a chasm of distrust between media professionals and scholars, but because it encourages the latter to place the inner workings of media industries into a 'black box' and, at worst, to draw simplistic conclusions about what goes on inside the 'black box'. The net result is a continuing difficulty for political economists in tracing the connections between the levels of (macro) political economy and (micro) text and reading, and a general lack of awareness of the perceptions, experiences, judgements, ethical and other dilemmas faced by professionals, with negative implications for soundness of theory construction and relevance of research. Yet without the perspective of political economy there is little hope of sound theorizing of the political and economic dynamics that currently attend processes of global expansion.

Finally, there is the cultural studies camp, to which I have already referred, at one time dedicated to the study of popular and mass culture and their role in the reproduction of social hegemony and inequality but now more generally concerned with how media texts work to create meaning (on the basis of careful analysis of the texts themselves), and how (culturally situated) people work to gather meaning from texts (increasingly based on observation of viewers, readers, listeners). This camp had considerable influence in the 1980s; its discovery of polysemic texts (the potential for readers to generate their own meanings from texts) fitted well with a politically conservative era and the re-invigoration of liberal capitalism which accompanied it, as well as with an academy that had grown embarrassed by its own radical past. Cultural studies has a great deal to offer in the study of how global texts work at a local level, of the features of locally produced texts for local and export consumption, and of local consumption practices which mediate media influences of any kind. Thus it offers routes to answering questions about how Western media products are perceived, how they compete with or relate to locally made products, and whether local products are innovations or mere copies.

Though contested by every academic discipline, by the media, economists and politicians, and subject to widely divergent opinion as to whether it is negative or positive, it may be less than fanciful to see in the concept of globalization, therefore, a discourse which has the potential to resolve some of the tensions between positivism, political economy and cultural studies, and perhaps even between administrative and critical research. Increasingly, we need to study media in their global as well as local context. This is a task which calls not only for global coordination between academics in establishing research projects, but increases the dependence of academics on the data-gathering of specialist and professional journals around the world and the 'administrative' research that is retrievable from the communications industries themselves. This in turn requires that academics engage in critical interrogation of such data and their sources. The positivist and administrative traditions of conventional research can be harnessed to theory development in establishing the broad political-economy parameters, while the use of qualitative techniques for analysis of global texts and audiences may be more practicable at the academic level.

The concept of globalization commands attention to issues of overall power and control, and therefore to the increasingly transnational character of media (stimulated by processes of digitization, convergence, consolidation and globalization of market reach (Hamelink, 1994a) – often detectable only through data which often tend to come from the industry and from specialist journals. While at the same time, because the local becomes more culturally heterogeneous in response to global forces, globalization theory must also be sensitive to the diversity of local meanings, practices and uses where often it is academics who may be best placed to study them. The very challenges of studying media in global context highlight the importance of holistic attention to media production, text and audience in their (globalized) economic, social and political contexts.

While arguing that 'globalization' presents an opportunity to resolve tensions within what had previously been described as 'international' communication, it is also possible to argue for the continuing relevance of studies of the international just as it is possible to argue (indeed protest) the continuing significance of the nation state. (Those who doubt this might be advised to talk to an audience from mainland China about the declining nation state of China!) In some of the 'information age' discourse that is peddled by 'technophil' enthusiasts of modern media technology, the 'globalization' concept has been hi-jacked precisely for polemic invective against the nation state in a wish-fulfilment bid to prevent a disliked but still powerful creation of modern Europe from intervening in the free-market realization of technological potential. Yet the nation state survives. It survives administratively, at the level of iconicity, identity, defence, policing, education and diplomacy, even if it must now compete with and is in part constituted by what may be a more prolific range of super-national and sub-national claims on individual identity, and a loosening regime of planetary regulation for trade (largely engineered by the world's great nation states in their own interests or in the interests of their nationally dominant alliances of capital). Indeed, the anti-nation state normative use of the concept of globalization may obscure precisely those alliances between political and economic institutions that still allow us, without overlooking the significance of transnational corporation activity, to attribute great power to the entities that we call, for example, the 'United States of America', or 'Germany' or 'Japan'. Nor is it unhelpful to observe that similar entities that we call 'India' or 'China' or 'Brazil' are edging ever closer to the top of the world's largest economies. If we could not observe such things, it would be much more difficult to appreciate the magnitude of some of the changes that have become apparent in the closing years of the twentieth century. And even if the nation state did not survive in its present cartographic form, it is difficult to imagine that it would be replaced by anything that did not look remarkably similar to it, even if of different size and with different degrees of intensity in the extent of its integration with other similar units.

Present directions

Looking at 1990s scholarship we encounter globalization as a discourse that takes full account of the many facets of human experience that can only be explained through reference to dimensions that are not sensibly or usefully contained within the frame of 'nation states', while still recognizing the ideological and physical reality of the nation state. However we define globalization, the media play an important role in it: media represent the world to the world; media products are exported beyond national boundaries often on the basis of capital resources drawn from corporate actors of several nation states; the attraction of media products enhances demand for such things as electricity, electronic hardware and software; this in turn has implications for local production and import; supply of electricity leads to demand for other electrical goods; the media are vehicles for advertising, and the advertising of products often stimulates demand for them, both internally produced or imported, and this in turn is an important stimulant to international trade. Media may be harnessed by national economic, political and military elites for engagement in international warfare or propaganda against other states. Media are vehicles for the expression of values, and the imparting of information which may sometimes be imported, and which will engage local viewers, listeners, readers and users in novel and perhaps unpredictable ways. Electronic networking offers a potential for communication and alliances of peoples and interests across nation states, of an immediacy and flexibility that is quite new. Tehranian and Tehranian, in Chapter 6, discuss the contradictory roles of media as sources of resistance to globalization, as protectors of capitalism, as agents of democratization, as vehicles for advertising and commodification, and as tools for 'glocalization', the processes whereby transnational corporations customize products for local markets. Are the media industries themselves, or those who lead them, now part of a distinctive new global elite class of the super-rich, perched above the many and varied manifestations and functions of their industrial practices, and can there be any transformation of society that does not have to negotiate with or seek to overthrow the global media aristocracy, or is there here another hegemony which has sown the seeds of its destruction through the potential of its own technologies?

If the concept of 'globalization' is to have a dynamic and positive influence as a tool for the advancement of the study of international communication what else must happen, what must change? The concept itself might seem to some to exemplify the fuzziness that gives 'social science' a 'bad name'. Whether one attributes such a view to a corruption of intellectual precision that can be laid at the door of 'non-scientific' cultural studies (Halloran, 1995) or simply to the arrogance and tendentiousness of self-proclaimed 'critical' theorists, it is timely to reassess the strategies for truth-claims in a postmodernist and truth-denying climate, and which 'globalization' as an analytical tool must overcome. The positivist tradition has a great many faults, serious faults, that have rightly condemned it to a measure of derision in at least some areas of social science and humanities over several decades. It asked only the questions that could be answered quantitatively; it preferred trivial quantitative questions to profound qualitative questions; it preferred reliability to validity; it was insensitive to the rich texture of social context, historical change and dialectics; yet on the basis of such evidence it was given to alarmingly assertive propositions. In one mode it might proclaim that media cause violence (on the basis, perhaps, of some correlation between exposure to incidents of 'violence' in film, and subsequent aggressive play, measured in laboratory conditions and in terms of context-independent counts of certain kinds of representations of 'violent' acts). In another mode it might proclaim that media do not cause violence (perhaps based on identification of the broad range of different variables associated with any given feature of behaviour). These debates persisted for years before radical alternative approaches were considered: was violence to do with aggressive incidents or with the overall character of a plot?; how could it or should it be identified?; might it be synonymous with 'arousal'?; might screen violence be more likely to induce fear rather than aggression, and could this, in turn, be related to processes of social control? Detailed analysis of the actual content of films shown in controlled experiments was rare to non-existent; likewise, the cultural and discursive practices that shape the ways in which viewers may make sense of television texts, or attention to immeasurable factors at the psychic level related to fantasy, sexuality and identity.

Notwithstanding such embarrassments, the rejection of positivism may have thrown out the baby of intellectual rigour with the bathwater of pretension (i.e. pretension to the methods of 'natural science' according to a model of such science that was itself a poor representation of actual practice). An outstanding feature of positivism is its insistence on formulating investigation in the light of precisely defined questions, questions which derive from theories and which shape judgements as to the appropriate evidence needed to answer them. Its procedures were largely transparent and open to refutation on the basis of logic or rival investigation. This is a far cry from research which does not unpack its key concepts, which has no unambiguously articulated questions, which rests on unexamined premises, does not charge itself to define and to examine alternative questions and explanations and which is restless without self-proclaimed political position or motivation. I do not want to make an argument about absolute right or wrong in research, but to make an argument about the procedures and strategies in research and its presentation that are most likely to sustain credibility over time, and for a wide diversity of audiences.

This argument has nothing to do with 'natural' versus 'social' science: just 'science', in the sense of applying, in a systematic, transparent manner, to particular questions or concerns the methods and procedures that are most appropriate to those questions or concerns. If we want to know whether men and women typically engage in distinctive ways with television texts, we can observe, interview, or survey them in a variety of different ways and in different contexts; if we want to know about the features that help texts to 'work' effectively, we can, in addition to researching actual audiences, borrow from the concepts and insights of literary criticism, linguistics, film studies and so on – concepts and insights which we would be unlikely ever to encounter through the positivistic route. We do not need to argue that moral and political concern is out of place in research. On the other hand, if the only questions that are asked are questions that relate to the researcher's preferred political model, then research is an extremely limited (and very definitely a non-'critical') exercise. If, for example, we confine our attention only to the negative implications of global media flows for, say, the stability of cultural identities in given countries, but we never enquire whether there might also be positive implications, the research in question is potentially misleading and dangerous. If we confine our attention to the implications for economic development (however we choose to define it) of television, but never bother to enquire whether there might be a relationship between telephony and development, then that too is potentially misleading and dangerous as a statement of the relevance of media for development. Or, again, if we examine only the implications of international satellite programming for local media markets but do not take into account the counter-strategies which state-controlled broadcasters may take in reaction to such programming, we have missed the dialectics of the situation and possibly the heart of it. If we confine our attention to innovative ways of utilizing television technologies by small minority groups, but somehow disregard wider processes at work that will assimilate such groups into the mainstream, perhaps, or exile them to less favourable conditions, again we have missed the point. To make such connections does indeed require a 'critical' imagination, but serious researchers cannot pick and choose between connections; they must be open to all that are relevant, and none of these connections will be established without a respect for the need for systematic data-gathering.

The current literature on globalization has spawned a variety of interesting issues, issues which also surface in this volume: is globalization new or old?; does it pre-date modernization or is it a consequence of modernization?; is it primarily about the compression of space or of time?; is it economic, cultural or political, or is it really all about technology?; is it liberating or is it repressive, and for whom?; is it synonymous with the decline of the nation state or does it sustain the nation state through a new era of global economic connectedness?; is it the same thing as capitalism or Westernization?; is it, alternatively, the defeat of Westernization (or the weakening of a Western sense of identity – the loss of centre) and the celebration of cultural hybridity?; is it perhaps about the emergence of the 'tiger' economies of the Pacific Rim and the fears which this has inspired in the West?; is it about the end of the 'cold war' and of the 'second world' and the development of new, more complex patterns of international alliances differently configured across different industries, cultural organizations and groups?; is it a discourse about homogenization (and cultural convergence) or heterogeneity (cultural fragmentation) created through opposition and resistance to global forces, opposition which (like Islamization) is itself globalized?; or is it a discourse about a standardized range of cultural heterogeneity that is globally encountered?; or is it, as Tomlinson argues in Chapter 7, about a collapse, through the compression of space and the decline in importance of geography, of the myths that once sustained a (mis)perception of difference and otherness where there was in fact similarity?; does it depend on media and information technology?; does it suggest greater access for individuals and groups to the skills, tools and channels for cultural expression, or more restricted access?; does it signify the disappearance of 'modernist' social divisions such as social class in favour of newer ones based on diasporic ethnic difference, technology 'haves' and 'have nots', the electronically connected and the unconnected (or exclusive privately connected versus inclusive publicly connected), 'new age' versus established belief systems?; or, alternatively, is it about the emergence of enormous new middle classes in countries like India, with an insatiable appetite for Western-style goods and services?; is it about continuity or about change?; does it inspire optimism for the future or pessimism?; are all of these developments the consequence of modernization?; and does it matter and why?

If these questions are asked with a serious intent that they be answered, then they will require much more than arm-chair speculation pitched at a universal level of generality on the basis of secondary sources. Yet I suspect that literature of this kind accounts for most of what is written around the concept. It is here that something may be retrieved from positivism to do with the refinement of questions – not in order to reduce them to things that can be measured, but to specify them to the point that they can begin to be answered, and at a sufficient level of detail that will permit us to identify distinctions and conditions and contingencies as between different media, contexts, groups, functions, and historical periods. This calls for greater inter-disciplinarity (history, economics, sociology, social anthropology, politics, linguistics, together with professional studies), and it calls for greater inclusiveness (telecommunications as well as television; language and literacy as well as newspapers; computers and electronic networks as well as film), and it also demands a sharper focus on media, the forces that act on or through media and upon which the media act, and the implications or significance of what they do, very broadly defined. Yet the research agenda that is required for a comprehensive understanding of international communication in the context of globalization will not be satisfied as long as it is left only a minor role within a myriad of sub-specialisms of larger and more established disciplines, such as sociology, taking its place as merely one range of social 'texts' among others.

A distinctive research agenda for the study of globalization is one which can also link with the possibility of moral and political concern. For example, we can say of the 1970s NWICO debates that they were among the very few occasions when the world of international diplomacy has recognized that the media are profoundly international in their constitution, representations of the world, and their markets. With respect to such concerns as increasing concentration, monopolization of markets, declining diversity, high barriers to market entry, NWICO asserted a case for more robust and comprehensive international legislation and regulation. Not all who have studied the NWICO debates are likely to be aware of the extent to which NWICO was but part of a complex history of the UN struggle to legislate in defence of a (multi-faceted) *human right to communication*, which is recounted by Hamelink in Chapter 5. This history directs us to a substantial philosophical and legislative foundation for future progress in this area, one of the very best available international forums for generating concern and articulating issues; however unfashionable it may at present seem to want to engage in such thinking within a forum constituted by deeply unfashionable 'nation states', there is no other credible route available for the resolution of significant media issues in the twenty-first century, unless we are prepared to believe that the 'free' market is the best regulator. Negrine's analysis (in Chapter 3) undermines the credibility of any such belief, and points instead towards the evident and intensifying need for 're-regulation' at an international level. The narrative of deregulation and re-regulation that began with the Reagan–Thatcher axis has ironically exposed the extent to which countries once thought to exemplify a lack of regulation (e.g. the United States) turn out to have (once) been models of regulation by contrast to its absence in countries further South in the Americas. Mohammadi, in Chapter 4, queries whether the market, and whether issues of market regulation can ever be sensibly divorced from politics and the real distribution of global power and the infusion of global power relations through international organizations such as the World Bank. If globalization is about the decline of the nation state, is this decline equitably distributed or are some nation states 'declining' for the benefit of others that are declining more slowly, if at all? If international agencies like the World Bank play a significant role in the construction of a globalized world which will suit some more than others, what should we make of the statistics which they yield and on which they build their constructions and which are absorbed by an academy of high porosity? Such questions further underline the significance of the study of international communication within the context of globalization.

The future

In the dawn of the twenty-first century we are living in a world where technology has resolved the constraints of time, space and distance, at least for the benefit of a privileged minority. Whether we believe we live in a world that is better, in consequence, or worse than the world as it was experienced in earlier phases of human history before these constraints were conquered, it is incontestable that we still confront profound problems, of which many are related to communication. These principally have to do with the control and commodification of culture and image, the relationship of media to economic and national development, the means of national and international regulation, the responsibilities and moral obligations which media proprietors choose or do not choose to observe, the opportunities and the threats of digitization, and diversity and representativeness of expression. Last but hardly least, we should then ask what space is there within a research agenda that is appropriately informed by political economy and cultural studies, for issues of quality and aesthetics: can academics afford to stand aside from such concerns, to leave a moral and normative vacuum at the very heart of their enterprise when so few others are inclined to stick their heads above the parapet? From traditional academic analysis through to aesthetics, perhaps we will be more encouraged to ponder the implications of globalization and its texts for the kind of people we have become and could be, and for the energy, inclination, and personal space that we are capable of mustering if we wish seriously to engage with the forces that are constructing this world.

Further questions

1   As you know, technology has resolved the constraints of time, space and distance. In your opinion, what should be the major focus of research in international communication and globalization in the twenty-first century?
2   What forces were the cause of the development of communication research from its inception in the United States?

2

International Communication Research: Opportunities and Obstacles

James Halloran

One of the key issues in communication research in general, and in the field of international communication in particular, is the art of asking the right question, an art crucial for excellence in social science research. In this chapter, Halloran not only focuses on the question of research in the field of mass communication as a whole, but also emphasizes the international dimension of communication, which, through the rapid development of communication technology, has established itself in a field known as international communication.

In this chapter we find out about the different approaches of European communication scholars towards research in international communication, as well as the history and development of research in relation to UNESCO. The final part of the chapter focuses on issues of morality and the lack of concern for the needs of the less developed world, especially as needs are shaped by the processes of deregulation and globalization. Halloran calls our attention to two key lines of questioning, critical for the end of the twentieth century:

- *How will it be possible to achieve goals of citizenship in the absence of appropriate information and communication systems? Aren't such conditions necessary to provide opportunities of access for, and participation by, all citizens?*
- *As the gap between the 'haves' and the 'have nots' is now growing much faster than half a century ago, is there not a moral obligation to demand that meaningful research programmes be undertaken in order to improve the quality of international communication for all? Isn't closing the gap between the developed and the less developed world more important than acceding to the present nature and speed of the globalization process?*

In posing the questions in this way, Halloran is clearly aligned with the 'critical' tradition of communication research. He is, throughout this chapter, strongly critical of the more orthodox tradition for what he sees as complicity with the existing holders of power in the world. The research agenda of much international communication research, he argues, serves, consciously or unconsciously, the interests of an unjust world order.

> Research is not initiated, organized, executed or applied in a social/political
> vacuum. A true understanding of the nature of research and its application
> calls for an understanding of the historical, economic, political, organiza-
> tional, professional and personal factors which impinge on the research
> process in so many ways. (Halloran, 1987: 135)

> If they get you to ask the wrong questions they don't have to worry
> about the answers you provide. (Halloran, 1991: 22)

The General Conference of UNESCO, at its fifteenth session in November
1968, authorized the Director-General, in cooperation with appropriate
international and national organizations, governmental and non-governmental, to undertake a long-term programme of research on technological
progress in means of communication, and to promote study on the role and
effects of the media of mass communication in modern society. In June
1969, with the assistance of the Canadian National Commission for
UNESCO, the Director-General convened a meeting of experts in Montreal
to examine the actual and potential role of mass communication in society,
and to advise the Secretariat on recent developments and probable trends in
communication research as a guide to future action to be carried out, or
recommended, by UNESCO. Towards the end of 1968 I was asked by
UNESCO to prepare the working paper for this meeting, draw up an
agenda, and make suggestions as to the experts who might be invited to
participate. The working paper, according to UNESCO, presented 'a
general view of the impact of the means of mass communication on the
modern world, and of the present state and organization of communication
research and the need for research in new fields'. It also indicated 'fields for
cooperative research activities at both national and international levels'
(UNESCO, 1970). An extended version of the paper, the proceedings of the
meeting, and recommendations for future action were published by
UNESCO (UNESCO, 1970). The Montreal meeting, the publication, and
another UNESCO publication which stemmed from the meeting, *Proposals
for an International Programme of Communication Research* (UNESCO,
1971), have been described by both those who favoured the development
and those who criticized it as marking 'a watershed' in international communication research, particularly as far as UNESCO was concerned. If the
'watershed' description is valid, then clearly one might expect that whatever
came from and after the Montreal meeting, no matter how short-lived,
would differ substantially from what had gone before. Indeed, although I
cannot be certain about this (chance has often been prominent in the
development of mass communication research), I can only surmise that I
was asked to prepare the working paper because key figures at UNESCO
decided that they wanted something different from what had gone before.

The Montreal experience was my first real contact with the politics of
international communication research. I had not published in this specific
field prior to Montreal, although it would have been clear from my early
publications in the general field (Halloran, 1964) – as later reflected in the
working paper – that I was in favour of a more critical, sociological,

holistic approach than had hitherto prevailed. At the risk of oversimplification, in addition to asking 'How can we get the message across more effectively?', I wanted to ask about the nature of the message. Was it worth getting across? What functions did it perform for giver and receiver? Whose interests did it serve? What needs did it meet? and so on. To that point, as clearly manifest in the list of UNESCO publications, (1970, 1971) these questions had not figured prominently in the international research agenda. The earlier approach is well illustrated in the book *Mass Media and National Development: The Role of Information in the Developing Countries* (Schramm, 1964).

The overall approach to research, and the underlying thinking in this international field, as illustrated, in their different ways, by Schramm, Lerner, Pool, Rogers and others, has come in for a great deal of criticism (Golding, 1974). This criticism need not be repeated in detail here; suffice it to say that in research lacking in theory, historical and sociological perspectives and being heavily ethnocentric, progress and development at all levels, from material resources to the industrial work ethic, were inevitably conceived in Western industrialized terms. The type of research referred to above was confined to this restricted framework and, consequently, it offered little challenge to the international status quo. In fact, directly or indirectly, explicitly or implicitly, it served the vested interests of the established powers.

It was no surprise, therefore, when those powers adopted a hostile attitude to the more critical approach emerging from Montreal, which offered a challenge to the existing order and some of the communication/media myths which sustained it. There is an important lesson to be learned from this opposition to critical research, for it illustrates how the results of research are received by the established powers, and criticized and disseminated by their media agents.

It is as well to remember that research in this area is not a game for remote academics engaged in research for the sake of research. Once the critical stance is adopted and responsibilities as independent researchers, scholars and intellectuals accepted, the researchers almost inevitably will find themselves in conflict with extremely powerful national and international forces, which are convinced that they (and the world at large) have nothing whatsoever to gain from critical investigations. They believe that they know all they want to know about communication and the media. The status quo suits them fine, and its maintenance or extension is what they seek. Alternative forms of thinking are not welcome because they might lead to alternative systems. What is more, they are most favourably placed to defend their position because, to a large degree, they are able to set the agenda and control the discourse. It is important to note in this connection the massive, well-orchestrated counter-attack mounted by the international media establishment against the previously mentioned critical research, which had exposed the nature and inequity of the international information order and suggested, *inter alia*, how the imbalance might be redressed. This critical research questioned and sought to change the lack of balance in the international information order. In rightly taking this line, however, researchers must not leave themselves open to attack from the international media establishment because of the lack of balance in their own research activities, or because they have failed to define the problems or apply their critical criteria within a wider universal context. Unfortunately, critical researchers have not always been as disciplined and respectful of evidence as they might have been. The hostility is there – it does not need to be reinforced.

Of course, selections have to be made from many areas of possible enquiry, and it is perfectly legitimate to establish research priorities and make choices accordingly. But it is neither legitimate nor responsible for the critical researcher to be partial, blind, or perhaps just simply naïve, to such a degree that an outsider might assume that there were parts of the world so perfect that critical criteria, say with regard to access, participation and manipulation, need never be applied. We need balance in research as well as in other communication areas. Unfortunately, critical research has not always been balanced.

The orthodox counter-attack

A good example of the defence, counter-attack and smear tactics employed by the vested interests in international communication to fend off the critical challenge is to be found in Rosemary Righter's International Press Institute (IPI)-sponsored book, *Whose News? Politics, the Press and the Third World* (Righter, 1978). Righter refers to the Montreal conference and the 'watershed' as marking a shift from 'a theoretical approach into an international action programme' (Righter, 1978). For anyone familiar with mass communication research, this interpretation is bound to seem somewhat strange for, as already noted, the pre-watershed research was characterized by theoretical paucity.

The research programmes, projects, reports, etc. which were seen as stemming from the post-Montreal approach were criticized and at one level dismissed by Righter because she considered most of them as 'wholly irrelevant to the actual problems of communication in the societies UNESCO exists to help' (Righter, 1978). But Righter would appear to want it both ways. She regards the work as useless and riddled with jargon, but 'to dismiss it for that reason would be to ignore the purpose of the new research programme' which she sees (without any obvious enthusiasm) as being essentially geared to informing policy-makers and as deliberately including 'all aspects of the communication process as an integral total'.

The new direction and emphasis was not welcomed. That researchers should want to ask questions about media ownership and control, the formulation of communication policy, decision-making in policy formulation, journalistic values, qualitative analyses of content, the agenda-setting function of the media, the role of the media in the formation of social consciousness, the relationship between the media and other institutions, and between the communication process and other social processes, about international communication patterns, inequalities, imbalance, exploitation and the erosion of cultural and national identities were all treated with suspicion by Righter. She grudgingly accepted that there could be legitimate reasons for these questions and for such kinds of research. But clearly her main concern was not with a disciplined, social scientific approach to media and communication questions, or with genuine attempts to study systematically complex processes and institutions so that policy may be better informed. Her preoccupation was with her perceptions of the political/policy implications of the research developments at that time, particularly those associated with UNESCO, and which questioned the status quo and the accepted ways of doing things.

It is interesting to see how Righter apparently regarded with approval the conventional research approaches that prevailed before Montreal. Incidentally, these approaches, which are still in evidence in some quarters, were reflected in some of the activities that were mounted as a counter to the UNESCO-sponsored and related research. This counter-research was not accidental, and it appears to have been conceived as an integral part of a well-orchestrated attack on UNESCO and anyone associated with research which it was feared might produce results critical of the prevailing international media system. In fact, some would argue that it represented a good example of the direct relationship between ideology and research. Moreover, it was not unconnected with the withdrawal from UNESCO of the United States and the United Kingdom.

As I saw it, the main hope of quite a number of researchers at that time (as expressed in the Montreal working paper, conference report and other publications) was that some form of critical approach – not homogeneous, not representing any given ideological position, but diverse and pluralistic, in fact a form of critical eclecticism – would take over from the conventional research which, up to that time, had characterized both the field in general and UNESCO's research policies and programmes in particular (Halloran, 1983).

As indicated earlier, this type of research had far-reaching policy implications for, on the whole, it tended to legitimate and reinforce the existing system and the established order, and in the Third World it tended to strengthen economic and cultural dependence rather than promote independence. It is also worth noting that many people previously unconcerned, or perhaps not aware of the problem, began to realize with regard to such issues as 'international communication', 'media and development', 'free flow', 'new information order', etc., that the Third World had a good case. But who, before the results from this new research were made available, was able to support the case with hard evidence, and who was able to challenge the myths about the universal benefits of freedom (freedom to select from a strictly limited agenda) which appeared to be readily accepted by the news agencies, their clients and supporters? What part did the vociferous advocates of 'free flow' play in facilitating free and informed discussion on this question? What research or enquiries on this score did they ever sponsor? They only became interested, they only sponsored research, when challenged – when their interests were threatened – and, of course, it was intended that such research would produce results that would help them in their defence.

On the other side, so to speak, it has been argued (even by some of those sympathetic to the Third World) that 'the virtues and benefits of the present system are in danger of being ignored in the current debate'. This may be so, but we must remember that it is only relatively recently that anyone questioned the prevailing system at all. Balance did not always figure in the debate. The virtues and benefits of the prevailing system were taken for granted, although not always specified or substantiated. What some of us regard as obvious inadequacies were wrapped in a cloak of silence for years. Although the cloak is still there for some, the lifting of the cloak is regretted by many of those who speak and write in terms of 'freedom'. It is not without significance that those who lifted the cloak with their research were attacked, and still are attacked by those who so obviously benefited from the silence.

This is no doubt why Righter and her allies suggested that UNESCO research should be shifted away from such questions as 'the right to communicate' to 'more concrete problems'. But what are these 'concrete problems'? The same as, or similar to, the safe, 'value-free', micro-questions of the old-time positivists who served the system so well, whether they realized it or not? All this represented a definite and not very well disguised attempt to put the clock back to the days when the function of research was to serve the system as it was, and not to question, challenge or attempt to improve it. This, then, is an example of the political arena in which international communication research operates. It is not that research suddenly became politicized, as some would claim; it is more a question of the emergence of a balance, as latently politicized research is challenged by more overtly politicized developments.

I have just referred to researchers serving the system 'whether they realized it or not', and elsewhere I have written in terms of direct and indirect influence, and of the explicit and implicit. The end product stemming from any given action may well be the same whatever the conscious purpose, or whether intended or not. It is not my purpose here to divide researchers into those who were fully aware and those who were not aware of the nature and implications of their work, nor to evaluate research in terms of its quality. It is as well to remember, however, that irrespective of intention or quality, research may, and often does, serve clearly identifiable political purposes.

The murky origins of research in communication and development

In this connection it is worth studying the article by Rohan Samarajiva on 'The murky beginnings of the communication and development field: Voice of America and "The Passing of Traditional Society"' (Samarajiva, 1985). The paper, which would appear to be appropriately titled, provides an historical and contextual analysis of the origins of the communication and development field in the United States in the 1950s, with specific emphasis on the seminal work, *The Passing of Traditional Society*, (1964) by Daniel Lerner, and the research project on which it was based. Relying in part on original documents, apparently not always readily made available, Samarajiva makes a strong case that *Traditional Society* (and this really was a most influential work) was a spin-off from a large and clandestine audience research project conducted for *Voice of America* by the Bureau of Applied Social Research, and funded by the Office of International Broadcasting of the US State Department. Despite its influence in the developmental field, this work had more to do with the Cold War politics of the time than with issues at the heart of development communication. The original focus was not on the relationship between empathy and media participation, but on radio listening behaviour.

Samarajiva argues that:

> The influence of these geo-political factors on communication research of the time is clearly manifested in the following excerpts from Harold Lasswell's contribution to *Public Opinion Quarterly* (1952–53: 498–500). . . . We can see in communication research a positive factor in the laborious and time-consuming process by which the non-Soviet world is being transformed into a unified body politic. Essential to the consolidation of a body politic by methods short of conquest is the growth of a common attention structure. . . . Research on communication has its most direct function to fulfill by modifying the attention structure of the non-Soviet world at strategic points. . . . [a] common frame of world attention . . . will clarify the identity of genuine allies and enemies in the actual and potential alignments that arise in the building of a united body politic for the free world. (Samarajiva, 1985: 5)

The influence of economic and commercial forces on the development of communication research was mentioned earlier. Here, in addition to stressing the importance of the geo-political factors, Samarajiva also draws our attention to the influence of psychological warfare work and, in particular, to the relevance of Lerner's attachment to the Psychological Warfare Division of the US Army in the Second World War. He quotes Lerner:

> In its 'cold war' with the Soviet Union . . . the United States is offering mainly dollars . . . to produce more 'good things of life'. . . . Should it turn out that . . . the 'good things' we offer are not adequate competition against the 'better world' offered by the Soviets, we shall need to consult the intelligence specialist (the social scientist) the communication specialist (the propagandist) rather than, or in addition to, the diplomat, the economist, and the soldier. (Lerner, quoted in Samarajiva, 1985: 6)

A point is also made of the similarity in the categories used in classifying Nazis to those used in Lerner's Middle East work.

Additionally, it is argued that this seminal work poses several ethical problems, including the nature of sponsorship, the disclosure of sponsorship, the infringement of national sovereignty, the exploitation of co-workers, publication rights, and so on. These, important though they may be, are not our main concerns here, although it is worth noting that sponsorship was not disclosed by Lerner in *Traditional Society*. Our main concern in the context of this chapter is with formative forces and in this connection Samarajiva's research reinforces the case that:

> Different areas of communication were influenced by different phenomena in varying degrees. While marketing and audience research were the dominant influences on domestic media studies, psychological warfare appears to have been the major formative influence on the field of communication and development. This may help explain why the 'hypodermic needle' theory of communication and the Lasswellian formula flourished longest and best in this field. (ibid.: 21)

Interestingly, he goes on to state that:

> Recent criticisms of the 'old paradigm' of communication and development have identified its manipulative, unidirectional nature as a major shortcoming. What is not realized is that what is now a shortcoming in a field that has been demo-cratized and internationalized, would have been one of the main selling points for legitimacy and funding in the early years. (ibid.: 21)

He concludes by suggesting that:

> Exploratory work on the early period suggests a pattern of net influence flows as follows: marketing research to communication research; marketing and com-munication research to psychological warfare; and from psychological warfare to communication and development. (ibid.: 22)

Such, then, are the pure and neutral beginnings of our field of interest! We might well ask 'Who are you neutral against?' However, in view of these murky beginnings we perhaps need no longer be surprised at the expressions of concern and dissatisfaction, or at the hostility which is generated by any attempt to challenge and criticize the status quo, the conventional wisdom, the established ways of looking at things, and the vested interests associated with, or responsible for, these.

Whatever the underlying causes, the predisposing factors, the intentions or the degree of awareness, there can be little doubt that different interpret-ations of the nature of social science, its limitations and possibilities, which stem from the very nature of social science itself, led to the formation of 'warring schools', which adopted fundamentally different approaches to media and development, and international communication generally. Although intellectually the war was won almost before it started (in fact, there was no real battle at the intellectual level), we should note that intellectual bankruptcy does not preclude influence. Error persists, and has been and still is used, both directly and indirectly, to prevent change, maintain the status quo, and serve other political ends.

An interesting aspect of this problem is that conventional researchers who like to consider themselves as scientists and scholars, often accuse critical researchers of politicizing research and engaging in polemics. In the process of doing this they demonstrate a profound ignorance of the nature of critical research, often claiming to support their position by setting up and attempting to knock down straw men that genuine critical researchers would not recognize as brethren. The intellectual blindness of their position would appear to prevent them from recognizing that all communication research has always been, and always will be, politicized in one way or another. Research (just like the media and communication systems) is not conceived, designed, executed and interpreted in a social/political vacuum. As we have seen, whether appreciated or not, it is firmly embedded in a system which it inevitably reflects.

Research which does not recognize this, and the importance of power and historical and sociological perspectives, while claiming value-free neutrality, scientific purity and objectivity, certainly cannot be classified as scholarship. No amount of references to the categories to be found in the conventional methodological textbooks can mask the fact that most of this work focuses on doing rather than thinking. There is little evidence of the building up of a corpus of knowledge which might be regarded as the *sine qua non* of scientific endeavour. Instead, we find numerous fragmented exercises, uninformed by theory; a plethora of allegedly definitive statistical statements about the irrelevant, the inconsequential or the plainly invalid. Methods have been begged, borrowed and stolen from the natural and physical sciences which are just not capable of dealing adequately with social/political/cultural relationships and situations. Validity and reliability are emphasized without any apparent realization that, in our field, in certain situations the two may not be compatible. Reliability (which receives much more attention) is often achieved at the cost of validity.

International comparative research

Let us illustrate this by taking some specific examples from international comparative research. At the risk of oversimplifying the issue, it may be said that, over the last thirty years or so, there has been a greater willingness, although by no means a complete acceptance, that in international comparative research there was no need for all the participating countries to rigidly and mechanically apply the same agreed instruments and that a more flexible, sociological orientation which recognized national, cultural, social and linguistic differences, and the implications of these differences for design and data collection, had its advantages. Put briefly, it was recognized that, except in the most simple of categories, different questions, or at least differently presented questions (reflecting differences in culture, language, etc.) – not the same questions – would be necessary to evoke the same type of information in the different circumstances. Moreover, in addition to this, it came to be accepted that, in order to do justice to the complexity of the subject matter, it would be necessary for each country to include special segments in their enquiries which, among other things, would facilitate a deeper understanding of national differences.

One final point in this connection was that the hard/soft quantitative/ qualitative, hierarchical dichotomy with regard to data should be rejected. Wherever possible we should blend the two. For example, quantitative data could be enriched and refined by data gained from more ethnographic and anthropological approaches – both being equally valid and useful. (It needs to be emphasized that this was not a 'majority movement'.)

It is also necessary to look in a little more detail at the significance of this shift in the mode of enquiry. A few researchers have recognized for some time that international comparative research was bedevilled not only by understandable and inevitable problems (practical, logistical, policies, research interests, resources, etc.), but also by misconceptions and mis-understandings about the very nature and potential of this type of research. Above all, it was felt that there was a need to ask what was really meant by comparative studies, and what should be the essence of the units of comparative analysis?

The units of analysis selected in any given project are essentially deter-mined by the nature of the research and its aims and objectives. Unfor-tunately, this is not always clearly understood. For example, in one project in which I was involved, which focused on producers and their knowledge of their audience, the point was raised, as a criticism, that the children in the different countries were not all of the same age. Age may be central in some studies, but the important factor in this particular study was that the main unit of comparison was not young people of the same age in different countries, but the relationship between the broadcasting institutions and broadcasters on the one hand, and their target audience (which might be 13/14 years in one country, 12/13 years in another) on the other. The match, or lack of it, between the two and the factors that influenced both provision and reaction to provision were what mattered, and what had to be analysed.

With regard to another project it had to be emphasized that compar-ability should not be confined to simple, and somewhat obvious, com-parisons of age, sex, etc. The aims of the research in question meant that it was not adequate to compare the media behaviour of, say, farm workers in Hungary and fishermen in Canada. It was necessary, in this particular case, that the comparisons should centre on the way in which the different media systems were organized and the differences in what was provided, how the provision was used by different groups within the society (e.g. farmers and fishermen), and what were the consequences of that use in the different countries in relation to the selected objectives of the research. It is absolutely essential to be clear about what, precisely, is being compared. Yet so often this is not clarified, and the situation is further complicated and obscured by the introduction of conventional variables (sex, class, age, educational background, etc.) which could be totally irrelevant as far as the main aims of a specific project are concerned.

There used to be many researchers – in fact there are still some – who automatically accept that even in the type of research discussed here, the carbon-copy, blue-print application in different societies of pre-tested questionnaire items, in a highly structured research instrument, is capable of providing data suitable for genuine comparative analysis. The position held here is that unless the 'analysis' is confined to very simple categories this approach is meaningless, and is likely to produce invalid and misleading information.

It is important to stress that language does not develop in a vacuum, and that words, phrases, sentences, questions, etc., have meanings only within given cultural, or even sub-cultural contexts. Consequently, it would be a mistake to attempt to produce uniformity in the verbal stimulus (questionnaire items) in a universe which is likely to be characterized by linguistic-cultural pluralism. The task is to make sure, in the various societies/cultures in which the research is being carried out, that the verbal stimulus or question used in the interview or survey, or the coding category in the analysis of news, is the one most capable of eliciting the precise type of information that the objectives require. Real comparability is obtained at this level of analysis, not at question item level. In different cultures, because they are different, different questions have to be asked (in different ways) to obtain the same sort of information. Comparing the answers to allegedly identical questions asked in different countries is not necessarily comparing like with like, as some would have us believe.

In any kind of comparative research it is not very useful simply to provide an item-by-item inventory of similarities and differences from the various participating countries. The studies from the various countries need to be integrated or compared in relation to some model or set of guidelines. These guidelines make it possible to impose some sort of meaning and coherence on what would otherwise be a relatively meaningless collection of snippets and fragments. In other words, to be useful data have to be classified, analysed and interpreted in relation to a chosen set of principles, for data never speak for themselves. But, of course, there is not just one model, or one set of principles – several may be available, so choices have to be made, and there are often fundamental disagreements about the choice of model. In the circumstances this lack of consensus is almost inevitable. What matters is to be clear as to what guidelines or models have been used, and to articulate this and specify the reasons for the choice. In studies such as these there is no room for spurious objectivity. It is important to note that the above comments about the integration of data in accordance with selected guidelines or frameworks is more of a statement of an ideal than an accurate description of what normally happens in comparative research.

The reference to these methodological problems leads us to some of the basic issues in relation to social scientific research which are central to our problems. Moreover, these problems and issues create certain difficulties with regard to the dissemination and acceptance of research results and, as will be seen, they are also relevant to any considerations as to the possibility of carrying out research in Third World countries (Halloran, 1990).

Communication research and the Third World

Let us then focus on two main aspects of a very crucial issue – crucial to the nature and scope of social science and, in particular, to the application of social science, including mass communication research, to Third World situations. The first has to do with the lack of consensus in mass communication research, and in social science generally. The simple division into critical and non-critical (conventional research) is an example of this. Although these gross categories may conceal as much as they reveal, for they are by no means homogeneous, they reflect the main basic divisions between the Aristotelian hermeneutic approach and the Galilean positivistic approach, the latter characterizing so much of conventional communication research.

At this stage our main concern, without taking sides or without dismissing any of the approaches as illegitimate, is with the implications of this lack of consensus of these 'warring schools', and the 'ferment in the field' in an allegedly scientific exercise. The situation becomes even more problematic when we add geo-cultural and stage-of-development components to those contributing to the lack of consensus, and to the discontinuities already mentioned. There is ample evidence in mass communication research to suggest that cultural, regional and national differences profoundly influence the research effort at all stages and levels.

But why should we expect to be free from such influences? It is not surprising if, in a situation of conflicting ideologies and other geo-cultural differences, we find disagreements across a wide range of relevant factors, including aims, purposes, needs, theories, conceptualization, design and methods. The different schools actually look for evidence (selectively defined, of course) in different places, and employ different criteria in assessing its validity. In such circumstances dialogue, meaningful exchanges and constructive debate are extremely difficult, if not impossible. The necessary common referents and agreed basic assumptions are lacking, as is the overlap in the respective fields of discourse which is essential for effective communication. Yet we talk of 'social science', emphasize the importance of scientific method, and in many cases act as though, once we have progressed beyond the understandable confusion and uncertainty associated with the embryonic stage of development, we shall be able to rid ourselves of the conflicts, contradictions and discontinuities and reach the holy grail of consensus, allegedly the hallmark of 'real science'.

But, realistically, what are the chances of this? Of course there are differences within the natural and physical sciences, but on the whole they are not of the kind which make constructive dialogue well nigh impossible. If consensus is a mark of scientific maturity, as some would claim, then the social sciences are not very mature. What is more, it is possible that, by their very nature, the social sciences will never be able to grow up or mature in this way. This could mean that new criteria of development and maturity are required – perhaps 'healthy, critical dissensus'! The continued use of natural science as a model for social science may not be appropriate.

In suggesting this I am by no means wishing to signal the end of communication research or international comparative studies. Systematic, disciplined, fruitful studies can still be carried out within an eclectic framework, and assessed accordingly. This is not an escape from rigour, but an acceptance of an approach (albeit as yet by no means a fully developed approach) which is capable of doing justice to the complex set of relationships, structures and processes which characterize our field of study. The so-called scientific approach is incapable of doing this on its own. The adoption of complementary perspectives is essential.

Another point, very closely related to the previous one, centres on mass communication and media research in Third World countries. What are we exporting from the so-called developed world in research? How suitable are these exported models, theories, concepts and methods derived from Western industrial experiences for the conditions it is intended that they should address? Are political, commercial, cultural and media imperialisms being followed by research imperialism? What forms of indigenization are required, and to what degree should they be applied? These are just a few of the questions which should be asked, both directly in relation to communication research, and more generally and more widely with regard to the question of universality and relativity in the social sciences.

Wherever we look in international communication research – exports and imports of textbooks, articles and journals; citations, references and footnotes; employment of experts (even in international agencies); and the funding, planning and execution of research – we are essentially looking at a dependency situation. This is a situation which is characterized by a one-way flow of values, ideas, models, methods and resources from North to South. It may even be seen more specifically as a flow from the Anglo-Saxon language fraternity to the rest of the world, and perhaps even more specifically still, within the aforementioned parameters, as an instance of a one-way traffic system which enabled US-dominated social science of the conventional nature to penetrate cultures in many parts of the world which were quite different from the culture in the United States. As the United States emerged as a superpower in social science, like it did in other spheres, even what little input there was from other sources tended to be excluded.

To me (although there would be considerable opposition to this stance), there is no doubt that much of what was exported from the United States, post-Second World War, and the implications of these exports were on the whole detrimental. I argued earlier that the exports certainly did not serve to increase our understanding of the Third World and its communication requirements, nor did they facilitate development in any way. I suggested that Daniel Lerner's extremely influential work on *The Passing of Traditional Society* was a prime example of this, irrespective of whether or not it is regarded as an artifact of the Cold War politics of that time. Moreover, what is more important is that this is not simply a matter of unsuitable exports. It is a much more fundamental matter of bad social science *per se*. The point being made here is that the principles and models underpinning Lerner's research (and much more research by others in similar vein) would not have been adequate in any situation, including the situation in the United States. To export such models simply compounded the felony, so to speak. It was not solely a Third World problem – it was a social science problem.

This takes us back to the questions already raised about the very nature, potential and universal applicability of social science, now matter how free it may be from the aforementioned conditioning. We have plenty of basic problems at the national or regional levels, as we have already noted, but we must now ask how can we possibly deal with the increasing diversification within our general field of communication research which inevitably stems from the extension of our investigations to cultures outside the cultures within which our ideas and tools were conceived, developed and articulated?

In general terms, the answer frequently given to this question is 'Indigenization at Several Levels'. Unfortunately, this proposed solution is often put forward without any apparent recognition that, in certain circumstances, it could lead to increasing dissonance and discontinuity, and a further weakening of the consensus which many still regard as the hallmark of social scientific maturity.

The global cry for the indigenization of social scientific and mass communication research cannot be dismissed, but it needs to be treated with reserve in certain areas, particularly in relation to some of the ways in which it has already been applied. We may readily accept the need for emerging nations and regions to determine their own research policies, priorities and strategies, rather than having them externally imposed, as was the case so often in the past. The need for home-based institutions, housing native staff capable of carrying out the necessary research in their own countries also appears to be generally acceptable – at least on the surface. I insert this 'surface' qualification simply because, for many years now, the case has been fiercely argued that the situation would improve to the benefit of Third World countries if the nationals of those countries were given the opportunity, and the resources, to enable them to carry out the research. Fine, up to a point, but it could be far too simplistic. Our experience makes clear that many of these nationals have been trained as conventional researchers, mostly in universities in the United States, and seem unable to free themselves from the ideological shackles of their educational and professional mentors. In this way they tend to exacerbate the situation and perpetuate the error by giving the 'alien import' a national seal of approval.

The heart of the problem is at the level of language, conceptualization, models, paradigms, theories and methods. In our field one cannot even take for granted the universal applicability of all that is frequently associated with so-called rational scientific approaches. The main task (assuming that the aim is still to pursue a form of universalism rather than encourage parochialism or complete relativism) is to identify, recognize and accept emerging indigenous phenomena in their own right, and then attempt to integrate them into a more universalistic framework. This would be done sympathetically and systematically, but with a full recognition of the inevitability of eclecticism in the foreseeable future.

The problem will not be overcome by confrontation and exclusion, and certainly not by a blind, unchanging adherence to simplistic notions of science and detachment. The solution might possibly be in a move towards a universality, which would take into account the diversity of cultural identities. The problems of universality and relativity of values, of individual liberty and life in community, of autonomy and solidarity cannot be avoided, and must be resolved.

The first part of this chapter focused on what might be called the external obstacles to research, and then went on to discuss the internal obstacles, namely those inherent in the very nature of the social scientific exercise. But the two sets of obstacles and problems are not unrelated. How can we expect policy-makers, broadcasters and other media practitioners to take us seriously when a researcher may be found to support almost any point of view or policy? On the other hand, even in the unlikely event of consensus and harmony coming to characterize communication research and researchers in the future, it would be unrealistic and optimistic to think that this would automatically lead to research results being incorporated in policy decisions, or even informing the public debate. The problem remains of the dissemination of research results, and the application and impact of research. The conclusion of the research project is the beginning, not the end, of the educative task – a task which, as we have seen, becomes very difficult when the outcome of research challenges the beliefs, interests and mode of operation of those whom we would seek to influence.

The return to Montreal (1992)

It is with this in mind that I wish to return to Montreal. The story told in this chapter started in Montreal in 1969, and it is interesting on several counts to finish it there, at least for the time being, almost a quarter of a century later.

In September 1992 the annual conference of the International Institute of Communication (IIC) was held in Montreal. The theme was 'globalization and nationalism'. The IIC, which was established in the late 1960s, is a genuine international body which provides a forum for top-level people concerned with communication in its many aspects. It started out as the International Broadcast Institute (IBI), and although broadcasting is still well represented in its membership, increasingly both membership and

programmes have reflected a wider interest in the information society –
technologically, economically and politically.

In its earlier days the IBI showed some interest in independent research,
and it was one of the first in the field to support a comparative international study of news. The Institute's association with this study offers a
good example of how the attitudes of media practitioners towards research
may change when the unanticipated results of the research present a
challenge to the status quo, prevailing professional values and conventional
media mythologies.

In the particular cases I wish to analyse, although the original agreement
between the IBI and the researchers gave the IBI a first right to publish
(but no veto), the publication option was never taken up. The reasons for
this lack of enthusiasm for what became a widely acclaimed, critical,
empirically based, theoretically sophisticated book (Golding and Elliott,
1979) should not be difficult to fathom. Moreover, it would appear that the
above was not the only example of its kind. Olof Hulten, a Swedish
researcher, was also commissioned in those early days of the IBI to carry
out research on 'communications satellite tariffs for television'. Hulten felt
that the IBI did not like his report because it did not give them what they
had hoped for. In this case, although Hulten also eventually found a
publisher for his work, the IBI took his material and gave it to two
economists in the United States, who then published a booklet using
different models. Hulten was not informed about this development.

Research, although of a different kind from the above, is still supported
by the IIC, and although I am not familiar with the details of projects in the
late 1970s and 1980s, it seems, particularly after the Montreal conference on
globalization and nationalism that IIC-related research, and contributions to
the conferences and programmes were more likely to be industrially,
technologically and economically driven (albeit different industries from the
early 1970s) than socially, culturally or morally inspired (Halloran, 1993). It
is also worth noting that when, in writing on the first twenty-five years of the
IBI–IIC (Halloran, 1994a) at the Institute's request, I included references to
the above-mentioned occurrences, and other remarks that may have been
seen as critical, these were edited out, without any consultation. Needless
to say this was all done in the interests of space! The media, and the
communication/information industries generally, have ways of protecting
themselves.

But let us return to Montreal. The way the theme of the IIC Montreal
conference in 1992 was addressed reminded me in some ways of the earlier
conference held in the same city some twenty years before. As already
detailed, this earlier conference came to be regarded as a 'watershed' in the
development of the study of international communications because, among
other things, it drew attention to the fact that the 'free flow of information'
inevitably reinforced dependency and exacerbated the differences and
inequalities between the 'haves' and 'have nots'. It also illustrated that the
workings of international communications contributed little, if anything, to

the development of Third World countries. Development was thought of, and even assessed by research, in Western industrialized terms. Many contributors to the 1992 conference made it abundantly clear that, at least on this score, little had changed over the years. References either to this dependency, or indeed to any sense of historical perspective, were conspicuous mainly by their absence. A comforting social/cultural myopia prevailed. One might have thought that it would have been obvious that the theme of the conference could not be understood outside the historical framework provided by an imperialist and colonial past. The terms and classifications used are ideologically tainted and the media, technological development, communication flows and even research inevitably represent forms of superimposition and dependency. Of course, to recognize this does not square very easily with the unbridled optimism and technological determinism which characterized so many of the conference contributions.

That the conference was in Canada also forced me back, some twenty years or more, to the hey-day of Marshall McLuhan. Without fuelling the controversy that surrounds the man, it is worth recalling that in McLuhan's work the blend of idealism, technological determinism and sociological naiveté led to a monocausal, media/technology emphasis which, in turn, encouraged an unquestioning faith in the benefits of technological progress. That this blind faith still exists was amply confirmed at the conference.

Although McLuhan did not conceive of his global village as an harmonious paradise and allowed for discord and conflict, his lack of sociological perspective meant that the significance of nationalism, race, ethnicity, class and other social/cultural groupings did not figure prominently in his thinking, any more than they did at the conference. It would also appear that this approach prevented a recognition that technological developments in communications might have other than global implications, and that in certain circumstances they might even facilitate and reinforce the group, the local, the regional, the ethnic and the national.

There was no agreement on what was meant by 'globalization'. The term was used without appropriate distinctions being made as to the different levels of impact. There are different dimensions of global cultural flows (people, technology, finance, media, ideas, culture, etc.) and these need not be seen as occurring at one and the same time, at the same rate or to the same degree. The situation is much more complex and problematic than the optimistic advocates of technological development would have us believe (Appadurai, 1993).

The theme of the 1992 conference linked globalization to nationalism, and called for an examination of the relationship between them. Several contributors argued that there was no necessary incompatibility between the two, and that one tendency might complement the other. It was suggested that we should attempt to reconcile – in fact to 'dovetail' – the two.

These may be laudable sentiments, but they are not well founded. They reflect a lack of understanding of nationalism, as well as confusion about globalization. Several scholars have argued (Galbraith, 1989; Phillips, 1990) that the 1980s, in addition to representing a decade of greed, self-indulgence and false prosperity, fostered disintegration and the decline of community. The ideal of the melting-pot gave way to a splintering into racial and ethnic groups which are more concerned with group identity and interests than with integration.

But, as well as being the decade of deterioration, the 1980s was also the decade of deregulation, privatization, increased competition, supremacy of market forces and the rolling back of the public sector. All of these tendencies were favoured and energetically advocated by several of the speakers at Montreal. They spoke primarily – at times solely – in terms of the benefits (unspecified) that 'will inevitably stem' from technological developments. The possible wider social, cultural and political implications were ignored, as were the possible relationships between the two aforementioned sets of tendencies.

Globalization and the Third World

Turning to the Third World – the target of many of the strategies of the conference participants – we must bear in mind that the technological developments in communications and elsewhere, which it was claimed would improve the quality of life, do not take place in a vacuum. They are conceived, planned, funded, organized, facilitated, operated and exported (ideally so, according to the contributors) within a deregulated free market system. It is this system which 'gives globalization its dynamic' (Rio Conference, 1991). It operates at several levels and consists of interrelated parts, of which technological development in communications is but one. But the parts are not exported and do not travel in watertight compartments. They have their value components which are an integral part of a larger economic/social cultural package which both reflects and reinforces the total system. These issues are at the very heart of globalization, and should have been central to any discussion on the conference theme; but they were not articulated in Montreal.

The ideologies and conditions that obtain in powerful countries have implications far beyond the shores of those countries. The Houston Summit of 1988, in dealing with farm surpluses, subsidies and dumping, provided a powerful example of how the free market doctrine leaves the developing world still hungry. Experience indicates that globalization, via the operations of transnational companies, is frequently inappropriate to national needs in Third World countries, primarily because market-place criteria prevail.

More recently, the Minister of Health in Brazil, speaking of the unbalanced nature of public development, referred to an alienation linked to priorities that were 'more material than social, more private than public'. A recent, well-researched study in Brazil, *Cultural Genocide* (Oliveira, 1991), in illustrating the primacy of consumerism, shows specifically how radio, which began as a channel for culture, was taken over for economic gain. The conclusion of this detailed work is that the media make use of a public good (the electromagnetic spectrum) in order to serve the economic interests of elite groups, ignoring the needs and privations of the poor.

Noam Chomsky (1992) widens the debate about the role of the media from agents of international consumerism to the total manufacturing of consent. The media are seen as subtly mobilizing public support for special elitist interests, homogenizing a narrow spectrum of 'thinkable thought', and creating tacit approval for exploitation. Not everyone would agree with Chomsky, but the Montreal conference provided plenty of evidence in support of his case.

At the time of the Montreal Conference in 1992 there were many countries far worse off than Brazil, and whatever figures one wishes to use (GDP, trade, industrial capacity, debt, use of energy, education, health, domestic savings, military spending, etc.) the imbalance and inequalities between the 25% of the world population who had and the 75% who did not have were quite astounding. The rich paid only 4% interest on debt compared with 17% paid by the poorer nations. In 1990 the net annual outflow from South to North in debt repayments amounted to US$ 50 billion. Moreover, despite promises from the richer countries, the situation is not improving. In 1992 40 countries were worse off now than they were a decade ago. Inequality is on the increase. From 1960–91 the share of the world's poorest population fell from 2.3% to 1.7% while the share of the richest 20% increased from 70–85%. This means that the ratio of equality doubled across the world in thirty years – the years that marked the introduction of 'globalization'.

The effects of globalization are not uniform and the economics of inequality at this level are by no means clear. However, despite the experience of some East Asian countries there are other countries (China, Chile, Mexico, Sri Lanka, to name but a few) where inequality has increased as the economies have been liberalized. It is also worth noting that not only do such inequalities stifle economic progress, they can also be a serious threat to social and political stability and render progress unsustainable.

These problems were high on the agenda of the Earth Summit held in Rio de Janeiro in 1991, and once again the world leaders promised to help the developing world. But it now appears that the chances of the promises being kept are very remote. Debt continues to drain the 'have nots' – sub-Saharan Africa in particular – but there have been few, if any, signs of writing off debts, or that these issues were considered relevant for the Montreal 1992 conference agenda.

As far as trade is concerned, the protracted dispute between the EEC and the United States on GATT was also to the detriment of Third World interests. Currently, northern protectionism costs the 'have nots' more than they receive in aid. An examination of the international scene provides a depressing picture of a global class system in which the sands of gross poverty are carried on the winds of change and development (Harrison, 1993).

Towards a new agenda

Research into international communication, globalization, media and development which refuses or fails to recognize this inescapable arena – the economic and power structures of the world – is not of this world. It is not scholarly, but academic in the pejorative sense of that word. No amount of references to conventional methodology and claims to value-free, scientific neutrality can hide its sterility and irrelevance.

What we basically and urgently require is a globalization of moral responsibility (although one prominent member later wrote that he could not see the relevance of this concept at all), and a research programme which accepts this. In the first instance this might enable us to diagnose the problem correctly. This is an essential first step, the prerequisite of the equally necessary education and action which could then follow.

In addressing the conference, the Secretary General of the International Telecommunications Union (ITU) called for new concepts, new terms and new modes of thought in order to meet a developing and challenging situation. But it turned out that these 'innovations' were confined to the benefits of deregulation and to the advantages stemming from the unimpeded play of market forces. The aim was 'to promote telecommunication growth and expansion, i.e. a comprehensive information technology development throughout the world' (Ras-Work, 1992). There was nothing about wider social/cultural implications, and certainly nothing about accountability or moral responsibility. This approach represents a discredited ideology, and has nothing in it whatsoever for the real needs of the Third World.

The situation demands public concern, public involvement and public accountability, although to adopt this position is not to advocate one extreme to counter another. The practical solution might be a socially pragmatic combination of private and public activity. However, those who do not believe in the benefits of unfettered free enterprise, and wish to explore further the concepts of responsibility, accountability and democracy, might look at Dahrendorf's concept of citizenship – 'a system of rights and entitlements which will embrace the whole of society' (Dahrendorf, 1990).

Dahrendorf outlines three sets of basic rights, namely those concerning justice and equality, normally associated with the rule of law; basic political rights, including voting and freedom of expression; and elementary social rights, including 'the right not to fall below a certain level of income, and the right to education' (Dahrendorf, 1990). Obviously, these elementary rights include vital information and communication components, the *sine qua non* of effective functioning in the information society. But these rights, which are universal, are rarely met. Inequalities mark most societies and so far, despite vociferous claims to the contrary, there has been little evidence of a trickle-down effect at either national or international levels. In fact, we have marginalized underclasses which undermine the very principle of citizenship.

This approach at least provides us with some principles to discuss in relation to globalization and nationalism which have clear links with communication systems and with the conference theme. Unfortunately, these principles were sadly lacking in the Montreal proceedings, and rarely figure in current research strategies.

As the information society develops it will not be possible to achieve the goals of citizenship in the absence of information and communication systems which provide the information base and the opportunities for access and participation for all citizens. Accountability and responsibility demand that those who espouse development and globalization take this into account. We must also realize that, if we wish to alleviate the conditions of the many 'have nots' – particularly in the Third World – then some form of self-sacrifice on the part of the 'haves' is essential. The acceptance of this form of moral responsibility, with all it implies, should figure prominently in any discussion on globalization and nationalism, and must be taken into account in any meaningful research programme.

Further questions

1 What are the major obstacles to research in international communication? Be sure to clarify and explain the political context of each problem thoroughly.
2 What do you think are the main differences between the European and North American traditions in international communication research?

Part II

AN OVERVIEW OF COMMUNICATION TECHNOLOGY, DEREGULATION POLICY AND THEIR IMPACT ON THE DEVELOPING COUNTRIES

In the first section of this book we looked at the directions and contradictions of communication research, and the problems with, and obstacles to, international communication and globalization research. In this section we take a look at communication technology and the rapid changes which have occurred in the field of international communication and globalization process.

The recent convergence of computers and telecommunications means moving from communicating via a wire telephone network to very sophisticated electronic-based communication. Negrine's chapter looks at the development of information technology and the various changes which digital signals brought into operation, facilitating data flow and image processing. It is argued that in cyberspace life, we have come to the limits of our industrial thinking, because it is now very hard to figure out cyberspace by using a linear cause-and-effect logic. In order to manage information flow for the twenty-first century we need new skills. Everyday new software and innovative knowledges are being created about 'know how' information technology and its application. The changes are so rapid and the competition so tense that the adaption of new communication technology becomes inevitable.

Negrine provides an overview of the impact and importance of communication and information technology in the globalization process. He briefly addresses how the process of liberalization of the market, and the encouragement of competition between different systems, have both contributed towards rapid globalization.

The second chapter of this section focuses on the globalization process in the context of the Third World. As we move towards the end of this century, the changes which result from communication technology cause tremendous concern among communication scholars. The powerful flow of cultural commodities – information, news and various television programmes – saturate world markets as they become more and more accessible via satellite-broadcast television in the developing world. In this context, developing countries are facing a serious challenge as to whether to hook up with telecommunication systems available on the world market, or to avoid such integration in order to protect their culture from direct influence of such powerful cultural commodity flows. If Third World countries are interested in being part of international communication technology, they need to borrow from the World Bank. In order to qualify for loans, they have to accept World Bank prescriptive policies – conditional loans. Mohammadi examines the conditional loan policy of the World Bank as well as the kind of interference of the International Monetary Fund (IMF) in the internal economic policy of developing countries. He also shows how, in the end, many Third World countries have no choice except to follow the prescriptive policy of the world financial institutions. He offers a detailed case study of one country in the South to illustrate how the globalization process erodes the autonomy of nation states.

3

Communications Technologies: An Overview

Ralph Negrine

Today we are living in a silicon-chip society. It makes information processing incredibly easy. Through innovative use of silicon boards in a variety of forms and techniques, a revolution in information technology is taking place. By the year 2000, telecommunications will be more privatized, and arguably more accessible. Competition to provide services will not only be tense, but also fragmented – the need factor as a consequence of information revolution may be world-wide.

In this chapter, Negrine provides an overview of all aspects of communication technology, an updating of regulations and communication policies and a summary of state-of-the-art communication technology. He also explores many of the new systems of communication in a broader context and identifies the disparities between countries, regions of the world, and between the North and the South. Negrine examines how the introduction of cable systems helped fax machines and mobile telephones come into operation and how the advent of satellite communications was the beginning of the very positive prospect of nations being able to speak to other nations beyond their geographical borders. The spread of images and voices of one nation to and over another nation or culture is very exciting, but we should bear in mind that the impact and flow of messages in only one direction and without cultural consideration is not necessarily a healthy process.

> Distances 'shrink' with faster and improved connections between places. Distances mean little and direction means less. Relative location is more important than absolute location in a tightly connected and integrated world. Absolute location, via, where you are, has much less meaning today. What is more important as markets, societies, cultures and governments are becoming more connected is whether one is 'connected', how far one is from other places in time not in absolute distance, and how much one is connected with other places. (Brunn and Leinbach, 1991: xvii)

> If you are not in [the network], you are out of business. (P. Chan, Managing Director, Singapore Network Services, 1993)

Introduction: only connect?

In the rapidly changing world of technology, it is notoriously difficult to keep apace of developments. As one form of communication is overtaken by another, and yet another, the inherent possibilities of more varied forms, and patterns, of communication become ever more complex. It is worth recalling that it is only since the early 1980s that computers have become so commonplace, and have become transformed from the bulky and carefully closeted 'mainframes' to the stand alone, personal pieces of equipment populating many a desk. When one adds to this the ways in which computers can now be connected to each other via, say, electronic mail networks (e-mail) or facsimile modems, the potential for faster and more efficient forms of communication is obvious.

The convergence of computer and telecommunications facilities is thus of relatively recent origin, and it signifies the transition from the more traditional and commonplace forms of communication via the wire-telephone network to a sophisticated system of communication which links together three essential features, namely, computers/microprocessors, telephone systems (including mobile telephony) and satellites. To this one needs to add the development of the necessary software to control the processing and switching of data on, and between, the communications networks. In essence, the convergence of technologies of communications means that the distinctions between systems of telecommunications, systems of broadcasting and systems for the storage and processing of information are becoming less relevant as data can be moved across from one to the other. The cable and telephone network can now carry voice traffic, television signals and data; satellite systems can transmit a range of services to many, as well as single, points; and computers can assist the processing of information traffic, as well as enhancing the value of the information which they handle. These developments are further facilitated by digitalization, wherein all information is converted into digital signals and is then capable of being processed by sophisticated electronic hardware, such that text, images and sound can all be reproduced and processed by, say, CD-ROM machines linked to computers.

One result of this erosion of the boundaries between different networks, or systems, of communication is that 'we can talk about a wider electronic communications infrastructure rather than separate technologies which each happen to transmit information' (Communications Steering Group, 1988: 1). Indeed, there is now much discussion about the construction of 'superhighways' of communication which carry all forms of communications. By way of illustrating the significance of the creation of 'electronic communications infrastructures', one can describe the way in which a person in Britain can write a document on her word processor, and send it by electronic mail via a telephone wire and routed via a satellite, to the United States. Such activity is not out of place in many businesses and academic institutions; for that matter, neither are facsimile (fax) machines which also permit the instant transmission of documents across land and sea. Indeed, the computer and the fax machine allow for whole newspapers to be set up in one country and printed in another. The most obvious example of this is the London *Financial Times* which is written and edited in London but printed in a number of different European locations. Other examples would include the Arab newspapers currently being published in London.

Not surprisingly then, the technological flow of events has set its own pace, albeit aided in no small way by governmental policy and commercial considerations. As Abler observes, 'we should recognize that the technical and economic forces expressed in the geography of telecommunications hardware are in fact a secondary and decreasingly important explanation of the maps of telecommunications. . . . *regulation* . . . fundamentally determines the shape and operations of telecommunications systems' (Abler, 1991: 35–6). The issue of regulation, and especially *changes* in regimes of regulation, is but one of several which begins to identify the development of communications structures world-wide. The other issues are those of privatization and liberalization. Before these are explored in a little detail, it is important to bear in mind that a considerable part of the ensuing discussion is tangential to a large number of the world's nations. More precisely, poor countries with minimal communications resources are unlikely to take advantage of either the new regulatory regimes currently being promoted, or of the new communications technologies being made available. Put differently, the reforming zeal of the last two decades, which targeted the controlling power of the traditional monopolistic national telecommunications entities in order to by-pass it, may be inapplicable in those countries where there are minimal facilities and few reasons to provide alternative systems of communications. Yet even these statements need to be treated with caution. The urban–rural divide in less developed countries, for example, can still allow for the urban centre to be, in Brunn's terms, well connected in contrast to the unconnected and technologically isolated rural areas. One need only recall that a considerable amount of the communication between the members of the Palestine Liberation Organization in the recent (1993) peace negotiations with Israel was conducted via fax machine linking the West Bank and Tunis, parts of the world not known for their wealth or rich telecommunications facilities.

Changes in regulatory regimes, plural networks and disparities

What have been the consequences of the changes in regulatory regimes? Briefly, and with the issues of regulation, privatization and liberalization treated as a loose triumvirate, the changes brought about as the consequence of overturning the hitherto central role occupied by monopolistic post and telecommunications entities can be identified as follows (and in no particular order):

- The fragmentation of service provision into functionally separate entities (e.g. posts, telecommunications, national versus international service provision, and so on).

- The privatization of hitherto publicly owned entities (e.g. British Telecom, the proposed privatization of Greek telecommunications).
- The encouragement of competition between service providers.
- The encouragement of competition in the construction of fixed networks (e.g. the creation of Mercury to compete with British Telecom).
- The liberalization of the supply of terminal equipment for interconnection to the public network.
- The encouragement of competition between different systems (e.g. satellite vs cable networks).
- The licensing of resale of transmission facilities so that organizations other than the traditional telephone companies can offer access to, and services on, the network.
- The use of regulatory structures to determine the relationship between service providers, including the price structures of inter-connections between such service providers.

Other changes can surely be added but they would merely underline the manner in which the experience of communications in the immediate post-war period with, say, the aim of encouraging the widespread adoption of television and the telephone by the whole population has given way to enticements to create multiple systems of communication and services which service specific groups within the larger whole. The British academic who e-mails her American colleague is, like the general builder or plumber with his mobile phone, connected to one of the many complex and plural networks of communication. Each has adapted to a different way of keeping 'in touch' with a specific network of people, be they academics or clients.

Such changes as documented above have not necessarily been adopted wholesale by every country. The pattern of change in regulatory and technological regimes has been uneven, with some countries permitting, say, competition in services but not in the construction of fixed networks. Overall, though, the philosophy embodied by the loose triumvirate has been such as to encourage the loosening of the grip of the traditional monopolistic posts and telecommunications entity, and the advent of competition and innovation. In Europe this process will culminate with the full liberalization of the EC telecommunications market by the year 2000 (Adonis and Hill, 1993).

But such changes are neither accidental, nor a positive fall-out of technological progress. They are a by-product of telecommunications policies in an era of rapid technological change; more specifically, they are a product of an unwillingness to define a dominant physical structure of communication. What was to become the British policy towards the communications 'infrastructure for tomorrow' typifies this approach. It was premised, for instance, not only on the promise of competition, so that

[F]rom the user's point of view it is competition which enables users to make ongoing choices and to vary opinions. Competition also provides a continuous pressure to improve the nature and the quality of services offered. (Communications Steering Group, 1988: 8)

but it was also based on the view that technological developments were so rapid and unpredictable as to defy a priori planning; options *had* to be kept open.

If the technical barriers that exist between delivery systems can be broken down, the opportunity which technological convergence brings to meet service demands flexibly in ways best suited to individual requirements can be realised. (ibid.: 22)

As Eli Noam, a specialist in the field of telecommunications policy, predicts,

in the future it is likely that specialised global networks will emerge for a variety of groups that communicate with each other intensely. Their relation to each other is functional rather than territorial, and they can create global clustering of economically interrelated activities in much the way that, in the past, related activities clustered physically near each other. (Noam, 1991: 432)

Such plural networks come about, according to Noam, because of growth in the volume of communication, differentiated requirements, as well as perceived savings which can be made when such large users are grouped together (Noam, 1991: 432). While it is undoubtedly true that savings can be made, it is also true that the savings are not distributed equally across all sectors of society. Just as pressure for change comes from certain quarters, it benefits only those who can exercise power from their heavy use of, and privileged access to, the telecommunications infrastructure. So it is perhaps not surprising to find that the most noteworthy developments in international communications over the past decade or so have been to the benefit of those large corporations and wealthy users of communications systems who are well able to organize themselves so as to benefit from them. In other words, change has privileged profitable and business uses of telecommunications over and above more socially responsible ones. Thus, according to a recent report from the British National Consumer Council, British Telecom 'slashed the price of international calls primarily to help business users, . . . while increasing local cheap rate calls by 82% since privatisation [in 1982] by hoisting the cost of calls from phone boxes, used primarily by the poor' (Erlichman, 1993: 5).

If one places these points within the global context, the source of the impetus for the present directions for change in telecommunication structures emerges very clearly. There is, for instance, no doubt that US dominance and commercial considerations are important determinants of the adoption and patterns of diffusion of telecommunications facilities. As Sussman and Lent observe, 'while some benefits rebound internally to global economic interests, the most profitable uses of communication technologies are preempted by demands of transnational banks and other financial institutions, manufacturing and trading firms, communication and transportation operations, tourism industries, and foreign governments, including their militaries' (Sussman and Lent, 1991b: 17–18). The 'transfer' or 'adoption' of new communication technologies in less developed countries is thus helpful to Western governments, Western telecommunications companies, and transnational corporations – a triumvirate which benefits from better, faster and more inclusive systems of communication.

John Langdale is more succinct in his observations. 'International telecommunications', he writes, 'is a key infrastructure underpinning the emergence of the global economy.' He continues,

> larger [information] flows occur in the business and governmental areas, since rapid information flows are vital for the effective operation of transnational corporations (TNCs) and governments. *The global information highways are primarily emerging to meet the needs of these large organizations.* (Langdale, 1991: 193, emphasis added)

This analysis points to the existence of a well 'connected' communications hub made up of governments and corporations, as well as, conversely, the lack of facilities in other areas, geographically and commercially. Those at the periphery suffer most because (i) being at the periphery places them along 'thinly trafficked routes' and routes which are hardly used and therefore at risk of disappearing altogether, and (ii) being on 'thinly trafficked routes' also means it is more costly to become 'connected' in the first place and to maintain that connection (Langdale, 1991: 199).

Although this chapter will explore many of the new systems of communication currently on offer, it is essential to place these within the sort of broader context offered above. It is also essential to place these within a context which does not ignore the fact of inequalities of access to such systems of communications. At the risk of stating the obvious, this is the case at a number of different, and easily identifiable, levels. Thus,

● There are disparities within countries as between, say, rural and urban inhabitants, or rich and poor.
● There are disparities between countries as between, say, the United States and less developed countries.
● There are disparities between regions of the world.

One of the most obvious ways of illustrating many of these points is by simply observing the global spread of telephones (Tables 3.1 and 3.2). These tables confirm the existence of deep disparities. Or, as Boafo graphically described it, 'phone connections in black African countries is 2 per 1,000 people; the city of Tokyo . . . is said to have more telephones than all sub-Saharan African countries' (Boafo, 1991: 106–7). But a more worrying aspect of this disparity is the continuing inequalities within countries and particularly between rural and urban areas. For example, Lent records that Manila has 13% of the population of the Philippines 'and 80% of the country's telephones' (Sussman, 1991: 58). Similar examples can be found for numerous black African countries. But this disparity is perhaps compounded by the fact that those who have access to communication facilities, usually the rich urban elites and the political leadership,

Table 3.1   *Telepower: distribution of telephone main lines, 1990*

Country	%
North America	30.5
Western Europe	30
Eastern Europe and USSR	11
Japan	11
Asia	7
Middle East	2
Africa	1.5
South America	3.5
Australia and New Zealand	1.8

Source: Staple, 1992: 58.

Table 3.2   *Number of telephone lines in selected countries, 1991/92*

Country	Lines per 100
Argentina	10.9
Australia	47.1
Austria	41.8
Brazil	6.3
Chile	6.2
China	6.2
Denmark	56.6
France	45.0
Germany	49.0
India	0.6
Indonesia	0.5
Malaysia	8.9
Mexico	6.0
Philippines	1.1
Poland	10.0
United Kingdom	44.6
United States	54.9
Singapore	44.0

Sources: Staple, 1992: 61; Dowler, 1992: 43; British Telecom, 1993.

make strenuous efforts to maintain their positions of dominance (Boafo, 1991). An even more extreme example of enforced political domination combined with a rural–urban split is the case of satellite communication, including television, in Indonesia. Although it is illegal to buy or install satellite-receiving equipment, this ruling is ignored by the governing elite.

However, the clear existence of inequalities of access to communications facilities needs to be considered apart from the much larger question of the nature of technological change *per se*. Though the inequalities illustrated above mirror, and may in fact compound, other inequalities, they are not a product of technological change *per se*. To return briefly to our example of the British academic, her access to advanced telecommunications facilities presupposes a solid and comparatively well-funded educational system which provides such (personalized) facilities, and which probably also has a large and well-stocked library. We may wish to decry the absence of similar telecommunications facilities in other educational establishments in Britain, Eastern Europe and Africa, but this is perhaps no greater a disadvantage than a badly stocked library full of out-of-date books and journals. Nevertheless, it remains the case that her access to telecommunications facilities does allow her to be 'connected' to like-minded colleagues to the disadvantage of others. Does this compounding of inequalities mean, though, that changes in telecommunications should be obstructed, encouraged or tampered with? How does one deal with such issues? These sorts of questions have been at the heart of much recent comment on the promise of the new infrastructure of communication. The next section will explore this area by focusing on the emergence and development of satellite and cable communications.

Satellites and cable: the 'new' media

New technologies present new possibilities as well as new threats. Satellite communications can supposedly 'shrink' distances because of their ability to cover large expanses of the Earth's surface. A broadcast-satellite footprint, for example, usually covers a great many countries with the greatest of ease, and it thus becomes a very cost-effective way of reaching large populations spread across large areas at the same time. But it can also highlight problems of national sovereignty, cultural integrity and deepening inequalities because the ability to engage in such communication systems is clearly limited by financial constraints. The result, as with telephone systems or other systems of communication, is a pattern of availability and use which mirrors the imbalance of financial and sometimes political power: CNN, Murdoch's satellite news services, and the BBC's World Service Television are available across large swathes of the globe with no reciprocity of services from their target markets.

As has already been hinted, there are parallels in relation to the introduction of cable systems, fax machines, or mobile telephony. Yet the pace of technological change, and sometimes the promise it contains in the vision of global communications or the availability of sophisticated communication systems for all, does continue to inform one of the many ways of looking at contemporary analysis of the emergence and adoption of new technologies. Tehranian lists four such ways of exploring technological change. There are, according to him,

- *Technophiles*, i.e. optimists who herald the coming of a new type of society.
- *Technophobes*, i.e. pessimists who question the promises of technological change.

- *Technoneutrals*, i.e. those who assume a neutral position in order to please those who fund them.
- *Technostructuralists*, who argue that technologies are by themselves neither good, nor bad, nor *neutral* . . . their impact is always mediated through the institutional arrangements and social forces, of which they are a part. (Tehranian, 1991: 5–6, emphasis added)

One can in fact add to this quartet. Some commentators conceive of technology as '*inanimate* . . . it does not act or choose, *people* and their organised representatives do' (Sussman and Lent, 1991b: 15) (though this is an argument reminiscent of the US Gun lobby's 'guns don't kill, people do'). And there are those who see technologies as already encompassing dominant interests in society so that, for example, computers were designed for more efficient data processing as an aid to business (Robins, 1983).

The significance of this list of divisions lies not only in the quite different interpretations of technological change, its causes and impact, but particularly in the ever-present tension between continuity and change. On the one hand, we have an unrelenting pace of development of new and different means of communicating across the globe, and, on the other, we have a continuing concern about the impact and implications of those developments.

We can observe this in reactions to the development of cable technology at the beginning of the 1980s (Negrine, 1987). A counter-attack was mounted in numerous critiques against the privatization of cable systems in Europe, and against the private- and entertainment-led development of cable, particularly in the United Kingdom. This has done little to turn the tide in any meaningful way. In fact, a dozen years after the first official (British) encouragement of cable television and cable systems, these are now fairly well established and arguably complementing the terrestrial broad-casting system (Table 3.3). Admittedly, there are still concerns about the quality and diversity of the available content but the essential fact of change cannot be doubted. As Collins perceptively observed over ten years ago,

Pessimism about technological change and cultural decline are, of course, endur-ing British tropes. Lord Reith's, in retrospect, hysterical Jeremiad against the introduction of commercial television, only continued the long and mistaken tradition of inveighing against 'illth' (the undesirable) and innovations in cultural forms. . . . [However, this] does not necessarily mean that cultural pessimism is misplaced . . . or that concern for the nature of programming is the prerogative of the middle class. (Collins, 1983: 293–4)

The view expressed by Richard Collins highlights the tension between continuity and change referred to above. There are, on the one hand, the Jeremiads – although it may be only in retrospect that they can be described as such – who railed against commercial television, cable systems, satellite broadcasting, and the privatization of telecommunication entities, and, on the other hand, there are those who advocate the coming into existence of ever-newer systems of communication. That the two sides – unrelenting technological change pitted against concerns about that change – occupy,

Table 3.3 *Cable in selected European countries, late 1992*

Country	Cable homes connected (000s)	Cable penetration (as % of total TV homes)
France	1,358	6.5
Germany	15,987	48.3
UK	1,630	7.2

Source: *Cable and Satellite Europe*, January 1997.

broadly speaking, the same terrain they did well over two decades ago when the first of many new means of communication, in this instance, satellite communication took on a very public profile (see, for example, Schiller, 1970; Schiller and Nordenstreng, 1979), should offer us a lesson of one kind or another. It should teach us, perhaps, that in a world now increasingly dominated by the ethos of competition and capitalism, those propounding better and ever-more efficient means of communications for profit and commerce are not overly concerned with the musings of the doubting Thomases or the Jeremiads around them. For it is like doubting Thomases, or more sadly prophets of doom, that detractors of change come to represent.

The advent of satellite communications offers a good example of this. The exploitation of the geo-stationary orbit, in which the satellite orbits above the earth at 12,000 miles and so has the appearance of remaining stationary, therefore offering continuous communications facilities, opened up the prospect of 'nations being able to speak unto nations', as well as of an instant and inexpensive way for a centre to reach a population spread thinly across a large land mass. The prospect of an ever-increasing stream of communication – of images and of voices – was, to many, very exciting. Others, however, viewed the matter quite differently. In an early discussion of the development of satellite communication, Herbert Schiller highlighted the emergence and consolidation of American interests and the implications of this for both developed *and* developing economies (Schiller, 1970). This general critique, and in particular its relevance to developing countries, was much more focused in a later piece on the implications of satellite communications. As Schiller and Nordenstreng were careful to stress:

the informational facilities and the flows that circulate, locally and internationally, are, with few and generally trifling exceptions, responsive to, if not at the disposal of, the power centres in the dominant national states. . . . in this historical period, then, the preservation of national sovereignty may be understood best as a step in the still larger struggle to break the domination of the world business system. (Schiller and Nordenstreng, 1979: 12)

. . . the 'new international information order' . . . is ultimately aiming at the 'decolonization' of information conditions in the developing countries, and in general advocating respect for the cultural and political sovereignty of all nations. (ibid.: xiv)

The location of this argument in the historical context of the 1970s does not lessen the concerns expressed. If anything, such concerns have continued to be at the centre of discussions about international communications and this is perhaps an indication of their universality (see, for example, Hudson, 1990; Mahoney, 1992; Negrine, 1987; Sussman and Lent, 1991a). Yet it may be necessary to modify the boldness of these statements in order to better appreciate the patterns of developments in the field of satellite communication.

On one level, Schiller and Nordenstreng are correct in highlighting the control exercised by 'dominant national states' over satellite communication. This has been done both by ensuring that they can gain easy access to the geo-stationary orbit, and by controlling the nature and content of the traffic via satellites, particularly of television traffic, as it moves from the developed world to the less developed countries. As Hudson put it,

> Only fourteen satellites serving developing countries were launched between 1980 and 1985. Even taking into consideration that Intelsat satellites are used by both industrialised and developing nations, satellites for the exclusive use of industrialised countries made up 72 per cent of the total. (Hudson, 1990: 263)

The detailed work conducted by Hudson led her to conclude that 'middle-income countries benefited most from the increased access to satellites for domestic and regional communications' rather than the less developed countries (ibid.: 263). Such middle-income countries clearly had the resources – both technical and monetary – either to lease transponders from Intelsat or to participate in the setting up of regional satellite systems; even though the willingness to partake of new systems of communications may sometimes reflect more of a willingness to take part in high-technology developments than in trying to meet some real and unmet need.

The example of Arabsat is a case in point. In 1976 a grouping of Arab countries established the Arab Satellite Communications Organization (ASCO). ASCO is thus made up of 22 members all drawn from the Arab world, including Algeria, Jordan, Kuwait, Saudi Arabia, Syria, the United Arab Emirates and the Yemen. The purpose of the organization was to find ways of meeting the increasing communications needs of the Arab world. In 1985, ASCO launched the Arabsat satellite system to provide for better communications and exchanges within the Arab world. However, the system is 'debt-ridden' and considerably under-utilized. One estimate is that 'it is utilized to only 40% of its total capacity', a fact which is in no small way related to 'Egypt's suspension [in 1979] from the Arab Telecommunications Union because of its dealings with Israel' (Wilson, 1990: 328). Though Egypt has since rejoined the Union, it still remains the case that religious, political and moral differences within the Arab world have made exchanges of, say, television programmes and films difficult (see Hudson, 1990: 187–9). Other regional systems such as the Palapa, linking Indonesia, Malaysia, Thailand, Singapore and the Philippines, and the Morelos satellite launched by Mexico, appear to suffer from similar problems of under-utilization. Part of the reason lies in cultural and religious differences between countries which prevent free exchanges of content, but there are other severe problems arising out of the lack of earth stations for picking up the signals and the absence of a high level of penetration of basic telephone services (see Table 3.2).

These differences in utilization, prospects and use notwithstanding, it remains the case that there has been a proliferation of satellite facilities and services in the last two dozen years. The capacity of the systems has also increased. Hudson's figures point to a 700-fold increase in the level of full-time international traffic carried by Intelsat between 1965 (Intelsat's first year of operation) and 1987. As for capacity, she notes that whereas Intelsat I (Early Bird) 'had 240 telephone circuits, Intelsat VI has the capacity for 40,000 voice circuits, or more than 200 television channels' (Hudson, 1990: 146).

The use of satellites for television traffic is perhaps the most obvious feature of the 'revolution' in communications in recent years. This traffic is carried on the 147 or so active satellites currently in geo-stationary orbit (Wilson, 1990: 46) and this is partly reflected in the explosion in the numbers of television services delivered by satellite, particularly across Europe. Whereas in 1988 one could identify around 35 to 40 satellite-delivered services across Europe, by 1993 that figure stood at nearer 130 (*Screen Digest*, May 1993: 105; *Cable and Satellite Europe*, September 1993). Not surprisingly, many of these services use imported material, usually but not always from the United States. Though detailed breakdowns are notoriously difficult to construct, and very recent ones are unavailable, *Screen Digest* felt secure enough in its analysis to note that of the 122 new television services started in the last decade, the vast majority of these being satellite-delivered services, only four 'claimed to have no imported material, one has two per cent and three have 10 per cent imports'. But, as it pointed out, 'as many as 75 per cent of new services rely on imports to fill at least half their screen time . . . almost half of new services use imports for upwards of 80 per cent of their output' (*Screen Digest*, 1992: 40).

The implications of this for cultural and political sovereignty, and cultural integrity in the European context, have been widely discussed elsewhere, as well as in the context of the Council of Europe and the European Commission (see, for example, Negrine and Papathanassopoulos 1990; Schlesinger, 1991; Sepstrup, 1991). Interestingly, similar changes and concerns have also been identified in relation to the development of satellite services in the Pacific region. Rupert Murdoch's take-over of the Hong Kong-based Star TV on Asia Sat in 1993 not only increases his control of media operations world-wide, but also allows him to enter markets to which he had previously had no access. Asia Sat's footprint covers some 38 nations from Egypt to Japan and from Indonesia to Siberia: a diverse collection of nations which operate different regulatory systems to direct the development of their domestic media. But with the advent of Asia Sat, the sometimes restrictive practices and broadcasting regulations operated by some countries, for example Korea and China with respect to satellite television reception, may need to be adapted to meet the challenge of programming from the Murdoch satellite system. Will they permit their citizens to install dishes to view broadcast material from outside and so risk the danger of exposure to undesirable influences? Will they seek compromises with satellite operators so as to minimize points of conflict *vis-à-vis* content? And how will they generally cope with the media 'explosion'?

The exploitation of satellite communications by commercial interests parallels the exploitation of other communications facilities. In this respect, the concerns of commentators such as Schiller and Nordenstreng are not misplaced since they point to the ways in which the less developed countries are unable to make a significant impact on the development of international systems of communications. Though such countries are able to exert pressure on decision-making bodies like the International Telecommunications Union (ITU), they lack the means by which to alter the agenda, an agenda set by commercial bodies.

Writing about the latest round of meetings to determine world allocations of radio frequencies, Liching Sung observed that WARC-92

> was more heavily influenced by commercial concerns than any other radio conference at the ITU (International Telecommunications Union). It was the first such conference wherein commercial interests and private sector initiatives dominated the issues addressed. The increased role that the private sector plays in telecommunication policy making largely reflects the global telecommunications and privatization trends. (Sung, 1992: 625)

Indeed, any description of current developments in international communication supports this view. The next section identifies some of the contemporary changes which are re-fashioning the world of communications.

The promise of the new

One of the easiest ways of making sense of contemporary developments in national and international communications is by utilizing Noam's idea of 'plural networks'. Thus, a company's head office may want to communicate with its subsidiaries across the globe; companies may wish to communicate with their clients speedily across the globe; banks may need to transfer data to other banks swiftly; and academics may want to contact others in other continents. Such examples can be multiplied yet they all emphasize two things: the existence of functional relationships for the heavy users of communication networks, and the diminution of the importance of delivering universal services to everyone.

While it is comparatively simple to plan for a universal network providing basic communications for all, the prospect, and the advent, of 'plural networks' is problematic: they cannot be planned for in advance.

Their development depends on many factors, including pricing, the availability of appropriate technologies, individual and company demand, and the like. One response to this regulatory dilemma – and it is a response implicit in the liberalization philosophy of the 1980s – has been to let the market decide the pattern of developments.

According to the consultancy discussion paper *Evolution of the United Kingdom Communications Infrastructure*, produced for the British government, 'developments in basic communications technologies are driven by *world-wide* trends, and that cost trends are driven by *world-wide* production volumes of which the UK forms only a small part' (PA Consultancy, 1987: 10). Indeed, there may be cost disadvantages in any one particular country 'going it alone': such an action may, in fact, be undesirable, since it may be too costly, it may lead to incompatibility, and it may close foreign markets to domestic producers. Although this is not quite a full return to Adam Smith's 'hidden hand' of the market, there is a sense in which this assumption plays with the notion of global trends narrowing available options in part by setting international technical standards, and dictating the pace of change. Yet, as the discussion paper also admits, 'global trends' are related to developments in specific, and powerful, producer countries which can effect changes by, say, shifting the scale of investment in specific technologies (PA Consultancy, 1987; 14). Japan, which produces most of the world's fax machines, is thus in a critical position.

Many of these factors are at play in the evolution of the mobile telephone. The mobile phone provides flexibility and mobility to all those who need to be in permanent contact with a specific base, or a clientele. Although it was a crucial accessory to the 1980s 'Yuppie', particularly if he/she was working in a financial institution, it soon spread across into other areas. There are currently some two million mobile phone users in the United Kingdom – 23 million world-wide (Taylor, 1993: 11) – and it is estimated that this will increase to 5.6 million, or 10% of the population, by the year 2000 (Bannister, 1993: 11) (see Table 3.4).

But it is short-sighted to conceive of the mobile phone only as a fashion accessory or as merely providing greater flexibility. The mobile phone represents an important shift in the nature of communications away from fixed connections. According to Paul Taylor, '[B]y the end of the decade half of all telephone calls world-wide are expected to originate or terminate on a mobile phone' (Taylor, 1993: 11).

This not only has significant implications for technical standards world-wide, but it also impacts on thinking about the provision of communication facilities for the future. As regards the former, it is interesting to note that European telecommunications organizations have agreed upon a common digital telecommunications standard (GSM) which will permit mobile communications across the continent. As regards the latter, it is now possible to conceive of an enormous expansion of mobile communication which side-steps the need for a full-wired network. Indeed, one project currently being developed by the American company Motorola, and named

Table 3.4   *Cellular telephones (per 1,000 population)*

Country	
Sweden	58
Norway	49
Finland	46
Iceland	20
Denmark	29
United Kingdom	19
France	5
Belgium	4.5
Netherlands	5.5
Germany	4
Italy	6
Spain	2.5
Portugal	1

Source: *Financial Times*, 19 June 1992, p. 14.

Iridium, proposes to use a series of low earth orbit satellites (Leos) to provide a global mobile telecommunications network. The benefits of such a system for less developed countries which do not have an existing wired network are obviously great.

The mobile phone, like the fax machine – currently with an installed base of some 20–30 million (Harnett, 1992: 7) – and the 'plural networks', all belong to a compendium of change which has provided flexibility of communications for, in the first instance, the business community. Other interests, like the academic community, have hung on to the coat-tails of these developments.

A roster of names and systems easily illustrates the greater flexibility which has become standard for the well connected. These include:

- Electronic mail which allows for communication via computer, wire network and satellites.
- Value added networks (VANs) which combine telecommunications and computing facilities to resell services by, say, processing data.
- Video conferencing.
- Electronic data interchange (EDI), allowing companies to have immediate access to all transactions across their branches.
- Virtual private networks (VPNs) which have the semblance of a private communications network but which are based on leased circuits. Companies can thus link up with their subsidiaries without having to create and install their own private network.
- Very small aperture terminals (vsats) represent the creation of private satellite communications networks whereby signals are received and transmitted via small terminals installed by specific corporations. Such systems of communication by-pass the PTTs which usually regulate

or control the uplinking of signals to satellites. One example would be the use of vsats by Volkswagen to connect all its dealers in different countries.

While each of these represents technical developments which allow for greater communication flexibility, underlying them is a pattern which reinforces the view that systems of communication are fragmenting in ways which mirror or 'connect' functioning groupings. Whereas twenty years ago, every communication had to be made via the public network, today it is possible to make connections in a number of different ways. In this respect, the role of the traditional centralized posts and telecommunications entity as a gatekeeper is not only under attack but under threat.

Conclusion

Developments in communications technologies have undoubtedly introduced numerous facilities which, to many, are now both useful and commonplace. From the electronic mailing system to the mobile phone, the fax machine to the very small aperture terminal (vsat), the new technologies have brought about newer, more flexible and speedier systems of communication. Those who are able to benefit from them will no doubt shed no tears for the old monopolistic posts and telecommunications entity.

None of these changes, however, overcome the full set of problems identified earlier with respect to the disparities in communications. For those with full access to telecommunications facilities, these developments clearly extend their reach. But they are still beyond the reach of the rural dwellers, the poor and those who simply cannot afford to participate in the computer and communications revolutions and who, as a result, cannot 'connect' with others. They are also out of the reach of those post-communist European countries who want to develop their telecommunications networks but lack the finance to do so. Dowler's comments on Eastern Europe are relevant to other countries also: 'the general case for modernising telecoms in Eastern Europe is . . . irrefutable. It is in the ways of achieving this aim that problems lie' (Dowler, 1992: 43).

By the year 2000, it is likely that many, if not most, of the hitherto publicly controlled and publicly run systems of telecommunications will move into the private sector and that the rules which govern them become progressively more liberal. The competition between system providers and service providers will become ever-more intense and there will be a continuing fragmentation of systems and services away from universal provision and to more specialized uses. But the detailed pattern will be, as always, complex, depending on the nature of the system. National and international systems of communication, be they telephone or television, will continue to exist as almost basic fare, alongside ever-more sophisticated technologies such as mobile systems of communications, or sophisticated and selectively available content such as music, films, news.

And as the state gives up its control over the patterns of development of such systems, the decisions about emerging technologies will be made by those who can benefit most from them rather than perhaps by those who have most need of them. In other words, one can expect the communications technologies discussed in this chapter to develop within a world system where the 'logic of capitalism' and the market reign (almost) supreme.

In the meantime, just as the less developed countries look enviously at the communications infrastructure of the West, so too does the Polish peasant look at the Polish entrepreneur or television producer who, clutching a mobile phone, can conduct conversations with colleagues around the world.

Further questions

1 What are the major consequences of a superhighway of communication on society?
2 Negrine suggests that by the year 2000 telecommunications will move towards the consolidated private sector. Do you agree? If yes, please explain why. If you disagree, discuss giving detailed reasons.

4

Communication and the Globalization Process in the Developing World

Ali Mohammadi

The purpose of this chapter is to examine the rapid process of globalization, its impact on the countries of the developing world and the changes which have emerged in the communication and cultural policies of these countries. The main focus is not only on the evaluation of deregulation policy, but also on the flow of capital and the drastic changes in communication technologies in the seven most powerful industrial nations of the world. The endorsement of both private sector and interest groups as agents with an active political role is considered and, furthermore, the empowerment of international institutions, such as the International Monetary Fund and the World Bank, as mechanisms of control, is examined. In order to study the impact of these rapid changes since the 1980s, the case of Iran as a developing country is studied. The chapter concludes by focusing on modifications made to Islamic cultural policy to accord with globalization processes, and some assessment of the contradictory impacts of the globalization of communications on developing countries.

> As the global plan advances, it increasingly demands a global depoliticization. Otherwise, the protests of the suffering majority may become too insistent. Our decoy politicians are the agents of such depoliticization. Not necessarily by choice, but by compliance. They accept the global market's projection concerning the future as if it were a natural law, instead of examining it for what it is. (Berger, 1995b: 4)

Since 1980, when the idea of involving the private sector in public matters became a crucial issue in Anglo-American media, the application of deregulation policy paved the road for the globalization process. In this context communication technology was accelerated faster than other sectors of the economy to dominate the world market. Deregulation policy had the effect of unleashing capital and allowing it to flow to markets that offered a minimum of government interference, better tax incentives and increasingly more profits. In other words, the transfer of capital no longer recognized nation-state boundaries in its constant drive for profit (Hills, 1994).

The period of deregulation during the 1980s

The concept of privatization stemmed from corporate America during the Reagan Administration. Market deregulation was pushed forward with the full support of the Thatcher government in the United Kingdom, and, through negotiation, with other industrialized nations. This finally achieved the 'free flow' of capital and effectively removed government boundaries from the world of global finance. At the same time, the flow of technology and its attendant forms of knowledge became the focus of the seven industrial nations (Hills, 1986).

The reduction of government intervention as a significant factor in businesses, especially in relation to their success or failure, holds a special place in the history of the United States' economy. The doctrine of deregulation has been successfully applied in the fields of banking, aviation, telecommunications and broadcasting for many years (Hills, 1986). However, the major vehicle of the success of the private sector was the full application of communication technologies, for example, the satellite linking of telephones and the expansion of the international computer network. For instance, the use of innovative communication technology by the New York financial markets has led to about US$180 billion being transferred and an estimated 50 trillion transactions being performed annually. This represents 96% of all financial transactions and asset movements (Spero, 1986).

In addition to the above, deregulation policy has led to the formation of a coalition between the conservative elements in the seven industrial nations. The Western Europeans and Japanese, however, had an experience and understanding of trade that was not tied to the doctrine of the free market. In Japan (like many developing countries), bureaucracy is regarded as more respectable than business, while in the United States it has totally different connotations. Thus, in the majority of Asian countries, the concept of 'we' is more important than that of 'I'. However, in the United States, the liberal approach highly valorizes the sovereignty of the individual consumer. The rhetoric of the 'freedom and liberty' of the individual is equated with the freedom of the market (Dizard, 1985; Hills, 1986).

Communication technology: a powerful tool for the globalization process

Rapid deregulation policy and the development of computer technology, including developments in broadcasting communications, formed a powerful tool in the globalization process. This has resulted in the domination of world markets by transnational corporations which face very little competition or resistance due to their overwhelming market force. Now multinationals based in the industrialized world have access to all parts of the world. It is estimated that the basic telecommunications equipment market of the South is at least $90 billion. The developing countries, with 71% of global population, possess only 17% of global GNP and a mere 7% of the existing stock of telecommunications resources, which are crucial for access to computer-based global markets and banking. The potential for the multi- and transnational corporations of the seven industrial nations to expand into the developing countries, and reap benefits, is enormous (Jussawalla et al., 1986). Table 5.5 on page 95 shows how extensive and vast the world communication market is. Based on 1992 statistics, the total estimated market is about $6 trillion and $200 billion.

Major changes in world trade and the increased accessibility to markets in the Third World were the outcome of the movement towards deregulation. Between 1980 (the starting point of deregulation) and 1992, the US market share in film and video in the European Community alone increased from 42% to 75% (*Screen Digest*, 1992). Such consequences of the deregulation process not only benefit the US government and businesses, but are also in the interests of the G7 group of nations as a whole. Realization of the objectives of deregulation reduced the ability of governments to interfere in private investment. It also served as a persuasive means of encouraging local firms to take advantage of expanding markets and become global corporations. Further, deregulation also set the agenda for the reorganization of public firms, placing them in the hands of private investors. Transnationalization has been 'a significant trend in the shaping of the world economy, becoming the driving force in recent years for global privatization' (Martin, 1993: 30). In Chapter 6 of this book there is a clear indication that globalization is proceeding without any resistance. The new transnational corporations have 'devised globalized strategies' in order to have control over the world market.

The conservative governments of the seven industrial nations introduced monetarist policies that regarded any socialist public sector policy as problematic for privatization. These policies were hailed as vital for economic recovery. Attempts were made to maximize private control of all economic sectors and to eradicate any socialist policy or article from the constitution and statutes of national governments. Budhoo, one of the IMF officials, resigned from the IMF. In his letter of resignation he referred to the Reagan Administration's recommendation of tough policies and its consequences towards developing countries as a clear indicator to 'go out and make the Third World a new basin of free-wheeling capitalism . . . toward this end we ignominiously created economic bedlam in Latin America and Africa in 1983–88' (Martin, 1993: 73).

Privatization or death as the name of the game of the Reagan/Thatcher prescription for the Third World

International institutions, such as the IMF and the World Bank, changed the entire policy of lending to the developing world. This resulted in a reduction of aid. The provision of aid was conditional on developing nations relinquishing economic sovereignty and adopting policies prescribed by the IMF and the World Bank. This actually meant

> a war being waged against the poor. Debt is enabling the rich to obtain from the poor what they might formerly have gained through the war. Since 1982, the world's poor have paid the rich some $450 billion over and above what they have received in aid, loans, etc. (Martin, 1993: 34; see also Mosley et al., 1991)

Deregulation also served to bring the influence of the private sector and interest groups into the active politics of government. The public sector was increasingly weakened and laws relating to monopolies and mergers were relaxed, allowing big companies to organize in global terms (Hills, 1986). The globalization process has resulted in the fact that 'eighty percent of foreign investment and seventy percent of world trade are controlled by 500 corporations that, between them, own 30 percent of the world's gross domestic product. They are mainly run from North America, Western Europe and Japan, and their profit returns to those places' (Martin, 1993: 30).

The criteria for accelerating privatization, described above, mean that companies can enjoy gains without frontier controls. As Martin clearly notes, '[T]his is about accelerating globalization in a way that further concentrates power and wealth with the already rich and powerful' (ibid.). A number of results by UNCTAD (UN Conference on Trade and Development) show that the consequences for some developing countries are devastating. It is not dissimilar to a 'garage sale' for favoured individuals, since some of the developing countries lack the solid infrastructure necessary for privatization. There are few detailed results on the success of privatized industry in the developing countries. The twelve case studies published by the World Bank from an inadequate representation, and their results, are of doubtful value (Martin, 1993).

Merging private and public was facilitated by the deregulation of advertising and the rapid development of communication technology. Advertising agencies are forming strategies that involve the global purchasing of media space (e.g. the emergence of McCann-Erikson as a world-wide company). They have developed sophisticated techniques to access the world's markets, including the development of commercial computer software. The McCann agency has invested in a new computer system that provides information on the audience reach and advertising rates of global media, country by country ('Organizing media deal', *New York Times*, 22 December 1986).

International computer networks are now an integral part of global communications – when an airline clerk makes a reservation for passengers in Warsaw or Tokyo, for example, their computer is connected to one in Atlanta where a large share of international flight reservations are stored (Dizard, 1985). Such technologies were first developed in the United States but other countries have been rapidly integrated. Strong communication networks are crucial for the United States in order to support its overseas interests. The export of communications goods and services is central for the question of development. The United States is very advanced in the communication sector. The expansion of world communication networks benefits multinational and transnational corporations based in the United States. World communication and information resources have been growing at over 15% a year in the last two decades (Carnoy et al., 1993; Dizard, 1985).

With the present rapid growth of communication sectors in the Western world, globalization is proceeding at an unprecedented speed. By examining the history of communications technology since the first commercial satellite was launched into space about thirty years ago, we can see that international trade in terms of exports and imports has increased from $293 billion to $7409 (IMF, 1988). World-wide ownership of television receivers has multiplied from 192 million in 1965 to 710 million in 1991 (A.S. Mohammadi, 1991). The summer Olympic Games were watched by 3.5 billion people around the world during 1992 and about 2 billion tuned into the World Cup in 1994.

Today, transnational corporations conduct about 70% of international trade; international capital markets process transactions worth around $75 billion per year (Jussawalla et al., 1986). Many of these transnational corporations are eager to overcome the telecommunications bottleneck. This would allow them to increase capital investment in the developing countries in order to expand their trade beyond the frontier settlement of mankind.

Some experts in the World Bank suggest that one way to reduce the North–South gap is to accelerate the development of telecommunications projects. This would definitely support transnational concerns. In China in 1985 the number of telephones in use was expected to grow from 5 million to 33 million by the year 2000. The expenditure for this project was estimated at over $30 billion (Dizard, 1985). The Tehranians, in Chapter 6, state that about one half of the world has less than one telephone per hundred people while over 71% of telephones are found in the rich countries. It is quite clear if this trend of expansion and hooking up to the telecommunications network was to continue in every country in the South, it would eventually stimulate the export of communications manufacturing goods from the North, thus benefiting the multinational and transnational corporations.

The most controversial area of Western information sales abroad involves the mass media – film, television, publications and news agencies. Most of the firms that are dealing with such cultural commodities are Anglo-American, but US mass culture is to be found all over the world, not only in film and television programmes but also in fast-food chain stores. The rapid expansion of communications goods and services by the United States, not counting products of the film industry, news, information and book trades, generates around $7 billion a year. This volume of trade in cultural commodities has set off alarm bells for cultural analysts around the world, particularly in the developing countries (Hamelink,

1994a). They have noticed that the United States has become a forceful instrument in establishing the First World cultural style (Dizard, 1985). It is important to note that the United States has become the major player in the business of international communications and information, its products ranging from manufacturing communication technologies to selling magazines, such as *The Reader's Digest*, all over the world. It is therefore clear to see why the US government is so concerned about the liberalization of the market. Since the early 1980s USAID and the State Department were advocates of the global privatization process and constantly sought to influence the World Bank, IMF, Inter-American Development Bank and other developmental finance agencies towards supporting a market-oriented privatization approach (George, 1989). Hills (International Association for Mass Communication Research, 1994) indicates that a push for privatiz- ation policy by the seven industrial nations was aimed at benefiting the demands of the North for increased access to export capital and goods to the South. She writes, 'Following the Gulf War and the crumbling of the Soviet bloc, the New International Economic Order is primarily about economic rather than military power and about the integration of a global capitalist market system' (Hills, 1994: 12). As a consequence of market liberalization and the enforcing of a privatization doctrine, the flow of capital has risen from 20% per annum (approximately $52 billion) to $133 billion by the beginning of the 1990s (Hills, 1994). And the World Bank is anxious to give loans to developing countries. The question arises, who will be the real beneficiaries of such investment? The alliance between multi- national corporations, local companies and powerful Western-oriented individuals in the developing countries serves the interests of the World Bank because privatization is a feature of the structural adjustment which is a prerequisite of World Bank loans (Martin, 1993; Mosley et al., 1991).

During the 1980s and early 1990s, the conservative governments of the major industrial countries, particularly the United States and the United Kingdom, were forced to cut public expenditure and borrow heavily from the private money markets. In order to control inflation they had to raise domestic interest rates, with the effect that productive investment was squeezed out. A rigorous insistence on monetary policy leaves a government facing a deficit with little choice other than to print more money and this risks increasing inflation. Over a decade of implementing monetary policy in the United States and the United Kingdom has left the two advocates of the free market in billions of dollars of debt. As a result, US monetary policy lost public support. Japan experienced a change of government and, in the rest of the industrial nations, the future of monetary policy is uncertain.

The privatization process in the developing world

Advancement of deregulation in the Third World and the former Soviet bloc, have often produced extraordinary results. In Eastern Europe, the black marketeers tried to legitimize and increase their ill-gotten gains. For example, in the Czech Republic in just one night a local entrepreneur made $600 million and took control of fifty-one firms. In order to increase the value of his holding, and based on USAID expert advice, he had to sack about one-third of his employees. In Mexico just thirty-seven local businessmen purchased one thousand enterprises. According to the World Bank report, foreign shareholders made about $12 billion out of the sale of Mexico's telecommunications industry. Then they increased telephone tariffs in order to add to the value of their assets. Such gains were made at the expense of the everyday users, the Mexican people (Martin, 1993).

The lack of any capitalist infrastructure or property rights in the Soviet bloc had a drastic impact on the emerging market economy in Russia, and the parliamentary election results showed the shortfall of monetary policy in general, and the privatization process in particular.

The consequences of deregulation and the free movement of capital led the two major advocates of the free market to influence the World Bank and IMF to adopt a conditional lending policy, both as an instrument to influence the internal economic policy of the developing world and to push the private sector as an important player within the economy. It is important to look at the role of the World Bank and IMF in this context because they are the major international finance institutions and they are the main providers of finance services for the South.

The World Bank and IMF

First, we must examine the role of the World Bank and the IMF since the Second World War. Without doubt, the World Bank and the IMF have been the most important financial institutions that the international system has been able to create.

The World Bank, also known as the International Bank for Reconstruction and Development, was established to provide loans for major infrastructural investments for which private bank loans were not available. The purpose of the original founders of the World Bank and the IMF, which have to this day governed the international economy, was to:

- Prevent massive unemployment in the West.
- Avoid international chaos in world trade.
- Minimize the influence of the former Soviet bloc.
- Support the spheres of influence, competitive search for markets, competitive devaluation and protectionism of capitalism (Payer, 1982: 22)

Since its conception, the main objective of the IMF has been the establishment of stable exchange rates, the creation of confidence in reserve currencies and the division of access to loans for countries facing short-term deficits in their balance of payments (Torrie, 1984).

In general, both of these giant financial institutions were designed to make international capitalism work. Their major concern was the Western world, of course, but following deregulation policy and the promotion of private sectors,

> the World Bank during the 1990s played an important role in promoting the concept of privatization, particularly among the developing countries. Furthermore, the World Bank acts as a prime node in the network of capital export from the USA and other Northern countries, promoting foreign direct investment on condition that companies have the freedom to repatriate profits back to the North. Almost all loans to developing countries are dependent on those countries fulfilling the policy demands of the Bank – policy which requires a redistribution of resources within the country itself in favour of the interests of those who hold capital and in favour of the integration of that country into the world free market economy. (Hills, 1994: 14)

The Third World emerged slowly in the early 1960s as an entity with which the international financial institutions were to be concerned. The IMF, the World Bank and the General Agreement on Tariffs and Trade (GATT) all modified their objectives to help the development projects in the developing countries in the mid-1960s, but the Third World countries called the modifications inadequate (Girvan in Torrie, 1984). The highlights of the changes that the financial institutions made to accommodate the developing countries' concerns were the introduction of compensatory financing facilities and the low conditionality of short-term finance. These were not beneficial to the poor nations in the long term, but they provided a temporary relief that served to further strangulate them in the international finance web (Torrie, 1984).

The World Bank, the IMF and the United Nations system are all organized in such a way as to secure the interests of the leading developed nations. The charters of both financial institutions firmly safeguarded Western dominance, in particular through US voting power in both the IMF and the World Bank. As one commentator has put it, 'World Bank funding is perceived as linked to the possibility of a revival in US exports to the developing World' (Hills, 1994: 13). The United States has always had the largest number of votes in the World Bank, with about 20% of total votes, the United Kingdom is in second place with 7% of total voting power, ahead of Japan and Germany. The United States continues to influence the policies of the World Bank, including the national allocation of credits within the international financial community.

As a result of the development strategy forced upon the developing countries by the World Bank, regardless of their internal economic conditions, their income distribution became more dependent on international lending institutions. This was especially the case in the smaller countries of Africa and Asia (Torrie, 1984). In the early 1970s the World Bank leadership enshrined export-oriented industrialization policies in the developing world. In general, the approval of loans was linked to the changing of internal economic policy based on the World Bank economic prescriptions. These included the requirement that companies which exported 70% of their products were to be rewarded with the following:

1   Permission for 100 percent foreign ownership.
2   Permission to establish a lower minimum wage than in the rest of the country.
3   Tax exemption privileges.
4   Low rents for land and waters.
5   Provision of finance to support the company infrastructure.
6   Accelerating the depreciation of fixed assets.
7   Legislation prohibiting strikes and all other forms of industrial action (Torrie, 1984: 165).

In 1992, a UNDP (United Nations Development Programme) report noted that both the IMF and the World Bank had failed to fulfil their original purpose of using the rich nations' savings to provide fair loans to improve the living conditions of people in less developed countries. On the contrary, the main outcomes of a one-dimensional policy were tremendous economic problems for the developing world and the placing of enormous financial power in the hands of the world's international financial lending institutions. Consequently, the escalation of interest rates and the accumulation of the less developed countries' (LDCs) debts became a coercive instrument of power for those countries that have influence in the World Bank and IMF. In the early 1980s, for example, the World Bank adopted a conditional adjustment lending policy in order to stop debt crisis in the Third World and to avoid the problems of the previous policy.

> Policy based lending was a double edge sword by the Bank. One was to persuade developing countries to change their internal economic policy based on the prescription of the Bank advisors; or in another word, the recipient countries should get rid of any policy that may be prejudicial to development. Second, the nature of the loans were designed to protect and shelter special interest groups, rent-seekers based on the rhetoric of efficiency and competition in the market. (Mosley, et al., 1991)

The implications of policy-based lending were examined in a number of studies in Kenya, the Philippines and Ecuador. The results were alarming and suggested that implementation of the new lending policy always favours the developing country's export growth and external account. The evidence shows that in many developing countries the living standards of the poor have fallen sharply. The withdrawal of food subsidies had an inflationary effect on food prices and caused tremendous social and labour unrest, all of which are the direct result of World Bank interference in the economic management of recipient countries. Iran, in order to qualify for a World Bank loan, has had to reduce food subsidies. Since 1990, as a consequence of the World Bank conditional adjustment loan policy, food prices have increased eight times.

The role of the IMF in the world economy is to monitor and regulate the international payments system in order to maximize international trade and promote growth in the world capitalist economy. So far, the strategy of the IMF has been to monitor balance of payments with regard to the free market, private enterprise and the open economy. This strategy provides growth but not development. It is obvious that the economic strategy of the IMF is different from that of recipient governments – to implement IMF policy is to abandon government policy. Further, such policies lead to the creation of a dependent capitalist economy under the supervision of the IMF (Mosley et al., 1991). By careful examination of cases in the developing countries, it is quite clear, that both the IMF and the World Bank are market-orientated and favour private enterprise.

So far, neither World Bank nor IMF approaches have proved able to help eradicate poverty or to help development. For instance, the debts of the LDCs in 1973 were around US$100 billion, but, ten years later, had increased to nearly US$900 billion (Martin, 1993). As a consequence of the rapid increase, it had quite the opposite effect on the process of development of LDCs, such as Tanzania, Kenya and the Philippines.

Many other countries in Asia and Africa are also cases in point (Torrie, 1984). The Human Development Report (1992) indicated that 'the existing distribution of global opportunities offers inadequate resources to poor nations. But worse than this, it takes significant resources away from them through debt servicing. In 1983–89, rich creditors received a staggering $242 billion in net transfers on long-term indebted developing countries' (Martin, 1993: 34). Bank leaderships believe sound progress should be more concerned with reducing poverty in much of the Third World. So far, in absolute terms, the number of poor people has risen dramatically. The World Bank estimates that in the developing world in 1990 there were 1.1 billion people living in poverty, about 8% more than in 1985. At the same time, the Bank is simply unwilling to withdraw support from those countries where the leaders simply pocket official assistance and transfer the loan directly to their Swiss bank accounts. The ousted president of the Philippines was a case in point (*The Guardian*, 29 April 1993).

The World Bank is always keen to send a team of experts to the developing countries to evaluate potentially loan-worthy projects. After thorough evaluation of an applicant country's economic performance and flexibility towards World Bank recommendations, the Bank will determine the loan prospects. In recent years the World Bank's major support has gone to those countries who are ready to transform their economy, regardless of their internal constraint. The Bank is also very eager to finance telecommunication projects in Asia, Africa and Latin America. According to the Stern Report on 'The World Bank's role in fostering telecommunications development', the Bank provides two kinds of loan for developing countries – one on a guaranteed basis and the other on a softer long-term payback basis. Currently, around US$2 billion of investment goes to telecommunication projects every year. The conditions attached to loans can be summarized as follows:

> The state monopoly of telecommunications should be changed to private ownership, as is the case in many industrialized countries. If developments in global communication create a new demand, then the market should create new enterprises to respond to that demand. The World Bank further insists that developing countries should adapt their economic policy to attract foreign investors. The

endorsement of the private sector is of primary importance, alongside major adjustments in the infrastructure and policy sectors. (Stern, 1986)

From a careful examination of World Bank policy in the last two decades, there is no concrete evidence that telephone investment in any developing countries caused development (Sussman and Lent, 1991a). Also, the case of the Philippines clearly supports the claim that the World Bank is not actually concerned with the development of Third World countries. In the Philippines the Bank promoted and supported the private monopoly of telephone ownership, favouring the expanding business district, supporting users of TNC and benefiting the United States, Japan and British investors who control 65% of all international circuits (Sussman and Lent, 1991a). The US Administration and USAID both expressed concern that export should be made a prerequisite, thus ensuring that US exporters have access to areas previously outside the sphere of influence of the '"old" colonial powers' (Hills, 1994: 16). Since the 1990s, USAID officials would visit developing countries and constantly promote the idea of privatization in major public sectors of the economy, such as telecommunications, finance and energy, in order to respond to the need of an integrated economy in global terms (Martin, 1993). The ongoing trend in the World Bank indicates that the privatization of telecommunication has benefited foreign investors and the manufacturers of communication technology in the North, but, in contrast, has had no impact on poverty or the process of democratization in the South (Hills, 1994). As members of some of the LDCs are struggling for the basics of survival, communication is not one of their priorities.

Deregulation of telecommunications

The deregulation of telecommunications in the South was essential for the integration of the developing countries into Western markets. Free competition would lead to the domination of such industries by Japan and the United States. One of the most important elements of communication technology is the technology for transferring information. Companies in the business of communication technology are integrated with each other in terms of software and hardware. For instance, AT&T is more concerned with data processing, while IBM is generally concerned with information transmission. Also, various other agencies are in the same business, but are shifting towards the provision of services, such as Reuter (recently involved in providing news resources for the Murdoch television network) and the airline and banking industries. The largest users of communication services are the car industries, such as US General Motors, who have taken over the information technology sector (Hills, 1986). As a result of the deregulation of the telecommunication industries, the US market opened to allow a few companies to export to the United States, but, at the same time, it has brought pressure from IBM and AT&T to have access to the World's largest market. As discussed above, the United States is very advanced in the field of communication technology. For example, IBM is responsible for over 70% of the installed capacity in Europe. IBM also enjoys a monopoly of the global data processing market and, as a result, is able to impose its standards on the rest of the world. The United States is the major producer and consumer of semi-conductors in the world. In 1989 the United States produced $20 billion, and consumed nearly $18 billion of them, while the rest of the world, except Japan and Western Europe, produced only $2 billion and consumed under $7 billion (Carnoy et al., 1993). The United States is also the largest manufacturer of satellites and fiber optic equipment in the world. It was always eager to have access to the global communications markets as computer and telecommunications exports are second only to agriculture in the balance of payments. Therefore, the transfer of international transmission markets from public to private control is in the political and economic interests of the United States.

The impact of globalization on the South

The impact of globalization on the South is crucially linked to privatization and the expansion of telecommunications. The developing countries represent an increasingly important market to transnational advertisers. This is mainly because their consumer activities are growing faster than those of industrial countries. The middle classes of the developing countries are expanding; in India, for instance, the constant growth of the middle class has resulted in 250 million new consumers. And the consumer markets have not yet been saturated with consumer goods. As a result, transnational advertisers are focusing on distributors and producers in these countries. Research has shown that the globalization of communication technology has played an important role as the key promoter of consumer goods throughout the developing countries. The bulk of media advertising is purchased by transnational firms to promote their products in these countries – firms such as Nestlé, Kodak, Kraft and processed food companies in general (Janus, 1984). As a consequence of the liberalization of the market, commercial advertising on television has increased rapidly. From 1976 to 1985 Italy experienced a 500% increase (Negrine and Papathanassopoulos, 1990).

So the globalization process has involved a boom in the advertising of consumer goods. This has created the incentive for countries in the South to develop their own television satellites or lease one and, in the worst cases, to accept the conditional loan policy of the World Bank.

As a result of satellite technology, video-cassette recording has been rapidly developed throughout the South, particularly in Latin America and the Middle East countries. As developing countries become a prime target of transnational advertising agencies, the important questions are:

- How can a sovereign nation protect itself from the penetration of persuasive consumer goods advertising?
- How can a government of the South keep up with the rapid changes in communication technology?
- How will the transnational corporations use the new technology to circumvent government restrictions on the commercial content of broadcasting?
- Is there any way to protect developing countries from entering into the global shopping centre and global consumerism? (see Mosco and Wasco, 1984).

In order to evaluate the impact of globalization clearly on the LDCs, it is necessary to look at the impact of US-based transnational corporations in Western Europe as a case in point. In 1989 America started directly challenging the distribution of INTELSAT's global network costs by agreeing to the private construction of satellites. These privately owned satellites on transAtlantic routes will fulfil several functions: they will accrue increased contracts for American satellite manufacturers and operators; they will provide a cheap communication service for American multinationals and defence establishments in Europe; they will allow US cable programme companies to penetrate European markets; and, finally, this will allow US companies to enjoy the profits from the busiest communications route in the world, one which at present is shared with the developing countries. The entry of private satellites into this telecommunications market will challenge the Western European PTT (Post, Telegraph and Telephone) monopolies. For many years the FCC (Federal Communication Commission) has attempted to deregulate the international market using cable facilities, but so far most Europeans have resisted private cable companies.

However, satellite broadcasting is not so easy for PTTs to control – the liberalization of current markets, the increase in the numbers of private carriers and the integration of private transmission with American equipment would make it considerably more difficult for any European government to introduce a full publicly integrated service network (ISDN). Short-term US interests lie in penetrating the markets of countries that have agreements with IBM and AT&T because of the technical compatibility and the benefits for the multinationals' digital network services. It is very hard to believe that IBM has been at the forefront of the movement for deregulation of telecommunications throughout the world. It is quite clear now that, as Hills puts it: 'the American efforts to release itself from the obligations of the INTELSAT treaty are in tune with its reduction in aid to the poorest countries, its growing protectionism, its withdrawal from UNESCO, its embargo of funding through the World Bank to those regimes with which it disagrees, and its imposition of strict monetarist policies on Third World debtor countries through the IMF' (Hills, 1986: 201).

Today, two-thirds of world telephone systems are owned by the nine major industrial countries. The other one-third are distributed unevenly. Originally, the interests of the industrialized and less industrialized countries seemed to coincide in the spread of telephone connections. It is particularly in the interests of the developing countries faced with the problems of inaccessible regions, dispersed populations and low literacy to have access to cheap voice and image communications. Small high-powered satellites could provide the technology which requires only chicken wire as an aerial for television reception and one-way conversation. But the interests of industrialized nations lie in low-powered satellites, increasing the circuits each transponder can hold, or in providing high-power satellites with digital time division multiplexing, an expensive technology.

So far, the globalization of telecommunication technology has been:

> the cause of ISDN and deregulation, with the emphasis on the data rather than voice transmission, which in practice squeezes out the interests of two-thirds of the world community in favour of big business in the West. Deregulation in the international market is a move by the rich against the poor, by emphasizing data over voice communication. When data still represents only a small minority of all transmission, it favours major companies in the industrialized world. (Hills, 1986: 203)

The force of globalization 'shifts power away from the sovereign governments to private capital in whatever market it takes place'. But the easy world-wide free flows of data 'make the global market a reality to the benefit of the strongest' (Hills, 1986: 203). Globalization of the market caused the freedom of exchange rates and financial markets and, coupled with the development of private data networks, made it easier for money and information to shift around the globe and more difficult for governments to control their economies.

The emergence of mega corporations

Privatization of international markets concerns the distribution of world power, not only in terms of whether that power should rest with governments or private companies, but also whether or not that power should be located in the United States. As globalization is proceeding, the rest of the world is gradually being drawn into the competition emanating from the American domestic market – competition between satellites and optic fibers, competition between IBM and AT&T, competition between private companies and European PTTs and competition between private companies and some of the developing countries' PTTs.

One of the crucial questions here concerns who will benefit from all of this competition, particularly if the access to electronic communication is restricted and information is in the hands of the private sector. As a consequence of the deregulation and market liberalization during the early 1990s, ten huge corporations emerged from the rapid mergers in the North and most of them are US- or Western European-based. Time-Warner Inc. is the largest corporation in the world. Its major business is information and cultural commodities, and it has subsidiaries in Australia, Asia, Europe and Latin America. When the two corporations Warner Brothers and Time merged, they became the leading information and entertainment corporation in the world.

It is roughly estimated that there are over 600 million televisions world-wide and this number is increasing every second. Since 1990 the new commercial channels demanded at least 500,000 hours of television programming every year (Middle East Broadcast Satellite, 1994). In the United States, every commercial channel can broadcast about 720 commercials a day. The expansion of US commercial television world-wide is inevitable because of the political power of multinational advertising agencies and the influence of the private sector. This will eventually help in the development of world-wide commercial television (Bagdikian, 1989).

At the moment, the shift towards commercial television in European countries is increasing very rapidly, particularly with the emergence of the media moguls in Western Europe commercial television. For example, the Murdoch family holds 37% of UK/US/Australia News Corporation; the Mohn family holds 89% of Bertelsmann in Germany; the Berlusconi family holds 100% of Fininvest in Italy; and the Marlis family holds over 50% of Hachette in France (Negrine and Papathanassopoulos, 1990). On cultural grounds, Schlesinger (1994) has indicated that the domination of the image factory known as 'Hollywood' has hastened the tendency to Americanization as a 'threat to European culture'. US audio-visual imports to Europe are US$3.7 billion, far beyond what European countries export to the United States. There is no doubt that domination of US cultural goods and the rapid trend of commercialization will eventually influence the media policy of Europe and of developing countries. They have little choice, if this trend continues, but to adopt a commercial policy and privatize sectors which have previously been under government control. These trends are expanding rapidly and the impact of commercialization of culture in Europe is alarming now.

In order to examine the impact of globalization on the Third World, it is important to look at one developing country to see how the policy-makers resist and adapt policy and how desperately confused they often are about the influence of 'know how' and the penetration of Western culture as a force of global market expansion. For this reason a case study of the cultural dilemmas of one Islamic country – the Islamic Republic of Iran – is important.

Iran in the age of satellite communication

Iran is one of the developing countries which is reluctantly going to allow private companies to produce film and television serials. They are doing this so as not to lose audiences to international television systems which are broadcasting their programmes via satellite. The satellite which carries international television broadcasting is part of INTELSAT, which is composed of representatives of governments of INTELSAT's member countries. These representatives normally meet every two years and the meeting includes all the investors in INTELSAT, either the member governments themselves or their designated telecommunications entities. The Board of Governors is largely composed of those representatives of INTELSAT who are the major users of the system. They are responsible for all decisions concerned with the design, development, construction, establishment, operation and maintenance of INTELSAT. About 117 countries were members by 1988, and this number is gradually increasing. The Executive Organ, with an internationally recruited staff, is headquartered in Washington DC. The INTELSAT system consists of sixteen satellites in synchronous orbit at an altitude of approximately 35,780 km over the Atlantic, Indian and Pacific Ocean regions. Earth stations' facilities consist of over 243 international communications antennas at 173 station sites in over 146 countries, dependencies and areas of other special sovereignty. Together with the satellites located above each of the three major ocean regions, these are providing over 1,107 earth station-to-earth station communications pathways. Now, INTELSAT is providing satellite facilities for more than 30,000 full-time voice and data circuits during the year and over 26,000 scheduled television transmissions. The demand for television transmission is increasing as a consequence of rapid globalization of the television broadcast industry (INTELSAT Annual Report, 1988).

Iran became a member of INTELSAT in 1969, using satellite for international communication, particularly to support existing microwave systems, broadcasting and telecommunication. In the early 1970s, when the Iranian National Radio and Television was established (radio started in Iran in the 1940s but in the 1970s joined with the newly established national television), the demand for satellite, both for the expansion of telecommunication and for the use of television broadcasting, became crucial. At this time a series of questions were raised about the developmental use of satellites in enhancing communication in transitional societies.

Iran as a transitional society

In the early 1970s Iran became a focus for the discussion of issues of rapid development in some Western universities. The debate on dependency and Westernization became a hot issue among communication scholars at that time. Satellite technology was an especially controversial issue, particularly in the mid-1970s. The developments in satellite applications in communication systems, since their beginnings in the mid-1960s had ushered in new possibilities as well as pitfalls for development strategists in the Third World in general, and in Iran in particular.

To be potentially effective in promoting development for those who will use these systems in the developing world, Third World media planners have to take into account some key questions:

- The dependence on Western hardware and software.
- The existence of traditional systems in the transitional society.
- The target/participants of the development strategies – that is, development for whom and what sector.
- The social, political and economic resources available for the incorporation of these new media into the transitional society.

By the mid-1970s, communication and development planners in Iran had become aware of the potential of satellite communication for development. It was at this time that Stanford University was helping Iran with a feasibility study on the use of satellite communication, not only for the development of education and health services but also for the expansion of broadcasting and telecommunication. There were, of course, major problems to be faced. The first problem was the intense competition between the newly established National Iranian Radio Television (known as NIRT) and the Ministry of Post, Telegraph and Telephone (PTT). NIRT was the more progressive organization because it had a very dynamic and competent leadership. NIRT was assigned by the government to do a feasibility study about the software and hardware development that was required for the satellite project, in cooperation with Stanford University. When the NIRT/Stanford study reported, the Iranian government decided that the issue required further study. The problem, understandably, was which satellite technology to choose. The government had (and still has) no science and policy-making study group. The field of satellite communication is not only very complex and advanced, but is also under the monopoly of a handful of companies which compete fiercely for advancing and improving satellite technology. These companies also strongly compete for the sale and leasing of satellite transponders to the developing countries. Finally, the Iranian government was not able to select the right technology. It decided to give a contract to General Electric for a 'know-how' analysis of tailor-made satellite technology based on Iran's present and future telecommunication and broadcasting needs.

After the Iranian revolution in 1979, Iran lost her place as a favourite nation in the shopping list of US corporations because of her anti-US stance. Furthermore, there was confusion and indecision among US foreign policy-makers towards the Islamic Republic, which was listed as an unfriendly government and subject to a US economic embargo. In these circumstances, the Iranian government was not able to continue her ambitious satellite project. Meanwhile, various other problems arose, such as the invasion by Iraq and the rapid migration of highly skilled workers to the United States.

The satellite project, like so many other development projects, came to a halt until the mid-1980s, when the first and the most important satellite earth station in Iran was bombed by Iraq. The Iranian government was in great need of satellite communication, not only for telecommunication purposes but also for broadcasting, which was vital during the war with Iraq. The newly established broadcasting authority known as VVIR (Voice and Vision of the Islamic Republic) urgently required broadcasting facilities and leased a transponder from the INTELSAT on a yearly basis.

The period of US policy shift

From the mid-1980s, US satellite policy also dramatically changed and endorsed competition within the INTELSAT system. Private companies began to compete for providing a cheaper and better service than those of INTELSAT, which was shared among 110 nations, providing services for 170 countries (Commercial Satellite Report, 1988). Some Third World countries became interested in buying a tailor-made satellite.

Such decisions raise major issues for Third World countries. The foremost consideration of any technology, including satellite communication, is whether it will serve as a healthy means of social innovation or a destructive and oppressive means of societal domination and control. Here the question of dependency cannot be ignored because one source of dependency problems is the importation of a foreign technology into a cultural environment where the values are at variance with those of the exporting country. The bias of the technology itself is complicated by the inability of the new environment to put the technology to use with its own software. The importation of technical/hardware leads to a need for compatible software. This in turn creates cultural dependency and, crucially, encourages cultural imperialism. Therefore, the ability to produce software for the technology, like television programming for satellite transmission, as well as the control to assure its distribution (i.e. ownership of the means of distribution) are the primary considerations for the successful utilization of satellite transmission.

As a result of the 1985 FCC decision, seven major satellite companies – Orion Satellite Corp., International Satellite Inc., RCA, American Communications, Cygnus Satellite Corporation, Pan-American Satellite and Financial Satellite – were established for commercial purposes. The FCC decision was based on a policy consideration of the Reagan Administration regarding the promotion of free trade in order to realize the US goals of further competition and market liberalization. This process involved nothing less than the privatization of Space.

Considering the impact that this would have, Demac (1986) correctly poses the following questions, particularly in the context of the developing World.

1   Does the surge of commercial activities imply a drain of capital away from Europe and the developing countries into the USA?
2   Is unlimited competition required to produce the highest cost efficiencies?

3 What commitment do the private investors have in global connectivity?
4 What signs are there that private interests will offer affordable rates to developing countries?
5 What is the risk of bankruptcy, and what impact would this have on the overall economic climate for international telecommunications services?

Schiller (1996) also noted how the wealthy multinational corporations would benefit from privatizing space because they have no allegiance or sovereignty to any nation or its people. They are privy to information and resources that are not available at the national level. The trend towards privatizing space gradually extends dependency and underdevelopment further and deeper into the Third World. As a developing country and the user of satellite services, Iran has no choice except to continue leasing the transponders or to finance a tailor-made satellite based on the needs of the country. All this would be according to availability and to the desires of the masters of communication technology.

The Venus Project

During the eight years' war with Iraq, a war that was supported by the West, particularly by the UK, US and French governments, the Iranian government was not able to finance a satellite project, because its priority was the immediate needs of war machine, refugees and war damage. When the war came to a halt at the end of the summer of 1988, the Iranian government again decided to study the satellite project. The then Ministry of PTT established a new office with a group of engineers who, however, were only to analyse satellite technology in order to determine what kind of satellite Iran should purchase from the international satellite market. (As already noted, this was with no critical appraisal of what was being studied and without the support of a national science and policy group.)

This project was called the 'Venus Satellite Project', and carried an estimated cost of about US$700 million. Two consulting agencies, one Italian and one French, helped Iran to develop a tailor-made satellite. This project was supposed to be ready by 1995, when the Iranian satellite 'Venus' was to be launched into orbit by the European space agency. It was estimated to have 120,000 channels for telephone, telex, teleconferencing, transmission of data and television broadcasting. In the first stage, the Venus satellite was to provide services to fifty-one rural areas and five urban areas in the five provinces of the country. The second stage of the Venus satellite, with the use of a second satellite was to be ready during this period, a number of earth stations which had been built in order to fulfil Iranian communication needs (Venus Report 1991).

As a consequence of the devastating eight-year war with Iraq and the economic embargo by the United States and its Western allies, major telecommunication projects with US-based companies had to be postponed. Some companies cancelled their contracts with Iran.

Since 1988 the Iranian government has started to follow the development projects of the previous regime without the help of foreign consultants. Companies have been faced with the hardship of finding necessary hardware at inflated prices and without enough technical 'know-how'. The Ministry of PTT is now far behind the demands of today's market at a time of rapid development in communication services. Iran, with a population roughly over sixty million in 1995, had only four million telephones, and there is increasing demand. PTT, however, has been able to decrease waiting lists from five years to three years in the urban areas, and increase the capacity of the telephone services by one million. Consequently, there are now five million telephones in use in the entire country. PTT's aim is to double this number in the next five-year development plan (1994/95–1999/2000). As a consequence of the communication technology explosion and rapid globalization of communication and information technology, PTT will be able to provide services for up to 10,000 mobile telephones in the first stage.

However, with the present population growth rate of 2.97% and the extensive expansion of housing and urban development, the growing demand of telephone services will be much higher than PTT had previously estimated. At the present time, the demand is four times more than what is currently available. In the area of broadcasting, Iran is struggling to keep up with the rapid mode of development in the region. Technological change in the form of satellite, computer-based information technology and, most crucially, the liberalization of the market and market forces, altogether allowed the expansion of television programmes as well as other cultural commodities such as books, music disks, cassettes and video tapes.

During the previous regime, Iranian National Radio and Television was the second largest broadcasting institution in Asia; however, after the revolution in 1979, because of the devastating purge with its enforcement of an Islamic ethic and code of appearance and conduct in all aspects of life, the process of Islamization became a first priority. The outcome of this harsh process was undoubtedly to have a devastating effect on the quality of broadcast programmes on radio and television in particular, and throughout the media generally. The strict Islamization of popular culture included the enforcement of veil-wearing for women on television, tough censorship of film and television programmes and a drastic change in media content. Instead of promoting a progressive Islam (enforcement of social justice, re-distribution of wealth, national health and equal access to higher education) and supporting domestic programming, Islamization brought the whole development of radio and television to a halt. The new cadre of Islamic television and radio producers, having no background in radio and television production and lacking 'know-how', had also a drastic impact on the quality and quantity of television and radio programmes. Approximately 47% of radio and television employees are high-school graduates, with no experience or proper training in the industry (VVIR Report, 1994). The restriction of programme contents of radio and television and eventually the change of broadcasting policy resulted in people no longer wanting to use Islamic radio and television.

Clandestine video clubs

The continuation of control over Iranian people's ways of life has caused further resistance to the total Islamization of culture. Gradually, a few entrepreneurs started to develop underground video clubs in Tehran and major provincial capital centres throughout the country. Young high-school graduates who were living in the south or north-west of the country, started to make pirate video recordings of interesting films or television shows from neighbouring countries. These were further copied and hired out for a small fee to neighbours or friends. The business of video piracy gradually became a very lucrative business. Within a short period of time, it had developed to such an extent that the government unleashed a group of Bassijis in order to stop the penetration of Western culture into the Islamic Republic of Iran.

Originally formed in 1980 to help in the war with Iraq, Bassijis are groups of bearded men or boys between the ages of fourteen and twenty who are now fighting against Western culture and its effects on Islamic life in Iran. They have the authority to confiscate and arrest anyone who carries video-cassettes or audio-cassettes with Western contents. The sudden re-emergence of the threat of Bassijis crushed the hopes of many Iranians of an opening to the West after parliamentary elections removed extremist deputies who opposed the president and argued for free-market reforms. (*New York Times*, 21 July 1993).

The protection of Islamic culture by force

Since the establishment of the Islamic Republic in Iran, the major concern of the government was the protection of Islamic culture from Western influence. Consequently, the policy-makers of the Islamic Republic have employed various measures of cultural protectionism in order to halt the flood of Western cultural commodities. Surveys show that all of the harsh cultural measures of protectionism have failed – video piracy and the sale of illegal satellite dishes are booming to an extent that the government is not able to control. This is particularly the case in the 1990s since the expansion of television satellite broadcasting has increased the potential access to international television. Iranians now have access to 129 television channels (Sorush, 1993). People gradually became more aware of the availability of alternative entertainment channels, and at the same time the government failed to see that international television, with a variety of interesting programmes on one hand and easy access by satellite dish on the other, made connection to international television a lucrative business for black-marketeers. Cultural policy-makers of the Islamic Republic were not aware of the internationalization of television and the rapid technological change in television broadcasting around the world; but even if they had been aware, they would not have been able to exercise control over such television programmes.

It was when the Islamic government realized it was powerless that it started to employ various methods of coercion. The fundamentalist group in the Islamic Council Assembly (Majlis) persuaded the religious seminaries of the Holy City of Qom to ask senior religious leaders to ban the use of satellite dishes on the grounds that the content of the international television programmes was ill-suited to the Muslim people of Iran. Among all the religious leaders only the very old and fragile Grand Ayatollah Arakey issued a communiqué based on the information that the fundamentalist group made available to him about banning the satellite dishes.

After this smart move, banning satellite dishes became the duty of the Islamic Council Assembly (ICA) which decreed that watching international television was 'a sinful act'. In December 1994, the ICA, after a long debate in several sessions, finally made a law banning the import, manu-facture and the use of satellite dishes. Meanwhile, in an interview, the head of radio and television of the Islamic Republic indicated that the Voice and Vision of the Islamic Republic (VVIR) was in the process of monitoring between fifty and sixty channels of international television, in order to select and dub some for re-broadcasting, pending the successful negotiation of copyright permission. He also gave priority to the privatization of television programmes and indicated that he had agreed to more than 750 private television production groups.

Conclusion

It is interesting to see how the liberalization of the market and deregulation of telecommunication policy on one hand, and the accessibility of inter-national television on the other hand, have affected the cultural policy of supposedly the most restrictive Islamic country in the world. When we attend to concrete cases in this way, it is not easy to evaluate the complex gains and losses which are involved in the globalization of communications, especially for developing countries. Certainly, there is a risk to cultural sovereignty from the merchants of culture. The influence of mega media empires erodes the cultural boundaries of nation states and this creates alarm and defensive reactions. On the other hand, coercive cultural policies at the nation-state level are made harder to enforce in the circumstances of globalization. Did the cultural protectionism of the Islamic state fail because the unenforceable ban on international satellite television pro-grammes alienated so many people? So far, the implementation of the harsh cultural protection policy has produced a double-edged sword.

Beyond this, it is unclear what the impact of transnational media, particularly television, will be on the culture of the countries in the South.

A developed entertainment culture carried by mass media is often new there. We are living in a world dominated by 'cybersociety'; it is often hard to assess if this is good or bad, but, for sure, the erosion of (attempted) cultural control by central governments is inevitable. In itself this is ambiguous. If, in the late twentieth century, we are proceeding towards not only virtual reality but virtual democracy, then no government in the world is able to keep its people away from the influence of international media. At the same time transnationalization and systematic world-wide deregulation make it more difficult for nation states to develop progressive social and economic policies which benefit the majority of their populations.

Yet this is only one effect of the new transnational media. As this study has shown, the most substantial effect over and again is that the gap between the 'haves' and the 'have nots' increases day by day. Developments in international communication are, from this point of view, one of the most important ways in which the fortunes of the poorer people of the world are dominated by transnational capital. It is not the case that the international free market in communication technologies, cultural goods and media messages is to the benefit of all: in many ways the inequities of the world simply gain some new dimensions.

Further questions

1 How did deregulations change the government boundaries relating to the world of global finance, and who were the major forces behind the market theory during the 1980s?
2 Can you analyse the major impact of globalization on the South and summarize the emergence of the mega corporation in the line of liberalization of the market? Do you think globalization will eventually benefit developing nations?

Part III

THE NEW PARADIGM
AND GLOBAL MORALITY

In this section of the book two issues are addressed. First, why a morality for the global market, with its new players in international communications, is essential. Secondly, why, in the last decade of this century, there is a need for a new paradigm or discourse for the world order.

In the first chapter of this section, Hamelink demonstrates how world communication has developed into a fast-moving and expanding marketplace which is controlled by a limited number of mega corporations. The major players in international communication are more market-driven. Under capitalist conditions this should mean the delivery of information and cultural commodities to everyone. He suggests, however, that world communication should adopt a common standard of achievement to support its conduct. He concludes that this standard should be driven by the morality of human rights.

Prior to a discussion of human rights, it is important to look at the factors which have caused sudden changes in the world market. The major factor has been the deregulation of the public sector, particularly in the communication sector, making privatization inevitable. Gradually, this whole process has brought about globalization.

In the second chapter of this part, Tehranian and Tehranian look at the need for a new paradigm for international communication in the post-Cold War era. This is an era which has swung from euphoric optimism to dark pessimism. It has ranged from Francis Fukuyama's declarations of the 'End of History' and the triumph of liberal democracy to Samuel Huntington's thesis on the 'Clash of Civilizations' between the Christian West and a Confucian–Islamic alliance. Tehranians' chapter offers a deconstruction of that discourse as an ideological reproduction of the traditional geo-political strategies of struggle between deterritorialized centres and peripheries.

Tehranian and Tehranian provide us with an alternative reading of an emerging world dis/order caught in the contradictions of combined and uneven development in an increasingly fragmented world system. They argue that in the last 10,000 years, the processes of rationalization and modernization have progressively incorporated the entire globe in seven successive, interlocking phases, waves, or tsunamis, encompassing rural areas, cities, nation states, empires, the planet, cyberspace and the universe.

The contradictions of premodern, modern and postmodern societies and sensibilities have been particularly sharpened by the fifth and sixth modernizations, the latest phase in the transnationalization of the world economy, accompanied by exploding global communication, totalization of surveillance, democratization of politics at the semi-peripheries, and tribalization of identities at the peripheries. This has led to globalization of the local and localization of the global. Historically, resistance has assumed a variety of forms and movements, including hyper-modernization, de-modernization, counter-modernization, post-modernization.

The accelerating compression of time and space, characteristics of modernization, is now facing a critical choice between technocratic and communitarian formations at the local, national, regional and global levels. This critical choice calls for a new paradigm. Tehranian and Tehranian illustrate historically the uneven modernization process and suggest how to tame the forces of modernity for the fulfilment of human needs beyond the year 2000.

5

International Communication: Global Market and Morality

Cees J. Hamelink

The rapid expansion of global markets is beyond the control of nation states because the transactional power of communication technology has made multinationals and transnational corporations major players in the field of the world market. In this chapter, Hamelink considers the implications of the spread of market relations for the key moral and political issue of human rights. He juxtaposes a view of the contemporary movements towards globalization, privatization and deregulation with the corpus of rights established in various decisions of the United Nations. In this way, he focuses on the morality of global markets. 'How', he asks, 'do the belief in the market and the morality of human rights confront each other?'

In order to draw our attention to the level of commercial activities in communication products, he first provides a series of tables about the flows of entertainment, voice messages, data, e-mail and consumer electronic goods. The volume of sales and the profit figures are astronomical, especially in the field of mass media products and communication hardware and software. Hamelink also touches on issues of deregulation policy and the doctrine of liberalization of the world market, particularly in the field of communication technology and the cultural commodities sector. This provides the context for the main aim of this chapter – to focus on aspects of human rights as a requirement for civil society. How can we alert civil society to guard its rights to information and culture?

International communication: the field and the players

Since the end of the Second World War world communication has developed into a rapidly expanding field with a vast number of players. Although there are numerous individuals and institutions using cross-border communications for non-commercial purposes, the *pièce de résistance* of the field is commercial activity.

World communication encompasses a variety of flows of different messages. These cross-border flows can be sub-divided into the following.

1 *The flows of international news* that are carried across the globe by the *major players* for print news – Associated Press, Reuter and Agence France

Press – and for visual news – the two leading agencies the former Visnews, now Reuters Television, and World Television Network. Reuters Television supplies television news to over forty broadcasters in eighty-five countries and reaches almost a half-billion households. In 1993 the Reuters Holding (UK) had sales of US$2,831 million and profits of US$452 million. World Television Network (WTN) provides services to a hundred broadcasters in eighty-five countries with an audience of some three billion people. In 1994 there were serious speculations that Reuters was planning to acquire WTN, thus reducing the two major players to one market leader.

Second in line for international television news production and distribution are BBC World Service and CNN. CNN distributes around the clock to over 200 subscribers. On an average day 160 items are broadcast, of which about thirty are international. CNN is available in over 700 million households world-wide and thousands of hotels. The Turner Broadcasting System (the parent company of CNN which is 20% owned by the Time-Warner conglomerate) had sales of US$1,922 million and profits of US$72 million in 1993. In the course of 1993 the news agency Associated Press announced that it was ready to enter the television news market in 1994. APTV could become the most serious competitor for Reuters Television and WTN.

Other major players in the flow of news include some large newspapers with their syndicated news services, like the *New York Times, Los Angeles Times,* or *Washington Post,* and the publishers of international magazines such as *Time* and *Newsweek.*

2 *The flows of entertainment and education materials* which include recorded music, feature films, textbooks, and television entertainment. The major players are the world's largest entertainment media companies. Table 5.1 shows the twelve largest firms in 1994.

3 *The flows of promotional messages* which consist mainly of commercial advertising carried by international newspapers, magazines and broadcast media across the globe. The major players are the world's largest advertising agencies (Table 5.2).

4 *The flows of data,* as in electronic data exchange, electronic funds transfers, remote resource satellite sensing, electronic mail and database searches. These flows are carried by networks such as the Internet, by the provider of financial data services such as Reuters Information Services, or by such inter-firm networks as the largest interbank network SWIFT which is now operated by some 1,000 banks and links more than 2,000 sites in sixty countries. The flows of electronic data across the globe are supported by a rapidly growing software services industry, with an estimated market value of some US$300 billion in 1995. Leading players are companies like Microsoft (US) with 1993 sales of US$3,753 million and profits of US$953 million.

5 *The flows of voice messages,* for both private and commercial applications, are facilitated by such major players as the world's largest telecommunication service providers. These are AT&T (with 1993 revenues of

Table 5.1 *The largest entertainment media companies in 1994*

Company	Sales in 1994 (Billion US$ country)
Bertelsmann	$10.9 Germany
Walt Disney	$8.5 United States
News Corp.	$7.5 United Kingdom
Time-Warner	$6.6 United States
Thorn-EMI	$6.5 United Kingdom
Havas	$6.2 France
Capital Cities/ABC	$5.6 United States
Paramount Communications	$4.3 United States
Reed-Elsevier	$4.2 Netherlands
Polygram	$4.0 Netherlands
Times Mirror	$3.8 United States
Reader's Digest	$2.6 United States

Table 5.2 *Advertising agency billings in 1990 in US$ millions*

1	WPP (UK)	18.09	(includes Ogilvy & Mather and J. Walter Thompson)
2	Saatchi & Saatchi (UK)	11.86	(includes Backer, Spielvogel and Bates)
3	Interpublic (US)	11.02	(includes McCann-Erikson and Lintas)
4	Omnicom (US)	9.70	(includes BBDO, DDB and Needham)
5	Dentsu (Japan)	9.67	
6	Young & Rubicam (US)	8.00	
7	Eurocom (France)	5.06	

Source: Advertising Age, 25 March 1991.

US$67.2 billion), the combination of British Telecommunications PLC and MCI Communications Corp (US) (with revenues in 1993 of US$33 billion), the projected combination of Deutsche Bundespost Telekom, France Telecom and the US-based Sprint Corporation (with combined 1993 revenues of US$69 billion), and the Japanese Nippon Telegraph & Telephone (with 1993 revenues of US$60 billion).

6 *The flows of text messages* which are transported through such media as telefax, telex and the mail services. The major players are the telecommunication service providers, the postal services around the world and the leading courier companies.

These different types of flows are organized around three components: the message producers, the operators of networks and the manufacturers of technical equipment, such as the large computer firms (see Table 5.3) and consumer electronics firms (see Table 5.4).

Together, the message producers, network operators and equipment manufacturers represent today a world-wide market of several trillion dollars (Table 5.5).

Around all three components a growing industrial activity has developed that is increasingly characterized by a trend towards consolidation. This

Table 5.3   *The world's largest computer companies in 1994*

Company	Sales in US$m	Profits in US$m per country	
IBM	62,716	8,101	United States
Toshiba	42,917	113	Japan
Fujitsu	29,094	349	Japan
Hewlett Packard	20,317	1,177	United States
Canon	16,507	190	United States
Digital Equipment	14,371	251	United States
Ricoh	8,974	88	Japan
Apple Computer	7,977	87	United States
UNISYS	7,743	565	United States
Compaq Computer	7,191	462	United States
Olivetti	5,497	296	United States
Bull	4,987	895	France
Sun Microsystems	4,309	157	United States
Casio Computer	3,557	49	Japan

Table 5.4   *The world's largest consumer electronics companies in 1994*

Company	Sales in US$m	Profits in US$m	Country
Hitachi	68,582	605	Japan
Matsushita	61,384	227	Japan
General Electric	60,823	431	USA
Samsung	51,345	520	Korea
Siemens	50,381	1,113	Germany
Sony	34,602	142	Japan
NEC	33,176	61	Japan
Philips	31,666	1,058	Netherlands
Alcatel	27,599	1,247	France
Motorola	16,963	1,022	USA
Sharp	13,810	295	Japan

Table 5.5   *The world communication market*

Mass media (including publishing)	US$3.8 trillion
Telecommunications	US$1.2 trillion
Computers	US$800 billion
Consumer electronics	US$400 billion

Source: Satellite News, 20 April 1992.

means that the major players are actively trying to get control over at least two of the three components. The emerging mega industries combine message production (ranging from digital libraries to television entertainment), the manufacturing and operating of distribution systems (ranging from satellites to digital switches), and building the equipment for reception and processing of information (ranging from HDTV-sets to telephones).

Illustrative is the Japanese company Sony which was already active in the equipment sector when it acquired, through Columbia Pictures and CBS Records, access to the message component. Consolidation basically means that companies are buying their competitors and thus concentrating market control in the hands of fewer companies. World communication has developed into a fast-moving and expanding market-place mainly controlled by a limited number of mega corporations.

The policy choices that the world community makes for the scope and the shape of the market-place are largely guided by the assumption that a free market under capitalist conditions provides an optimal distribution of information and communication resources in the world. As take-overs occur in the world communication market, mega corporations are emerging and their powers, by and large, are beyond national control. Who, then, will protect the public interest?

The keywords of this market-driven arrangement are deregulation, privatization and globalization. Increasingly, in many countries the political climate is very supportive of these processes. The creation of global electronic networks, for example, is largely facilitated through the privatization of public telecommunication services, the liberalization of electronics markets and the deregulation of tariff structures. There is world-wide a trend towards a shift from public-service type provision of information and telecommunication services to a competitive environment for the trading of these services by private market operators.

In response to recent economic and technological developments many countries around the world are revising their communication and information structures. In this process the leading stratagem would seem to be 'more market, less state' and the buzzwords have become privatization and liberalization. Whereas privatization refers to the complete sale of publicly owned companies to private interests, as well as abolishing regulations that prevent private entrepreneurs from going into certain economic sectors, liberalization refers to a de-monopolization of markets by introducing competition in the supply of information and telecommunication services. Privatization and liberalization occur in telecommunications, public libraries and public data banks.

Deregulation became the key policy orientation of the 1980s. This decade was characterized by a wave of telecommunications deregulation which found concrete expression in privatization and liberalization. In fact, the concept is somewhat misleading as deregulation tends to mean re-regulation and often leads to more rather than less rules. Deregulation also tends to refer to the withdrawal of the state from very special social areas. There is a trend in many countries to dispense with state involvement in the area of social welfare. At the same time one observes in the same countries increased state involvement and related regulation in the fields of technology policy and industrial policy.

The key policy issues in the recent GATT Round of multilateral trade negotiations – which ended in December 1993 – were market access around the world for providers of goods and services and the global adoption of a regime for intellectual property rights which protects the interests of the large, corporate producers of culture and technology.

In the debates on the creation of global information infrastructures to implement the global information superhighway, the strongest tendency is to delegate the realization of this project to the forces of the market. The closest the world gets to the projected global information superhighway is today the Internet – a public meeting place where more than 20 million PC users in some 150 countries exchange information, search databases, play games and chat. Internet is beginning to attract the attention of the international business community. *Business Week*, in its cover story of 14 November 1994, suggests that Internet is emerging as 'one of the most exciting places for doing business' (*Business Week*, 1994: 38). Internet has been guided by the rule of sharing information for free and has now been discovered as a major vehicle for commercial advertising. *Business Week* quotes Bill Washburn (former executive director of Commercial Internet Exchange) saying: 'With the Internet, the whole globe is one marketplace' (*Business Week*, 1994: 39). It may turn into a global electronic shopping mall. In brief, the field of international communication and its major players can best be described in terms of a commercial market-place driven by the belief that a free market under capitalist conditions guarantees an optimal delivery of information and culture to everyone.

Human rights as an alternative morality?

Parallel with the development of world communication – driven by the morality of the market – the world community has adopted a 'common standard of achievement' to guide its conduct.[1] This standard is driven by the morality of human rights.

On 10 December 1948 the General Assembly of the United Nations adopted through its resolution 217 (III) the Universal Declaration of Human Rights. This first comprehensive international standard on human rights was prepared by the United Nations Commission on Human Rights. It expressed the concern for the protection of human rights which emerged after the Second World War in response to the atrocities of Nazism. The first indications of this concern were signalled by the charters of the war tribunals at Nuremberg and Tokyo and in the United Nations Charter of 1945.

Article 55 of the UN Charter states 'the United Nations shall promote universal respect for, and observance of, human rights and fundamental freedoms for all without distinction as to race, sex, language, or religion'. The origins of the Declaration are found in European history – its philosophical undercurrent is the tradition of the eighteenth-century Enlightenment. Its prime mover was a European-initiated war and its first proponents were Western governments with strong European roots. In spite of this biased beginning and despite the continuing debate about the need to redress the European bias in human rights thinking, the Declaration is recognized by all member states of the United Nations as the 'common standard of achievement for all peoples and all nations'. The Declaration does not constitute binding international law but its universal recognition as a standard of conduct renders its provisions moral obligations for all peoples and all nations.

The adoption of the Universal Declaration signals the beginning of a dynamic development of human rights-based standards in world politics. It is common to refer to the classical civil and political rights as the first generation of human rights. These represent the freedom of citizens from state interference or their rights to perform certain activities while the state observes the duty of non-intervention. The historical roots of the first generation are the Magna Carta (1215), the American Bill of Rights (1787) and the French Declaration *Des droits de l'homme et du citoyen* (1789).

Economic, social and cultural rights are referred to as the second generation which represents the right to claim an active involvement in the state. The first and second generations of human rights are formulated as binding international law in two conventions that were drafted in the 1950s, adopted in 1966 and came into force in 1976. These are the International Covenant on Civil and Political Rights and the International Covenant on Economic, Social and Cultural Rights. Together with the Universal Declaration of Human Rights, these instruments constitute the International Bill of Rights. In addition to the Bill of Rights, the UN General Assembly has adopted the International Convention on the Elimination of All Forms of Racial Discrimination (1965), the Convention on the Elimination of Discrimination Against Women (1979), the Convention against Torture and Other Cruel, Inhuman or Degrading Treatment or Punishment (1984) and the Convention on the Rights of the Child (1989).

In the development of international human rights a third generation has also emerged. This addresses the question of the need for a separate category of human rights in which the dominant individualistic orientation of human rights instruments would be complemented by the recognition of collective rights. This would imply that peoples can be holders of human rights. It has been argued that this logically flows from the acknowledgement of an intrinsic link between the notion of human rights and the principle of collective self-determination. This principle is embodied in the UN Charter, Articles 1 and 55, and in Article 1 of the two human rights covenants.

These collective rights have been proposed:

1   The right to peace and security.
2   The right to development.
3   The right of minorities to their own culture and language.
4   The right to communicate.

The African Charter on Human and Peoples' Rights (1981) refers both to the rights and freedoms of the individual and those of peoples. Among the difficulties that the proposed collective rights raise is the identification of the holders of these rights. Related to this is the question of how far collective holders of rights can be seen as having the power to implement their entitlements and how far they can be held responsible if these rights are not enforced.

In the development of human rights it is important that the United Nations World Conference on Human Rights of 1993 has reaffirmed the right to development as a universal and inalienable right and has also decided to strengthen its implementation. The Vienna Programme of Action

> welcomes the appointment by the Commission on Human Rights of a thematic working group on the right to development and urges that the Working Group should promptly formulate comprehensive and effective measures to eliminate obstacles to the implementation and realization of the Declaration on the Right to Development. The working group must recommend ways and means towards the realization of the right to development by all States.

Collective claims to human rights are contested and are not normally incorporated into international arrangements. The emphasis in international law is on individual claims. Article 27 in the International Covenant on Civil and Political Rights, for example, provides protection to minorities, but through individuals who belong to these minorities. The collective rights recognized by the United Nations are the basic right to self-determination (United Nations Charter, Articles 1 and 55, and the International Covenant on Civil and Political Rights), the right to physical survival of 'national, ethnical, racial or religious groups' (Convention on the Prevention and Punishment of Genocide), and the right to development (Declaration on the Right to Development, adopted by United Nations General Assembly Res. 41/128 of 4 December 1986).

The core of international human rights law is the simple though powerful notion that 'all people matter'. This idea represents the fundamental novelty in world politics that was introduced with the adoption of the UN Charter in 1945. The Charter provided the basis for the recognition of the entitlement of all human beings to the protection of dignity, integrity, liberty and equality. Herewith, it proposed an 'inclusive' interpretation of human rights. Earlier human rights entitlements had always been defined in an 'exclusive' manner.

During most of world history most people did not matter. They were slaves, serfs, workers, women, children, aboriginals, blacks. They did not matter. For the political arena they were 'non persons'. When fundamental rights were awarded, there always was this category of 'non-persons' that was not included. The Bill of Rights of the State of Virginia provided in 1776 fundamental freedoms to the 'good people of Virginia'. The good people did not include the black slaves and the indigenous Indians.

Against the selection of human rights norms as common standard of achievement for the world community, a recurrent argument is that human rights have no universal applicability, since their implementation is related to specific cultural and historical spaces. The importance of accepting a

minimal standard of universal validity is precisely the possibility to intervene in situations where the victims cannot speak for themselves. It should
be borne in mind that the belief that there are no universally shared basic
moral concepts is usually proposed by elites that are not representative of
ordinary people.

The relativist argument is in most countries around the world easily
defeated if one only enquires among the victims of human rights violations.
As Donnelly observes, 'ordinary citizens in country after country in the
Third World have found internationally recognized civil and political rights
essential to protecting themselves against repressive economic and political
elites' (Donnelly, 1993: 35). This is what Ramcharan has called the
democratic test of universality. 'Just ask any human being; Would you like
to live or die? Would you like to be tortured or enslaved? If there is any
critic of universality who would argue that an individual would choose
death to life, and serfdom to freedom, let us hear from that critic'
(Ramcharan, 1989: 26). I would add to this that an even more convincing
test of universalism is the 'victim test'. If anyone is in doubt about the
desirability of the universal application of basic human rights, he or she
should ask the victims of human rights violations.

It is important that the United Nations World Conference on Human
Rights (1993) has reaffirmed the universality of human rights. The final
declaration states, 'The universal nature of human rights is beyond
question'. In the preparatory process of the Conference the universality
concept had been challenged by several actors.

In the Cairo Declaration on Human Rights in Islam (9 June 1993) the
member states of the organization of the Islamic conference made human
rights subordinate to Islamic religious standards. The Declaration provided
that the rights and freedoms it stipulated are subject to the Islamic
Shari'ah.[2] The Bangkok Declaration of the Asian preparatory conference
stated that in the protection of human rights differences in national,
cultural and religious backgrounds had to be taken into account. The
Declaration recognized that while human rights are universal in nature,
they must be considered in the context of a dynamic and evolving process
of international norm-setting, bearing in mind the significance of national
and regional particularities and various historical, cultural and religious
backgrounds. The Vienna Declaration recognized that universality does not
equal uniformity and reminded that 'the significance of national and
regional particularities and various historical, cultural and religious
backgrounds must be borne in mind'.

Human rights provide an international standard of legitimacy. Only if
policy choices measure up to this standard can they be considered legitimate. This pragmatic justification can be reinforced by the observation that
it is common practice to associate communication with human rights
values. As Pekka Tarjanne, the Secretary General of the International
Telecommunications Union has stated, 'From its very beginning the telecommunications industry has been closely associated with certain values –

most notably freedom of expression, reciprocity between individuals and universality of access' (Tarjanne, 1992: 45). In line with Tarjanne's remark, one can establish that many regulatory instruments on world communication contain explicit references to human rights standards.

The specific basic premise of human rights standards is that the interests of ordinary people should be accommodated. This premise proposes that communication structures and processes are not just an end in themselves. The most efficient, effective and universally available means of communication can be used for very destructive purposes. As Justice Kirby has phrased it, 'Dictators can build magnificent highways and sometimes provide sufficient telephones: all efficiently susceptible to official interception' (Kirby, 1993: 262). Therefore, if we accept that 'all people matter', it is imperative to assess communication policy choices in the light of their contribution to the protection and promotion of the dignity of all people.

How do the belief in the market and the morality of human rights confront each other? In response to this question, I propose to select a number of provisions that are pertinent to world communication, explore what essential requirements they imply for world communication and whether a market-driven morality can accommodate these.

Human rights provision on the freedom of expression

The UNESCO Constitution, adopted in 1945, was the first multilateral instrument to reflect the concern for the freedom of information. The Constitution was largely based on US drafts (Wells, 1987: 62). These drafts included among others a proposal stressing the paramount importance of the mass media and 'the need to identify opportunities of UNESCO furthering their use for the ends of peace'. To promote the implementation of the concern for the freedom of information, a special division of 'free flow of information' was established in the secretariat in Paris.

In 1946 the delegation of the Philippines presented to the UN General Assembly a proposal for a resolution on an international conference on issues dealing with the press. This became United Nations General Assembly Resolution 59 (1) which was adopted unanimously in late 1946. According to the resolution, the purpose of the conference would be to address the rights, obligations and practices which should be included in the concept of freedom of information. The resolution called freedom of information 'the touchstone of all the freedoms to which the United Nations is consecrated'. It described the freedom of information as 'the right to gather, transmit and publish news anywhere and everywhere without fetters'. Already freedom of information began to shift away from the concern about the individual's freedom of speech to the institutional freedom of news gathering by news agencies.

In 1947 the United Nations General Assembly adopted additional resolutions that were to be placed on the agenda of the Conference on

Freedom of Information. One dealt with measures against propaganda and incitement to war, the other was concerned with false or distorted reports. Already by 1947 the UN had indicated a concern for both freedom and social responsibility in matters of information. In 1948, at Geneva, the United Nations Conference on Freedom of Information took place from 23 March till 21 April. Fifty-four countries were officially represented and, on the initiative of the United Kingdom, also practising news people were included. The United States was interested only in a convention on news gathering. France was mainly interested in a convention on the international right of correction. The United Kingdom preferred a convention on freedom of information. Eventually, only the French text became a convention, but with few ratifications only. As Caroll Binder, a member of the American Society of Newspaper Editors, commented, 'our initial attempts to commit the United Nations to [the US concept of freedom of information] were successful beyond expectation' (Wells, 1987: 61).

As the United States had taken the initiative, the Soviet Union and its allies were put in a re-active position. They responded to the US proposals for a free flow with demands for regulation. They were a minority in the UN bodies and most of their motions to qualify the free flow standard were defeated. This was also a result of the emerging Cold War antagonism. The conference produced numerous resolutions and three draft treaties on the Freedom of Information (proposed by the British delegation), the Gathering and International Transmission of News (proposed by the US delegation), and the International Right of Correction (proposed by the French delegation). The six Eastern European countries voted against all three conventions, the United States abstained only from the Freedom of Information convention. This was based on the problems the Americans had with the list of limitations on the freedom of expression (Article 2) which they found too restrictive. The draft convention on the Gathering and International Transmission of News was modified and subsequently approved by the UN Economic and Social Council (ECOSOC) in Resolution 152 (VII), and then discussed at a meeting of the Third Committee of the General Assembly (at New York in April 1949) which decided to join the draft with the draft convention on the International Right of Correction. Then the joint texts were adopted by the United Nations General Assembly Resolution 277 (III)C in 1949 but not opened for signature. The Right of Correction draft was subsequently separated from the Gathering and Transmission text and was opened for signature in 1952. After ratification by six countries, the Convention entered into force on 25 August 1962. In 1993 there were only eleven UN member states that had ratified the Convention.

The third draft Convention on the Freedom of Information was adopted by the United Nations General Assembly in 1949 (UNGA Resolution 277 (III)A) after modification and adoption by ECOSOC and modification by the Third Committee that abandoned work on the Convention after approval of its preamble and five articles. The Convention was never opened for signature and got lost in protracted ideological confrontation. In 1959 ECOSOC, urged by the United States, drafted a set of principles as the basis for a Declaration on Freedom of Information. In 1960 the General Assembly received the principles, but took no action.

At the 1948 conference there were confrontations between those who advanced a largely liberal-economic position in defence of newspapers and news agencies and those who challenged this as a sanctioning of commercial monopolies and propagandistic practices. Serious objections were made by the Soviet Union against a concern for the freedom of information that was exclusively based upon commercial claims. The Soviet Union Minister of Foreign Affairs, Andrei Gromyko, claimed that the proposed freedom of information was in fact the freedom of a few monopolies. The doctrine of the free flow of information obscured, in his opinion, the interests of bankers and industrialists for whom Wall Street represented the summit of democracy. The Soviet Union also claimed that the freedom of information could not mean freedom for fascist propaganda. Other delegations equally stressed the need to prevent the establishment of news monopolies under the guise of freedom. Some nations, such as the former Yugoslavia, drew attention to the wide disparities in available means of mass communication and claimed that freedom should be linked with the standard of equality.

Following the 1948 conference, one of the articles of the Universal Declaration of Human Rights was dedicated to the freedom of expression. This became the well-known Article 19 which states,

> Everyone has the right to freedom of opinion and expression; this right includes freedom to hold opinions without interference and to seek, receive and impart information and ideas through any media and regardless of frontiers.

An important observation is that the authors of the article constructed freedom of information along five components. The first is the classical defence of the freedom of expression. The second is the freedom to hold opinions. This provision was formulated upon the American insistence on protection against brainwashing, the forced exposure of a political conviction. The third is the freedom to gather information. This reflected the interests of the US news agencies to secure freedom for foreign correspondents. The fourth is the freedom of reception. This has to be understood as a response to the prohibition of foreign broadcasts reception during the war. The fifth is the right to impart information and ideas. This is a recognition of the freedom of distribution in addition to the freedom of expression.

The Article 19 formulation became important guidance when later international documents articulated the freedom of information concern. Important illustrations are the European Convention for the Protection of Human Rights and Fundamental Freedoms (1950), the International Covenant on Civil and Political Rights (1966), the American Convention on Human Rights (1969), and the African Charter on Human and Peoples' Rights (1981).

The free flow of information remained a recurrent concern with UNESCO. In the debates (of the 1970s) on the Third World demand for a new international information order, the concern with the free flow became a leading controversial issue. Particularly under pressure of Third World representatives, the 'free flow' concept was broadened to include the notion of 'balance'. In the first years of the freedom of information debates the Third World countries were practically absent or had no common claims to offer. This began to change in the 1970s when Third World nations succeeded in getting UNESCO to change the 'free flow of information' formula to the standard of a 'free and balanced flow of information'. This shift first surfaced at a UNESCO conference of experts (representing sixty-one member states) in December 1969 with the recommendation to 'making the flow of visual news in the world more balanced, particularly with regard to providing news coverage to and from, as well as between, developing areas'.

The UNESCO Mass Media Declaration of 1978 used the concept of a 'free flow and wider and better balanced dissemination of information' and also referred to 'a new equilibrium and greater reciprocity in the flow of information'. These notions represent a reformulation of the earlier 'freedom of information' concept as the basis for a New World Information and Communication Order (NWICO). The UNESCO General Conference in Belgrade of 1981 stated, for instance, in its Resolution 4.19 among the basic principles of the NWICO: the removal of the internal and external obstacles to a free flow and wider and better balanced dissemination of information and ideas, the plurality of sources and channels of information, freedom of the press and information, and the freedom of journalists and all professionals in the communication media, a freedom inseparable from responsibility.

In line with the extension of the freedom of information with the notion of balance, new thinking also emerged that sought to extend the existing provisions into a 'right to communicate'. In the early 1990s freedom of information was highlighted on UNESCO's agenda through regional meetings to promote the development of free media. These meetings were held in 1990 in Windhoek, Namibia and in 1992 in Alma Ata. Special attention to the concern about freedom of information was given by the Conference on Security and Cooperation in Europe (CSCE) since 1975. In the Final Act of the CSCE in Helsinki, 1975, a great variety of issues on the CSCE agenda was distributed over three baskets. The first dealt with security matters, the second addressed cooperation in economics, science, technology and environment, and the third covered human rights, information and culture. For the concern on the freedom of information the Final Act contains the most important provisions in the third basket. The participating states expressed their conviction that

> increased cultural and educational exchanges, broader dissemination of information, contacts between people, and the solution of humanitarian problems will contribute to the strengthening of peace and understanding among peoples and to

the spiritual enrichment of the human personality without distinction as to race, sex, language or religion.

In the field of information the participating states acknowledged

that a wider dissemination of information contributes to the growth of confidence between peoples and therefore emphasize the essential and influential role of the press, radio, television, cinema and news agencies and of the journalists working in these fields. The participating States aim to facilitate the freer and wider dissemination of information of all kinds, to encourage co-operation in the field of information and the exchange of information with other countries, and to improve the conditions under which journalists from one participating state exercise their profession in another participating state.

In the Helsinki Final Act the states decided to continue the multilateral process and since 1975 a large number of CSCE meetings have taken place. For the freedom of information the Ottawa meeting (7 May–17 June 1985) on human rights and fundamental freedoms (no concluding document); the Cultural Forum (21–25 November, 1985, Budapest) (no concluding document); and, in particular, the Information Forum in London (18 April–12 May 1989) were important. The Forum was an exceptional exchange of opinions between diplomats and media professionals. There was no concluding document but there was a list of seventy proposals for the improvement of the working conditions of media personnel. Freedom of information was also addressed at the Conference on the Human Dimensions of the CSCE, held in three subsequent meetings at Paris (30 May–23 June 1989), Copenhagen (5–29 June 1990) and at Moscow (10 September–4 October 1991).

The final document of the Helsinki follow-up meeting in 1992 stated that the participating states decide that 'under the guidance of the CSO [the Committee of Senior Officials which was established at the Paris summit of November 1990], the Office for Democratic Institutions and Human Rights will organize CSCE Human Dimension seminars which will address specific questions of particular relevance to the Human Dimension and of current political concern'. In order to launch the new CSCE Human Dimension Seminars without delay, the participating states decided that the Office would organize the four following seminars: Migration, Minority Issues, Tolerance, and Free Media. All four were to be held before 31 December 1993. The seminar on Free Media took place in November 1993 at Warsaw, Poland.

Requirements for international communication

The provisions in international human rights law on freedom of expression have the following implications. First, people have *the right to freedom of expression of opinions, information and ideas* without interference by public or private parties. For people to exercise the fundamental right to freedom of expression there should be free and independent channels of communication. This means that media should be independent from governmental, political or economic control or from control of materials and infrastructures essential to the production and dissemination of newspapers, magazines, periodicals and broadcast programmes. Free media are pluralistic media. This means that monopolies of any kind are impermissible and that current trends towards the predominantly commercial provision of information and culture should be controlled.

People have *the right to receive opinions, information and ideas*. This implies that people have the right to be informed about matters of public interest. This includes the right to receive information which is independent of commercial and political interests, and the right to receive a range of information and cultural products designed for a wide variety of tastes and interests. According to the jurisprudence of the European Court, citizens have the right to be properly informed. In several opinions the Court has stated that not only do the mass media have a right to impart information, they have the task 'to impart information and ideas on matters of public interest', and the public has a right to receive such information and ideas. The Court has ruled that the media are purveyors of information and public watchdogs.

People have *the right to gather information*. This includes the right of access to government information and information on matters of public interest held by public authorities or private interests. There can only be restrictions on access to government and privately held information of public interest if such restrictions are necessary for the protection of a democratic society or the basic rights of others.

People have *the right to distribute information*. This includes fair and equitable access to media distribution channels and to adequate resources and facilities.

Human rights provisions on discrimination

Article 20 of the International Covenant on Civil and Political Rights contains a paragraph that states, 'Any advocacy of national, racial or religious hatred that constitutes incitement to discrimination, hostility or violence shall be prohibited by law'. This was formulated even more strongly in Article 4 of the International Convention on the elimination of all forms of racial discrimination (adopted as United Nations General Assembly Resolution 2106 A(XX), 21 December 1965). Here 'all dissemination of ideas based upon racial superiority or hatred, incitement to racial discrimination, as well as acts of violence or incitement to such acts against any race or group of persons of another colour or ethnic origin' was declared a criminal offence. Essential to this provision is that states are also required (in Article 4b) to declare organizations which promote and incite racial discrimination illegal. The UNESCO 1978 Declaration on Race and Racial Prejudice mentioned the mass media specifically in Article 5. The

Declaration provides a strong prescription for media conduct as it urges 'the mass media and those who control or serve them' to 'promote understanding, tolerance and friendship among individuals and groups and to contribute to the eradication of racism, racial stereotypes, partial, unilateral or tendentious picture of individuals and of various human groups'. The mass media are also told to be 'freely receptive to ideas of individuals and groups which facilitate communication between racial and ethnic groups'. International human rights instruments also contain normative provisions on discrimination against women.

The Convention on the Elimination of All Forms of Discrimination against Women (1979) provides in Article 5 that states parties shall take all appropriate measures: 'To modify the social and cultural patterns of conduct of men and women, with a view to achieving the elimination of prejudice and customary and all other practices which are based on the idea of the inferiority or the superiority of either of the sexes or on stereotyped roles for men and women.'

The provisions in international human rights law on discrimination have the following implications.

People have *the right to the protection by law against prejudicial treatment of their person in the media*. This right to be treated in non-biased ways implies that reporting by the media should refrain from the use of images that distort the realities and complexities of people's lives or that fuel prejudice by discriminatory descriptions of people and situations, and that neglect the dignity and ability of opponents in national, racial or ethnic conflict.

The media should also contribute to the modification of the social and cultural patterns of conduct of men and women, with a view to achieving the elimination of prejudice and all other practices which are based on the idea of the inferiority or the superiority of either of the sexes or on stereotyped roles for men and women. In line with human rights provisions one might expect that policy measures would be taken that combat the powerful stereotyping of the sexes in media entertainment and media advertising.

Human rights provisions on privacy

Article 12 of the Universal Declaration of Human Rights prohibits arbitrary interference with the individual's privacy and provides the right to protection of the law against such interference. The International Covenant on Civil and Political Rights provides in Article 17a that: 'No one shall be subjected to arbitrary or unlawful interference with his privacy . . . .' Also, the European Convention on Human Rights and Fundamental Freedoms provides in Article 8.1 the right to respect for private life.

The provisions in international human rights law on the protection of privacy have the following implications:

People have *the right to the protection by law against interference with their privacy.* The media should respect people's right to respect for their private lives. Privacy concerns private, family and home life, physical and moral integrity, honour and reputation, avoidance of being placed in a false light, non-revelation of irrelevant and embarrassing facts, unauthorized publication of private photographs, protection against misuse of private communication, protection from disclosure of information given or received by the individual confidentially.

Human rights provisions on the right to development

The right to development was first proposed in 1972 by the Senegalese lawyer Kebam Baye. It is founded on Articles 25 and 28 of the Universal Declaration of Human Rights and Article 11 of the International Covenant on Economic, Social and Cultural Rights.

In 1977 the UN Commission on Human Rights recommended to the Economic and Social Council to invite the UN Secretary General, together with UNESCO and other competent agencies, 'to undertake a study on the subject of "the international dimensions of the right to development as a human right in relation with other human rights based on international co-operation, including the right to peace, taking into account the requirements of the New International Economic Order"'. This study was presented to the Commission in 1979 and led to the establishment of a working group to study the scope and contents of the right to development and the most effective means to ensure its realization. The Working Group had nine meetings in the period 1981–84 and presented, in 1984, a report which was the basis for the Declaration on the Right to Development, adopted by UNGA Resolution 41/128 of 4 December 1986. A hundred and forty-six states voted in favour, there were eight abstentions and one state (the United States) voted against.

The Declaration proclaimed that: 'The right to development is an inalienable human right by virtue of which every human person and all peoples are entitled to participate in, contribute to and enjoy economic, social, cultural and political development, in which all human rights and fundamental freedoms can be fully realized.' The Declaration also states that: 'All human beings have a responsibility for development, individually and collectively . . . and they should therefore promote and protect an appropriate political, social and economic order for development.' The 1993 World Conference on Human Rights in Vienna confirmed the right to development by declaring in its final statement (Article 10): 'The World Conference on Human Rights reaffirms the right to development as established in the Declaration on the Right to Development, as a universal and inalienable right and an integral part of fundamental human rights.'

The provisions in international human rights law on the right to development have the following implications.

In the most general terms *world communication ought to be structured as an inclusive playing field.* This means that the existing and persisting international 'communication gap' ought to be resolved. Only when all people, either as individuals or as social groups, have equitable access to the use of communication resources can the basic human rights standard that 'all people matter' be met. In today's world communication – increasingly controlled by a decreasing number of powerful players – most of the world's people are excluded from most of the flows that make up the playing field. The low-income countries which have some 55% of the world's population have less than 5% of the world's telephone lines. In 1994 more than two-thirds of the world's households had no telephone. The Maitland Report of 1984[3] projected that in the early twenty-first century most people in the world would be within one to two hours walking from a telephone (Maitland, 1994). The International Telecommunications Union (ITU) has recently admitted that this target cannot be reached by 2010 (ITU, 1994).

In spite of the much publicized 'information revolution', today's reality shows an increasing gap between the world's information rich and information poor countries, and between information rich and information poor sectors within societies. Resolving the communications gap implies the design and implementation of policies that address the provision of an equitable distribution of communication resources to all people.

Human rights provisions on cultural rights

The most important international human rights documents propose that entitlements in the area of culture are considered as basic human rights. The Universal Declaration of Human Rights (1948) formulates the right to culture in the sense of participation in cultural life. Article 27 provides: 'Everyone has the right freely to participate in the cultural life of the community.' Article 22 states that everyone is entitled to the realization through national effort and international cooperation of the economic, social and cultural rights indispensable for his dignity and the free development of his personality.

Participation in cultural life has raised difficult questions about the definition of communities, the position of sub-cultures, the protection of participation rights of minorities, the provision of physical resources of access, and the links between cultural access and socio-economic conditions. Underlying some of these difficulties is the tension between the concept of culture as public good or as private property. These positions can be mutually exclusive in the concrete cases where historical works of art disappear in the vaults of private collections.

The inclusive nature of human rights ('everyone') implies a shift away from an elite conception of culture to a view of culture as 'common heritage'. Actually, the UNESCO Declaration on Race and Racial

Prejudice (1978, General Conference Resolution 3/1.1/2) founded the right to culture on the notion of culture as 'common heritage of mankind' which implies that all people 'should respect the right of all groups to their own cultural identity and the development of their distinctive cultural life within the national and international context' (Article 5). The right to culture thus implies beyond the participation in cultural life, the protection of cultural identity, the need to conserve, develop and diffuse culture, and the need for international cultural cooperation.

In 1968 a UNESCO conference of experts considered the question of cultural rights as human rights (Paris, 8–13 July 1968). The statement of the conference: 'The rights to culture include the possibility for each man to obtain the means of developing his personality, through his direct partici-pation in the creation of human values and of becoming, in this way, responsible for his situation, whether local or on a world scale' (UNESCO, 1970: 107). The Intergovernmental Conference on the Institutional, Admin-istrative and Financial Aspects of Cultural Policies (convened by UNESCO in 1970) decided that the right to participate in the cultural life of the community implies the duty for governments to provide the effective means for this participation. A series of regional conferences on cultural policies (in 1972, 1973 and 1975) provided important inputs into the formulation of a UNESCO recommendation on participation by the people at large in cultural life and their contribution to it. The recommendation, approved on 26 November 1976, aims to 'guarantee as human rights those rights bearing on access to and participation in cultural life'. The recommendation questions the concentration of control over the means of producing and distributing culture. Regarding the mass media, the text states that they should not threaten the authenticity of cultures and 'they ought not to act as instruments of cultural domination'. The preamble proposes that measures are taken 'against the harmful effect of "commercial mass culture"' and recommends that governments 'should make sure that the criterion of profit-making does not exert a decisive influence on cultural activities'.

There was strong Western opposition to various elements of the recom-mendation, such as the mention of commercial mass culture in a negative sense, and the use of the term 'people at large'. In the preparatory meetings and during the UNESCO General Conference, several Western delegations expressed their concern that the recommendation, if implemented, would restrict the free flow of information and the independence of the mass media. The strongest opponent was the United States.

> The USA asserted a belief from the outset that access to and participation in cultural life were not fit subjects for international regulation, took minimal part of the drafting process, sent no delegation to the intergovernmental meeting, urged the General Conference to turn down the proposed text and, after its adoption, announced that it had no intention of transmitting the Recommenda-tion to the relevant authorities or institutions in the US. (Wells, 1987: 165)

The Western countries were against, although to differing degrees, the developing countries and Eastern European countries that supported the text. In the drafting process there was little input from the cultural industries. The voting was 62 for, 5 against and 15 abstentions.

The preamble refers to the Universal Declaration of Human Rights, the UNESCO Constitution and the Declaration of Principles of International Cultural Cooperation and considers cultural development as a true instrument of progress. The recommendation links participation in cultural life with access to culture and claims that 'access by the people at large to cultural values can be assured only if social and economic conditions are created that will enable them not only to enjoy the benefits of culture, but also to take an active part in overall cultural life and in the process of cultural development'. It is recommended that member states 'guarantee as human rights those rights bearing on access to and participation in cultural life', 'provide effective safeguards for free access to national and world cultures by all members of society', 'pay special attention to women's full entitlement to access to culture and to effective participation in cultural life', 'guarantee the recognition of the equality of cultures, including the culture of national minorities and of foreign minorities'.

Regarding the mass media, the recommendation states that they 'should not threaten the authenticity of cultures or impair their quality; they ought not to act as instruments of cultural domination but serve mutual understanding and peace'. And member states and appropriate authorities should 'promote the active participation of audiences by enabling them to have a voice in the selection and production of programmes, by fostering the creation of a permanent flow of ideas between the public, artists and producers and by encouraging the establishment of production centres for use by audiences at local and community levels'; and 'encourage media to pay special attention to the protection of national cultures from potentially harmful influence of some types of mass production'. This line of thought was reinforced by the 1982 World Conference on Cultural Policies held in Mexico City. The Declaration on Cultural Policies adopted by the conference reaffirmed the requirement that states must take appropriate measures to implement the right to cultural participation. In recommendation 28 on cultural rights, the conference participants claimed that governments should take measures 'to strengthen the democratization of culture by means of policies that ensure the right to culture and guarantee the participation of society in its benefits without restriction'. An assessment of the implementation of the recommendation on participation in cultural life in 1985–86 showed that little had been done by many states and that these issues remained relevant.

Requirements for world communication

The provisions in international human rights law on the right to culture have the following implications.

1 World communication ought to contribute to a cultural environment that treats people as autonomous beings entitled to a respect for their integrity and dignity.
2 People have the right to a diversity of languages. This includes the right to express themselves in their own language. This implies the need to create provisions for minority languages in the media and the need to promote educational facilities to encourage language learning by all people without discrimination.
3 People have the right to protect their cultural identity. This includes the respect for people's free pursuit of their cultural development and the right to express existing cultural variety through the media as well as to receive a variety of cultural expressions.
4 People have the right to the protection of their local cultural space and provisions for the protection of cultural heritage should be established.
5 People have the right to an equitable use of the common cultural heritage. This right includes that no one shall be arbitrarily deprived of sources of knowledge. The right shall imply that all peoples and nations have the duty to share with one another their knowledge. The right also entitles everyone to benefit from the protection of the immaterial and material interests resulting from the production of knowledge.

Human rights and the market-place

When human rights morality meets the realities of the market-place we face a number of disturbing questions. I have selected the following cases.

Can the market-place guarantee the freedom of information which the exercise of human rights requires?

This question can be looked at from the requirement articulated by the European Court of Human Rights that people are 'properly informed about matters of public interest'. The market-driven direction of information media world-wide raises the serious prospect that the selection of ideas and information is more determined by the maximization of profits than by the wish to serve the information needs of democratic societies. Emphasis is more likely put on light music and advertising than on information and ideas that enable people to exercise the rights and duties of citizenship. However, for social communication to perform its public function it needs the realization that mass media have a fundamental duty to their audiences. They cannot simply equate them with consumers or commodities to be sold to advertisers.

A market orientation promotes the commercialization of information and culture and they tend to become identified as commercial services to which classical trade rules will apply.[4] The ensuing tension between public good and private commodity is increasingly resolved to the latter's advantage. Commercialization implies that increasingly citizens are required to pay for information services rendered by public bodies. In many countries governmental departments charge for information that is generated through public finance. They levy fees for the use of data collections or sell these through private on-line service operators. Whereas the trend towards global digital information utilities facilitates an unprecedented access to information, there is a good chance that deregulatory policies reinforcing commercialization would relate this access to the affordability of the service. Commercialization implies that price and not public interest is the decisive factor. This may lead to the peculiar phenomenon of more and more people hooking off the 'information society' as they can no longer afford the charges.

Commercialization also implies the erosion of the public sphere. Since the early 1980s a process has begun that increasingly erodes the public sphere in many societies through the penetration of corporate interests into terrains formerly protected by public interest, such as government information, public libraries, or the arts. Commercial sponsoring of more and more socio-cultural activities has become very popular and leads to the emergence of 'billboard' societies in which every location, institution, activity, event and person becomes a potential carrier of commercial messages.

The erosion of the public sphere by implication undermines diversity of information provision. Cultural diversity becomes the choice markets can offer, but markets offer multitude and more of the same, not fundamentally distinct goods; everything that does not pass the market threshold because there is not a sufficiently large percentage of consumers, disappears. That may be good for markets, but it may be suicidal for democratic politics and creative culture.

Deregulation also facilitates the development of markets for pay-TV type of operations. It is likely that in most pay-TV operations the dominant programme fare will be theatrical films made in the United States. This is so because the United States still maintains a strong competitive advantage in markets for motion pictures and pre-recorded video-cassettes. In any case, it would appear likely that the pressures of privatization will increasingly create commercial incentives for the creation of television products. This is bound to have an impact on the contents of the products and will render the public interest aspirations sought by broadcasters in many countries ever harder to attain.

Can the market-place guarantee people's right to culture?

Around the world the major cultural producers promote the creation of a cultural environment in which victimization, compulsive consumerism, loss of local cultural space reinforce forms of social and cultural dependency. Modern markets tend to keep their clients under control by inundating them with avalanches of non-stop distractions which suggest, as Aldous Huxley phrased it in *Brave New World*, 'everybody is happy now'. In these distractions sex and violence figure prominently. Violence tends to be presented in ways which make people fearful of becoming victims and thus paralyse them.

> Constant displays of violent power and victimization cultivate an exaggerated sense of danger and insecurity among heavy viewers of television. That is the most pervasive and debilitating consequence of daily exposure to television violence. What we call the 'mean world syndrome' contributes to a loss of sensitivity and trust, demonstrates power for some and vulnerability for others, and invites violence and victimization. (Gerbner, 1992: 1)

A massive choreography of violence has become an essential component of the cultural environment in which people live and children are born. This disempowers people since it creates deep feelings of dependence, particularly on those most likely to be portrayed as the victims: women and minorities. Television violence facilitates feelings of dependency as the resulting insecurity tends to lead to requests for the mechanisms whereby the power-holders control their environment: more prisons, more police, more repression. Global entertainment also employs on a grand scale gendered stereotypes that misrepresent and disempower women. These images portray women as second-class citizens, sexually available and dependent.

A special concern in the light of cultural rights is the reduction of local cultural space. Whether a community will be able to develop its own cultural identity (to empower itself culturally) will largely depend upon the local cultural space people can control. If people are to be 'beings for themselves' (Freire, 1972: 129), they need sufficient cultural space to define their identity autonomously. If this space is not adequately provided or acquired, they will be incorporated in structures of oppression that define people as 'beings for others'.

Local cultural space is a battleground. There are always hegemonic forces inside and outside the community intent on reducing this space and thus diminishing people's capacity for autonomous choice. Today, the local cultural space of many communities across the world is threatened by the process of cultural globalization. Facilitated by technological innovations, the enormous growth of international trade, and a very supportive liberal political climate, one observes the rapid transnational proliferation of mass-market advertising and electronic entertainment produced by a handful of mega conglomerates. There is a world-wide spread of commercially packaged cultural products. A uniform consumerist lifestyle is aggressively marketed across the globe. This process is engineered by forces intent on the reduction of local cultural space. This obstructs the local initiative and disadvantages the local cultural producers. It effectively silences local culture and hampers people's development as 'beings for themselves'.

Can the market-place guarantee the equitable access to the common heritage of knowledge resources that human rights require?

As a result of the trends towards deregulation and globalization, the market-place has become the leading actor in determining the direction and scope of knowledge production. As knowledge is created and controlled as private property, knowledge as common good is destroyed. This is the inherent meaning of privatization (private = to deprive). It deprives communities of access to their common heritage and renders this the entitlement of individual owners.

The emerging international intellectual property rights regime transforms common heritage into exclusive, private (corporate) property. A case in point is the world's biological systems which are common heritage, but which, through technological innovations (biotechnology), are now becoming private property.

Against the rather successful movement of Western states and transnational corporations to incorporate the protection of intellectual property rights in a GATT agreement, a large meeting of non-governmental organizations (NGOs) maintained that such an agreement would seriously hinder the diffusion of technical knowledge to Third World countries, hamper local technological innovation and benefit mainly transnational corporations. It would therefore obstruct the very development of science and technology in the public interest. The proposals aim at reserving the domestic markets of the Third World countries for the manufactured goods of the developed countries. The proposals would arrest the promotion of indigenous technological capabilities.

The global harmonization of protection of intellectual property rights (IPR) that is proposed by the emerging GATT agreement is supported with the argument that this will increase technology transfer to Third World countries and will facilitate access to advanced technology. Given their export orientation, many developing countries have accepted to change their IPR domestic regulation to a level defined by the industrialized countries. By now, many of them have adopted the draft GATT text on trade related intellectual property rights (TRIPs) which determines global minimal norms for protection. Several countries have already revised their IPR laws.

There is a clear shift from the earlier position taken by the Third World countries. Most of them feel now that only by adopting the proposed harmonization can they reduce the North–South technology gap. In connection with the technology gap, many countries have begun to focus on export strategies and the common expectation is that improved IPR protection will reinforce this economic policy through transfer of technology and cooperation in science and technology. It is still far from clear whether the shift in position will indeed benefit the Third World. In any case given the great differentiation among Third World countries, the effects are likely to be different across countries. It may well be that only very few countries will benefit through the new IPR regime and have more technology imports, more domestic innovation, and more research and development investment. The likelihood is, however, that the majority of countries will not see any such benefits and may even confront strong drawbacks. It is likely, for example, that prices for the products of biotechnological engineering will increase.

It would have been unrealistic to expect otherwise, as the global imposition of the new IPR regime is not motivated by a strong desire to share the world's knowledge and to reduce ignorance, but by the need to control expanding markets. The emerging regime for the global control of knowledge demonstrates the effective employment of the strategy of disempowerment for the benefit of the transnational corporate interests. The GATT TRIPs agreement allows the biotechnology industry to commercialize and privatize the biodiversity of the Third World countries. This industry uses the genetic resources of the Third World as a free common resource and then transforms them in laboratories in patentable genetically engineered products. In the process, the industry manipulates life-forms that are common heritage. This means that whereas formerly plants and animals were excluded from the IPR regime, biotechnology has changed this. Life can now be the object of ownership. This has many perplexing implications, one of which is that thousands of years of local knowledge about life organisms are devalued and replaced by the alleged superior knowledge of Western scientists and engineers.

Conclusion

Whereas the standard of human rights represents an inclusive and egalitarian perspective on world society, the global market-place tends to exclude people as it creates disparity in access to, and use of, resources. As Jack Valenti (the leading lobbyist for the US film industry) has explained, 'people with a lot of money have the best cars and people with the least money have the used cars, but nearly every one has a car – so what's the problem?' (Brown, 1994: 33). Applied to the 'information society', Valenti's argument implies that the rich will have lots of information, the poor will have little, but everyone has information – so what's the problem?

The problem is a highly inegalitarian distribution of a fundamental resource that influences people's daily lives in many different ways, enabling them to take part in public decision-making, shaping the quality of their lives and determining their educational chances or job opportunities. The problem is that if the construction of the global super information highways is left to the forces of the market, we may get the new Athenian democracy that US Vice-President Al Gore has spoken about. In his speech to the International Telecommunications Union's World Telecommunications Development Conference in Buenos Aires, 21 March 1994, Gore said 'I see a new Athenian Age of democracy forged in the fora the G11 will create'. It may have escaped the Vice-President, but democracy in Athens was a very restricted arrangement; it excluded such categories as women or slaves.

Moreover, if we leave the construction of the information highway to the private sector, this implies that the market will develop ways to pay for the projected information infrastructure. This will raise the (seldom asked) question about the type and quality of information the world may expect. The money-makers are likely to deploy at a grand scale the so-called 'killer' applications: video on demand, home shopping, video games and direct-response advertising. Their Global Information Superhighway may just amount to the global provision of pornography and the interactive shopping in the 'Mall in your Home!'.

The market cannot deliver equitable access to the world's common resources as it makes common heritage into a commercial commodity. The commodification of information and culture creates a price tag for access and use. As the capacity to purchase is unequally distributed in most societies and between societies, there is growing evidence that the market-place creates a growing disparity between rich and poor in and between societies in terms of access to information and communication resources.

A free market under capitalist conditions leads inevitably to a concentration of capital, growth of transnational corporations and forms of industrial oligopolization which are not necessarily supportive of everybody's interest and need. Market-oriented economic development implies diminishing attention to collective social provisions and invites the exclusion from this development of large numbers of individuals, social groups and even whole nations. In this process the market strengthens existing conditions of social inequity.

As a final point, what are the requirements of human rights for civil society? In a letter to the UNESCO Director General Julian Huxley, Mahatma Gandhi wrote in 1947: 'I learnt from my illiterate but wise mother that all rights to be deserved and preserved came from duty well done. Thus the very right to live accrues to us only when we do the duty of citizenship of the world.' It is an essential component of human rights standards that they relate entitlements to duties. If is thus the task of an alert civil society to guard its rights to information and culture. With so many people preferring second-rate services from broadcasters and print media, they seem to claim a right to ignorance. This is fatal for democratic societies that can only be established and preserved on the basis of people's desire for knowledge.

The promotion and defence of the morality of the market-place is the territory of the world's money-makers, largely supported by the world's political communities. The promotion and defence of the morality of human rights will have to be the concern of civil society. In the field of world communication this implies that people themselves begin to question whether the messages that world communication delivers serve their dignity, liberty and equality.

Notes

1   The preamble of the Universal Declaration of Human Rights states that the General Assembly proclaims the declaration 'as a standard of common achievement for all peoples and all nations'.

2   Shari'ah is the holy law of Islam.

3   Sir D. Maitland chaired the Independent Commission for World Wide Telecommunications Development which reported in 1984 to the International Telecommunications Union through a document entitled 'The Missing Link'. This was published in January 1985.

4   In this connection the decision of the European Commission to define broadcasting as 'service' and thus apply the competition rules of the EEC Treaty to this commercial activity is a telling illustration.

Further questions

1   How are human rights relevant to the question of international communication?

2   What are the main ways in which the market organization of international communication is inconsistent with the honouring of human rights?

3   How far does the organization of global communication promote democratic politics?

6

Taming Modernity:
Towards a New Paradigm

Majid Tehranian and Katharine Kia Tehranian

This chapter offers a comprehensive discussion about how to tame modernity and how to think about new paradigms as we approach the end of the twentieth century. The authors provide an extensive critique of the prevailing discourses related to the concept of development and modernization in the contemporary world

A brief look at the argument of the 'end of history' by Fukuyama (1989) and the discussion by Huntington (1993a) on the possible clash of civiliza- tions are the preliminary discourses of the first part of this chapter. The authors also discuss the need for a new paradigm in the light of the dissolu- tion of the Soviet Union in 1991 and the devastating conflicts in the former Yugoslavia, Tajikistan, Somalia, Rwanda, Haiti, and go on to criticize the 1990–91 Gulf War. They present a critical outlook on the current discourses on the new world order and provide an expansive historical and grounded view of current international continuities and discontinuities. Finally, they state that in the absence of knowing the shape of the future, we are living in a paradigm shift, so the emergence of a new paradigm at the end of this century appears likely.

Configuring the world divisions

In a remarkable passage, Isaiah Berlin has identified two contrasting paradigms in the understanding of the world:

> . . . there exists a great chasm between those, on the one side, who relate every- thing to a single central vision, one system less or more coherent or articulate, in terms of which they understand, think and feel – a single, universal, organizing principle in terms of which all that they are and say has significance – and, on the other side, those who pursue many ends, often unrelated and even contradictory, connected, if at all, only in some *de facto* way, for some psychological or physiological cause, related by no moral or aesthetic principle; these last lead lives, perform acts, and entertain ideas that are centrifugal rather than centripetal, their thought is scattered or diffused, moving on many levels, seizing upon the essence of a vast variety of experiences and objects, for what they are in themselves, without consciously or unconsciously seeking to fit them into or exclude them

from any one unchanging . . . at times fanatical, unitary inner vision. (Berlin in Rowe and Koetler, 1992)

This chapter falls somewhere between the two extreme poles of the dichotomy suggested by Berlin. It critiques both the modernist and post-modernist views that consider the world, respectively, as the arena for the unfolding of some inexorable law of 'Progress' *or* as a theatre of chaos and absurdity. It argues that the world may be more usefully viewed as a complex web of order and chaos, necessity and chance, determinism and freedom, resilience and fragility. In other words, the world is an open, adaptive, mutative, curvilinear system that is both manipulable and manipulative. The project of modernity provides a telling example of such order and chaos, necessity and freedom, anticipated and unanticipated consequences. The project began self-consciously with the European Enlightenment Movement in the eighteenth century and has now become world-wide. The philosophers of modernity saw the world as the arena for the unfolding of the natural laws of Progress, including the Darwinian theories of evolution, the classical-liberal views of market competition as the engine of economic progress, and the Hegelian-Marxist views of history as the arena for progressive expansions of human freedom. Modernity has, of course, brought about progressively higher levels of science and technology, wealth, income and consumption for those who have benefited from it. However, it also has led to the invention of weapons of mass destruction, the bloodiest century in all human history, holocausts and ethnic cleansing, environmental disasters, as well as rising expectations, frustrations, regression and aggression for those teeming millions who have been left behind in the twilight zones of tradition and modernity. The challenge lies therefore not so much in how to modernize as in how to tame modernity for those who have achieved it, those on the way, and those aspiring to its benefits.

The traditional geo-political or spatial divisions of the world into East and West, North and South, First, Second, Third, and Fourth Worlds, or Centres and Peripheries no longer ring true. Territories have been deterritorialized. The flows of goods, services, ideas, news, images and data have increasingly assumed a transnational character in a global economy and culture that values whatever is novel and affordable. Cheaper goods and novel ideas emerge perhaps as much from the traditional centres as from traditional peripheries. In the meantime, some centres have become peripherized (e.g. New York and Los Angeles slums), and some peripheries have assumed the status of industrial and financial centres (notably the four Asian tigers of South Korea, Singapore, Hong Kong and Taiwan). This does not mean that a new reign of world democracy has dawned. On the contrary, hard evidence shows that the world has become more differentiated and fragmented along growing gaps in social and economic equality (UNDP, 1996; Maitland, 1994; Tarjanne, 1992). But the globalization of the world economy has brought about a new deterritorialized system of centres and peripheries based on the levels of science, technology, productivity, consumption and creativity, regardless of location. The new centres and peripheries now reside in transnational organizations and *networks* wherever they happen to be situated.

The dynamics of accelerating, uneven, and self-contradictory global change can be therefore better understood in the light of a longer historical process that is still unfinished. For want of a better terminology, that process may be called 'modernization'. Although the term has accumulated a heavy baggage of theoretical biases with which we may not agree, it still continues to have analytic value. We use the concept here to mean a process of change that puts a primary value on scientific, technological, social, economic, political and cultural innovations in order to achieve progressively higher levels of productivity, wealth, income, consumption, democratic participation and cultural pluralism.

The European Enlightenment Movement provides the prime historical example of such modernization, but its fundamental assumptions can be questioned without rejecting modernization as a discourse or practice. A modernization project need not be conditioned, for instance, on the infinite perfectibility of humans, absolute power of Reason (often interpreted as instrumental reason), domination of nature, historical inevitability of progress, or total rejection of Tradition (whatever that means!). The capital letters 'R' in Reason and 'T' in Tradition are inserted here to mock the discourses that consider them as monolithic entities, one and indivisible, as if no tensions exist within the rational mind or a given cultural tradition. Reason can be viewed as torn among practical (our common sense), critical, communicative, and environmental reason. Most traditions are torn between their positivist and mystical interpretations focusing, respectively, on the letter or the spirit of the law. The discourses of scientific positivism, on the one hand, and religious fundamentalism, on the other, typify the cognitive tyrannies of a kind of modernity that privileges Positive Science or Positive Religion as the Natural Order. Contrary to their claims, however, successful modernization projects have often led to tradition in modernity, continuities punctuated by change, nurturing of nature, acceptance of the epistemological limits of human reason, and the recognition of the need for spiritual-mythological foundations in human communities. The tensions in human reasoning and cultural traditions may be thus viewed as creative sources for both continuity and change, stability and progress.

The forces of modernization have proved to be historically cataclysmic forces. They have torn societies asunder in successive acts of creative destruction. Since the sixteenth century, the project of modernity has gone through several phases, including a Sixth Modernization that currently appears to be the dominant trend. In the industrial centres of the world, the cultural resistances to its seemingly irresistible force have ranged from 'de-modernization' to 'post-modernization' movements. In the agrarian and industrializing peripheries of the world, modernization has been largely imposed from above by the colonial masters or the post-colonial elites. It has thus either launched 'hyper-modernization' campaigns to 'catch up', or it has devoutly resisted in 'counter-modernization' movements.

If there is a new world order, therefore, it can be better understood in terms of the paradoxes of a situation in which we are increasingly witnessing dazzling technological and economic breakthroughs without corresponding social, political and normative innovations. These epistemological lags are inducing economic growth without employment, political mobilization without political efficacy and cultural diversity without tolerance and civility. As Adam said to Eve, we are truly in an age of transition. We have lost our innocence by the Fall from the bliss of monoculturalism, but we have not yet gained an adequate knowledge of the complex shades of good and evil required for successful living in a multicultural world. In order to avoid the enormous risks facing us, the challenge lies perhaps in trying to bridge the widening chasms between the exploding technological opportunities, the currently unfulfilled human needs, and the social systems that attempt to fulfil them.

Deconstructing the discourse

The discourse of the New World Order is not so new. In a computerized search at the University of Hawaii, 125 items were retrieved, including books published around the two world wars, among them, Hitler's *My New Order* (1941). The roots of the discourse can be found in at least four major, competing theories of international relations, namely Realism, Liberalism, Marxism and Communitarianism. The Realists have primarily focused on the geo-politics of the struggles for power, employed the nation state as their chief unit of analysis, considered domestic and foreign policy as separate spheres of action, and argued that the pursuit of national interest in the context of a balance of power strategy is the safest and most 'realistic' road to international peace and security (Morgenthau, 1985; Kissinger, 1994). Realism has been the dominant school of thought both in theory and practice, focusing on peace through national strength, armament and balance of power.

The Liberals, by contrast, have pointed to the integrating forces of the world market as a new 'reality' that has created considerable international interdependency in the post-war period. They have argued that increasing levels of free trade, development, and the deepening and broadening of interdependency are the surest path to peace (Keohane and Nye, 1989).

The Marxists and Neo-Marxists, although in decline politically, continue to present powerful theoretical arguments that have an appeal in the peripheries of the world. They view international relations primarily in terms of class conflict within and between nations, and argue that since the sixteenth century the advanced capitalist countries have increasingly incorporated the peripheries of the world into a world system of domination and exploitation through imperialism, colonialism and neo-colonialism (Wallerstein, 1974; Schiller, 1976, 1989). The social revolutions in Russia, China, Cuba, Vietnam and many Third World countries have attempted to break away from the fetters of the world capitalist system. However, they are being reincorporated by an international regime (Krasner, 1983) orchestrated by the leading capitalist countries, the World Bank, the International Monetary Fund (IMF), the General Agreement on Tariffs and Trade (GATT), and its successor, the newly formed World Trade Organization (WTO). In the meantime, the Marxists argue, internal contradictions, wars and revolutionary struggles will continue to erode the world system.

Finally, the Communitarian perspective has been articulated by a perplexing diversity of political theorists and activists (Deutsch, 1966; Huntington, 1993a, 1993b; Tehranian, 1990; Tehranian and Tehranian, 1992). Although the ideologies of its proponents markedly differ, the idea of the centrality of institutions, culture, communication and community formation in international politics is what unifies this theoretical perspective. In the traditional literature of international relations, this school of thought is closely linked to the institutionalist perspectives emphasizing the processes of world integration. However, it also has manifested itself in a variety of anti-colonial, nationalist, tribalist, localist, ethnic and religious movements focused on the mobilization of the common historical memories of the peripheries to wage a cultural and political struggle against the centres. The Communitarians thus emphasize the centrality of political community in creating the conditions for a durable peace at local, national, regional and global levels.

Although each discourse has its own unique set of assumptions and conclusions, reflecting the competing interests in the international community, international communication has forced them into a grudging dialogue. This has resulted in a number of intertextual discourses conducted at international forums. Table 6.1 confines itself only to a genealogy of the more recent discourses and their metanarratives. It demonstrates how, like a chameleon, the slogan of the New World Order has historically changed its colours. Depending on who has used the slogan when, it has conjured up vastly different images. When a small group of oil exporting countries managed to quadruple the price of crude oil in 1973 through OPEC's collective action, it appeared for a while that the raw material exporting nations could now call for a new world economic order to redress the deteriorating terms of trade between the developed and developing countries. To the Group of 77 at the United Nations calling for a New World Economic Order in a 1974 General Assembly resolution, the new order meant a revamped international economic system to redress the terms of trade in favour of the less developed countries (LDCs). To UNESCO, which picked up the discourse in the 1970s and 1980s under the banner of a New World Information and Communication Order (NWICO), it meant *balance* as well as *freedom* in world news and information flows. The Brandt (1980, 1985) and MacBride (1980) Commission reports that emerged out of these efforts clearly set out those policy agendas (Frederick, 1993; Galtung and Vincent, 1992; Lee, 1985; Traber and Nordenstreng, 1992).

Table 6.1   *The New World Order discourses and metanarratives: a genealogy*

Dates and labels	Proponents	Opponents
1 The political discourses:		

1974–84   New World Economic Order   Group of 77   G7 led by US

The long-term deteriorating terms of trade between the industrial goods producing countries of the North and the raw material producing countries of the South have systematically deprived the LDCs of their chances for self-sustaining development. To correct these inequities, a New World Economic Order is needed to redress the terms of trade by collective bargaining, to provide access for the LDCs to the MDCs markets, and facilitate transfers of science and technology. Outcomes: the Brandt Report and North–South negotiations at United Nations Conference on Trade and Development (UNCTAD).

*1974–84   New World Information
and Communication Order*   Group of 77   G7 led by US

The media concentration in the hands of a few transnational corporations from a few advanced industrial countries has created a severe imbalance in the flow of news, images and data against the LDCs. The consequence of these imbalances is that the LDCs are often stereotyped as places where natural and man-made disasters are rampant. The genuine efforts of the LDCs for development are rarely noted. To correct these imbalances, a New World Information and Communication Order (NWICO) is needed in which the free flow of information is matched by a greater balance. In addition to South–South cooperation, the North has an obligation to assist the LDCs to build up their information and telecommunication infrastructure. Outcomes: The MacBride Report and the establishment of the International Program for the Development of Communication (IPDC) at UNESCO.

1989–93   The New World Order   US and Gulf War Allies   Iraq and sympathizers

The end of the Cold War has unleashed a variety of new threats to international peace and security by such small or medium powers as Iraq, Libya, Iran, North Korea and Serbia. To counter this threat and to establish a new regime of international law and order, the Great Powers through the United Nations or independently should police the world by active intervention in situations of conflict. Outcomes: UN intervention in the Persian Gulf War, Somalia, Bosnia and Haiti. The limited efficacy of such interventions has led to a decline of the discourse of 'the New World Order'.

2. The academic and policy discourses:

1945–present   Modernization Theories   Liberals   Marxists

As exemplified by the historical experiences of the West, the transition from traditional to modern societies is an inevitable historical process. The LDCs can best succeed by emulating that experience. The best policies to pursue are breaking the traditional cultural barriers to progress, democratizing their polities, liberalizing their markets, and encouraging foreign trade and investment.

*1945–present   Dependency and
World System Theories*   Marxists   Liberals

Capitalist penetration of the LDCs has progressively impoverished them materially and culturally, creating a dependency status for most. Some periphery nations such as Japan and South Korea have escaped this fate by joining the ranks of capitalist nations in a world system

continued overleaf

Table 6.1   *cont.*

Dates and labels	Proponents	Opponents

primarily run by the transnational corporations. Others may also join the ranks, but the system of capitalist exploitation will continue until socialist revolutions can abolish the class system.

1973–present Post-Industrial, *Information Society Theories*	Liberals	Marxists

In the advanced industrial countries, a progressive shift from manufacturing to service and information sectors has ushered in a new post-industrial society in which the greatest percentage of the labour force is engaged in the production, processing, transmission and application of knowledge and information. The resulting information economy and society is an international phenomenon facilitated by global transportation and telecommunication technologies. To catch up, the LDCs must follow a strategy of technological leapfrogging by the adoption of the latest industries and technologies.

1989–present End of History *and Clash of Civilizations Theories*	Fukuyama and Huntington

The end of the Cold War, the collapse of the Soviet Union and Eastern European communist regimes, and the introduction of market economies in the remaining communist countries, signals the global triumph of liberal, democratic capitalism. History as Hegel defined it to be the battlefield of ideas has thus come to an end. The rest will be devoted to the boring details of the global application of liberal democratic capitalist principles. This process, however, is encountering some resistance from other incompatible civilizations. The next world war may therefore be a war of civilizations between the Christian West and an emerging Confucian–Islamic alliance.

1980s–present Late Capitalism, *Postmodernist Theories*	Marxists and Post-Marxists

Late capitalism is exhibiting a number of features, including global expansion, flexible accumulation, deterritorialization, disorganization and displacement with postmodern cultural consequences. The process may be viewed either as potentially emancipatory in the unfinished project of the Enlightenment (Habermas) *or* as a new stage in the development of capitalism in which deconstructionist and anti-narrative strategies are most effective in leaving power no place to hide (Foucault). While the former strategy calls for a politics of meaning focused on creating alternative normative structures, the latter implies a politics of anti-politics.

Following the largely fruitless North–South negotiations of the 1980s, the discourse of the new order was resurrected by President Bush. To mobilize international support for a war effort against Saddam Hussein, Bush employed the slogan at the wake of the Persian Gulf War in 1990–91 with maximum effect. The discourse was thus turned into meaning a new international regime of 'law and order' under the aegis of the United Nations supported by the unanimity of the five permanent members of the Security Council. However, the brief consensus on the Gulf War came to an end by the rise of the domestic cleavages in Afghanistan, Tajikistan, Bosnia, Somalia, Rwanda, Chechnya and Haiti, where brute force continued to rule. International interventions in such conflicts have proved to be a mixed blessing. In the meantime, certain long-standing conflicts that had 'matured' into a new equilibrium for peace (those between the Arabs and Israelis, the Irish Protestants and Catholics, and the black and white South Africans) have successfully led to *rapprochement*. The post-Cold War world thus presents a contradictory picture of a new order punctuated by disorders that border on genocide (e.g. the Kurds, the Bosnian Muslims, the tribal feuds in Rwanda).

Francis Fukuyama's essay on 'The End of History?' (1989) belongs to the early phase of post-Cold war optimism. 'What we may be witnessing', he argued, 'is not just the end of the Cold War, or the passing of a particular period of postwar history, but the End of History as such: that is, the end point of mankind's [*sic*] ideological evolution and the universalization of Western liberal democracy as the final form of human government' (Fukuyama, 1989). All that is left to accomplish now is, according to him, the boring details of working out the implementation of the liberal-democratic capitalist agenda throughout the world.

This proposition was reminiscent of what Daniel Bell (1960) had argued a generation earlier. Unfortunately for the prophetic merit of both predictions, Bell's *The End of Ideology* and Fukuyama's 'The End of History' were published just before a new surge of ideological contestations on the world scene. The Cold Wars between the United States and Soviet Union, on the one hand, and between Soviet Union and China, on the other, characterized the 1960s. So did the counter-cultural movements in Europe and the United States. The 1990s are similarly characterized by the re-emergence of secular nationalism and religious resurgence to fill the ideological vacuum left by the end of the Cold War. The lesson seems unambiguous. Ideological contestations are a perennial part of human conflict. So long as conflict continues, ideologies will persist in order to embellish material interests with moral legitimacy while providing new myths for social solidarity and action. To be effective, however, ideologies have to cast their own particular myths into universal narratives. Hence, we have the narratives of 'End of History' and 'Clash of Civilization'. Both these myths, as all myths, have clearly some grounds in constructed realities.

The 'End of History' thesis points to the global expansion of the market economy and its liberal-democratic metanarrative. Huntington's 'Clash of Civilizations' (1993a) comes as the first phase of post-Cold War euphoria is giving way to a new phase of sober realism and even Hobbesian pessimism. He is appropriately sceptical of the triumph of liberal democracy. He ominously forecasts, however, that 'the clash of civilizations will dominate global politics. The fault lines between civilizations will be the battle lines of the future. The most prominent form of this cooperation is the Confucian–Islamic connection that has emerged to challenge Western interests, values and power' (Huntington, 1993a). The religious resurgence in the Judaic, Christian, Islamic, Hindu and Buddhist traditions, and the increasing economic and political cooperation between East Asian and Islamic countries, provide Huntington's thesis with some plausibility. However, to frame the complex and continuing gaps and conflicts of interests between the deterritorialized centres and peripheries in strictly geo-political terms is one-dimensional, simplistic and misleading. It may also serve as a justification for launching another Crusade, notwithstanding Huntington's call for peaceful coexistence. We define our worlds, and our worlds define us. What hard evidence there is also points to the fact that nations pursue their geo-political and economic interests more consistently than their presumed ideological pronouncements. The Iraq–Iran and Iraq–Kuwait wars were between Muslim nations. In Bosnia, the alliance of Catholic Croatians with Muslim Bosnians against Orthodox Christian Serbs supports a geo-political rather than a cultural explication. An emerging alliance of Russia, Iran and Armenia *vis-à-vis* Turkey, Azerbaijan and Western oil companies tells more about competing economic interests than cultural affinities.

If the articles by Fukuyama and Huntington were simple expressions of the optimistic and pessimistic temperaments of two solo scholars, there should have been no cause for concern. However, both articles have been celebrated by the US foreign policy establishment (the Council on Foreign Relations and its quarterly, *Foreign Affairs*, the US Institute of Peace, and a number of conservative, private think-tanks) as major intellectual breakthroughs in defining the post-Cold War era. While Fukuyama became the focus of much media attention in 1989–90 (Tehranian, 1989), the editors of *Foreign Affairs* compared the significance of Huntington's essay to another article published in that journal in 1945 by a Mr X (George Kennan). The latter had defined and shaped US policies in the Cold War for the next forty-five years. Just as Kennan's proposed 'containment' policy hardened the US position *vis-à-vis* the Soviet Union in the Cold War years, the Fukuyama and Huntington articles seem to propose a US hardening towards China and the Islamic world. The two articles serve several complementary functions. They fill the ideological vacuum left by the decline of communism by identifying a new ideological 'enemy'. While Fukuyama argues that the triumph of liberal democratic capitalism is inevitable, Huntington suggests that some residual resistance is still left (Chinese tyranny, Islamic bigotry) against that progressive movement of history.

The academic discourse on the post-industrial, postmodern, post-Fordist, information society has been equally controversial. The optimists and pessimists have similarly dominated the field. While liberal analysts such as Daniel Bell, Mark Porat and Yoneji Masuda provide generally optimistic scenarios, the Marxist world system theorists (e.g. Wallerstein, 1974, and others) present a rather pessimistic view of the emerging world order. At issue is the fate of the peripheries of power, whether situated in the urban ghettos of the First World or in the rural hinterlands of the Third World. While the optimists argue that a new phase of 'post-industrial, information society' will eventually 'trickle down' its benefits to the lower-income groups, the Marxists point to the structural impediments that will keep certain regions, societies and sectors of population perennially under-developing (So, 1990).

In the cultural arena, however, the left has become divided between the old and the new left. While the old left scholars tend to argue that the media conglomerates are homogenizing national cultures into the expanding global capitalist channels of consumer desires (Ewen and Ewen, 1982; Hamelink, 1983; Mattelart, 1983; Schiller, 1976), the new left points to the increasing participation of the peripheries in a global, multicultural, postmodernist pastiche of migrating meanings and identities. To capture the fluidity and irregularity of such transnational exchanges, Appadurai has suggested a number of channels, including 'ethnoscapes, mediascapes, technoscapes, finanscapes, ideoscapes' (1990, 1993). In the cultural arena, while the old left points to the narrowing of the public sphere of discourse (Habermas, 1984), the new left suggests that power is everywhere to be seized by the deconstructive hit and run tactics of postmodernism (Foucault, 1980). While the old left recommends a new politics of meaning focused on creating 'ideal speech communities' and 'alternative normative structures' (Habermas), the new left calls for a deconstructive politics of anti-politics (Foucault).

Mapping the New World Dis/Order

The new world order may be usefully viewed as a new phase in the progressive spatializations of power, that is as a succession of conquests of space by time (Soja, 1989). If we define modernization as the processes of compression of time and space to achieve progressively higher levels of productivity, the process has now reached nearly all corners of the globe. Time-saving (labour-saving) production techniques (assembly-line, robotics) and space-shrinking technologies (in modern transportation and telecommunications) have diffused modern ideas, technologies and organizations from the European centres to the rest of the world.

It is appropriate therefore to situate the problems of world conflict in the global processes of modernization and democratization that, since the sixteenth century, have led to growing material and cultural gaps between the centres and peripheries of power. Table 6.2 provides a schematic view of the unfolding of some 10,000 years of history. The table suggests (1) the combined and uneven development of the world in seven concurrent, contradictory and overlapping processes of modernization, democratization and communication; (2) reveals the collapses of time, space and identities in an accelerating process of history; and (3) implies a deterritorialization of the world centres and peripheries of development in a process of creating a new, global cognitive elite linked through common education and access to information via the global electronic networks.

The metaphor of tsunamis, or tidal waves, caused by sub-oceanic earthquakes is employed here to suggest the enormity of the creative destructions that the forces of modernization and democratization entail. Tsunamis also suggest the invisibility of the forces they generate. However, a few caveats are in order. First, Table 6.2 is constructed for heuristic purposes. The

Table 6.2 *Seven modernizations and democratizations: historical layers of global development*

Times	Spaces	Economies	Polities	Technologies	Ideologies	Communications
8000 BC –1492 AD	Agrarian empires	Agrarian revolution & multi-national bureaucratic empires	Feudal fiefdoms Democratization I: Direct democracy & Religious revolutions	Transmission of information: writing, ploughing, clay tablets, papyrus, roads, postal systems	Anticipatory modernization: Rationalism vs. Shamanism & religious dogmatism	Oral & written: Shamans Soothsayers, Poets, Prophets Priests, Temples
1492–1648	City-states	Commercial revolution (aka Mercantile Capitalism)	Rise of City-States; Democratization II: Protestant Reformation & Scientific Revolution	Mechanization of information: Print, Compass, Oceanfaring ships	Mercantilism vs. Feudalism	Print: Intellectuals, Scientists, Universities
1648–1848	Nation-states	Industrial revolution (aka Manufacturing Capitalism)	Rise of nation-states & Colonial empires: Democratization III: Liberal democratic revolutions	Mass production of information: Newspapers, Magazines, Books, Steamships, Trains	Liberal nationalism vs. Monarchical Absolutism	Elite media: Publicists
1848–1945	Industrial Empires	Banking revolution (aka Finance Capitalism)	Multipolar world system Democratization IV: Social democratic & Totalitarian revolutions	Electrification of information: Telegraphy, Telephony, Photography, Film, Radio, Automobile, Airplane, Paper money & banking	Imperialism vs. National liberation ideologies	Mass media: Ideologues

continued overleaf

Table 6.2 *cont.*

Times	Spaces	Economies	Polities	Technologies	Ideologies	Communications
1945–1989	Planet	Managerial revolution (aka Corporate Capitalism vs. State Capitalism/ Communism)	Bipolar world system Democratization V: National liberation revolutions	Digitalization of information: TV, Computers, Satellites, Transborder data flows, Electronic cash transfers, Atomic energy, Space probes	Globalism (Capitalism vs. Communism) vs. Nationalism	Big/small media: Technologues vs. Communologues
1989 –present	Cyberspace	Information revolution (aka Technocratic Capitalism)	Multipolar world system & Democratization VI: Localist, Ethnic, Religious, Feminist revolts	Integration of information ISDN & Multimedia DBS, Global Networks (CNN, MTV, Internet)	Ecumenicalism vs. Fundamentalism	Cybermedia: Technologues, Communologues vs. Jestologues
Futures	Hyperspace	Space revolution (Communitarian vs. Totalitarian Capitalism)	Cyborg planetary system Democratization VII: Underclass revolts against dehumanization	Totalization of information: Time-travel, Cyborgs, Genetic engineering, Spaceships & voyages	Totalism vs. Communitarianism	Hypermedia: Shamans, Soothsayers, Visuologues

dates, in particular, should be taken seriously but not too seriously. They suggest some important but arguable historical watersheds. Secondly, although it may appear otherwise, the table does not present a stage theory of history. In fact, history is considered here as conjunctural and curvilinear rather than progressive and linear. The table should be thus viewed as layering of history rather than stages of history. Thirdly, the long period of history lumped together in the first tsunami may be considered as *anticipatory modernization* during which significant accumulations of science, technology and capital in the ancient and medieval worlds took place. These provided the stock of knowledge from which the modern West heavily borrowed in order to pave the way to the Industrial Revolution. Fourthly, the last tsunami is entirely hypothetical, taking us into the realm of science fiction.

Let us now review Table 6.2 in its horizontal and vertical dimensions. Vertically, Table 6.2 can be read as a progressive collapse of time and space while, horizontally, it reveals a dual process at work towards homogenizing and differentiating human identities. The collapses of time have revealed themselves in the accelerating rate of major technological breakthroughs (Toffler, 1980). Scientific and technological knowledge is an additive phenomenon, feeding upon itself. It is not surprising, therefore, that it takes less and less time to move from one major technological breakthrough to another. Under the impact of rapid scientific and technological change, history also is visibly accelerating. It took, for instance, a century of struggle and two world wars for the edifice of modern European empires to collapse. But the Soviet Empire collapsed of its own accord in 1991 and within less than a decade. Similarly, the table shows that the succession of historical tsunamis is occurring at lesser intervals as we move towards contemporary times.

The collapse of space is also visible from the table. Modernization as a process is incorporating progressively larger spaces within its domain of power, from localities to cities, nation states, empires, the planet, the cyberspace of the global telecommunication networks, and the hyperspace of new dimensions of reality beyond the four of which we are aware (Kaku, 1994). In our own age of global communication, distances are being conquered by time. As in time travel, historical anachronisms also have become commonplace. Different historical epochs live side by side in the same spaces. As tsunamis collide on the surface of the ocean, so do civilizations and cultures. They borrow, steal and adapt elements from their friends and enemies in order to advance their own cause. That is how an uneven world such as ours survives, adapts, moves forward and backward. An African village could juxtapose some of the signs of premodern, modern, and postmodern lives in a single space, encompassing the plough, the automobile, Coca-Cola, and Madonna's songs and semi-nude pictures. Art also imitates reality. The new postmodernist art juxtaposes times, spaces and identities of different historical epochs in pastiches that shock and decentre our present sensibilities.

The fusion of identities is a more complex process but no less visible. The globalization of markets, communications and cultures has led, from a pessimist view, to a Coca-Colonization of the world while, and from an optimist view, it has resulted in global consciousness and citizenship. Whichever way we look at the phenomenon, it is certain that the awakening of progressively larger segments of humanity to historical consciousness and the increasing demands made by them to become subjects rather than objects of history has led to a differentiation of identities along religious, linguistic, ethnic, gender and generational lines. The debate between the primordialists and constructivists on identity formations has served to demonstrate that humans construct their identities out of both past memories and present needs (Anderson, 1983). The collective memories are, in fact, politically negotiated to construct an identity that suits the perceived present and future needs of human communities. The differentiation and integration of identities is thus a dual process in history that has accelerated with higher levels of modernization, democratization and communication. The individual and social constructions of identity have been thus facilitated by the increasing availability and projection of a rich repertoire of imaginaries from the past into the future.

These three historical processes have, however, given rise to enormous material and cultural disparities in the world, leading to a variety of conceptual maps. The social and political constructions of the world around such concepts as Occident and Orient (encompassing Europe and Asia), East and West (i.e. the communist and capitalist worlds), First, Second and Third Worlds (i.e. the capitalist, communist and non-aligned countries), North and South (industrial and pre-industrial nations), or Centre and Periphery (developed and underdeveloped countries) may all be considered as attempts to describe, analyse and sometime legitimate the world disparities in particular historical contexts. The complexities of the world, however, do not easily lend themselves to such conceptual schemes. To allow for the increasing orders of complexity, some authors (Galtung and Vincent, 1992) have even proposed a Fourth World that includes the newly industrialized countries (NICs) of East Asia (Japan, China, South Korea, Hong Kong, Taiwan and the ASEAN). One could add to that a Fifth World (the least developed countries), and so on, in order to account for the increasing differentiation among the world nation states.

The main problem with all of these conceptual maps is that they are basically territorial in conception. Global modernization and communication are, however, fast deterritorializing and informatizing the world. Some parts of the industrial world Centres (notably the urban ghettos) are fast becoming peripherized (witness the rise of the unemployed and unemployable underclass in advanced industrial societies, in the United States approaching 20% of the population), while certain parts of the pre-industrial Peripheries and industrializing Semi-peripheries are achieving the high standards of living of the Centres (e.g. Guangdong Province in China, the city-states of Hong Kong and Singapore, the urban centres of the

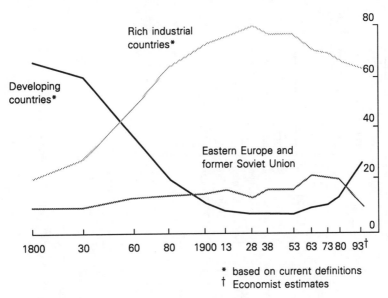

World manufacturing output, % shares

Figure 6.1 *The cycles of history*

Source: Woodall, 1994

NICs). As the engines of the global economy, the transnational corporations (TNCs) have little regard for territorial boundaries. They go wherever lower wages, rents, taxes and government regulation promise higher profits. The movements of capital and labour across the globe are further facilitated by the transportation, telecommunication and tourism (TTT) technologies that have made central and global strategic planning possible when, and if, it is combined with decentralized operations by the corporate subsidiaries.

As *The Economist* 'Survey of the World Economy' projects (Woodall, 1994), there is a possibility that sometime in the next century, the pendulum of history might swing back to Asia (see Figure 6.1). Around 1500, the adoption of the Chinese compass and the construction of oceanworthy ships by the Europeans led to the discovery of ocean routes to the Orient, opening the way for trade with and colonization of Asia, Africa and the Americas. The replacement of such land routes as the Silk and Spice Roads for world trade by the ocean routes weakened the Asians and strengthened the Europeans. The Asian countries lost their leading position in manufacturing to the European countries by the mid-nineteenth century. By technological leapfrogging and economic miracles, however, the Asians are now catching up. If the present rates of economic growth continue without any political mishaps, Asia may reach and possibly surpass the West by the year 2020 with China leading as the world's largest economy (see Figure 6.2).

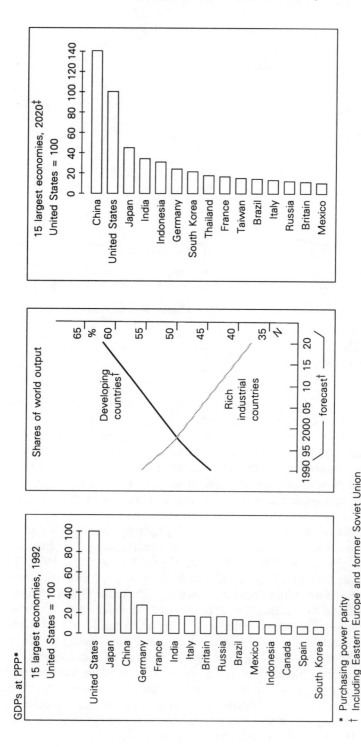

* Purchasing power parity
† Including Eastern Europe and former Soviet Union
‡ Forecasts assume countries continue to grow at regional rates projected in the World Bank's *Global Economic Prospects*

Figure 6.2   *2020vision*

Source: Woodall, 1994

Centres, Peripheries and Semi-peripheries, therefore, can no longer be seen as neatly and permanently defined spatial categories; they should rather be conceived as deterritorialized and informatized *networlds*. The social status of individuals can no longer be assessed by their spatial location. An individual can live in New York and yet be worse off than another individual living in Bombay. S/he should be considered as part of a periphery in Harlem rather than of the core at Wall Street. The critical question in the emerging global hierarchy is whether an individual is informationally linked with the technostructures of government, corporate and related decision-making institutions. Levels of wealth, income, education and network connections clearly correlate positively with these informational and communication links. The chief actors in this global hierarchy are those who stand at the apex of the information pyramid. That is why the information-rich are often the same as those actively engaged in the processes of global decision-making, while the information-poor are subjected to the consequences of those decisions.

Seven modernizations: the layering of history

Table 6.2 provides a schematic outline of seven interlocking phases in modernization as experienced by the advanced industrial world. In this adaptive process, the less developed countries (LDCs) are currently emulating and leapfrogging the more developed countries (MDCs). Capitalism initially started with the spatial integration of the modern mercantile cities moving successively on to the nation-state, imperial, global, and increasingly planetary and cyberspatial systems. If thus viewed, the processes of modernization can no longer be seen as a uniquely European phenomenon. Despite its dramatic results, modernization also cannot be considered as an abrupt change in the course of history. History crawls more than it leaps; it is evolving rather than making discrete departures from the past. Contrary to the traditional theories of modernization, history also does not move in clearly defined stages. Rather, new layers of economic, political, and cultural formations are added to the old. The Bazaars and the mosques in Central Asia, for example, did not die under the Soviet regime. They just hibernated and have now come back to claim their share of the economic and cultural life. Modernization should be thus viewed as an accumulative process of accelerating change achieved by successive applications of scientific and technological knowledge without necessarily obliterating tradition. The pace of that change has historically gained an exponential momentum. Given the elements of continuity and change in this process, however, 'punctuated evolution' rather than 'revolution' is a more appropriate metaphor.

Modernization I

In each successive tsunami, Table 6.2 draws attention to the times, spaces, economies, polities, technologies, ideologies and communication institutions and elites of modernization. Sometime around 8000 BC, a transition from hunting and gathering to agrarian societies must have occurred (Frankfort et al., 1963). That transition clearly required a higher order of complexity and organization than that of the earlier era. To tame the land, the domestication of animals and invention of agricultural tools were necessary. To assert the rights of individual or collective ownership to land and its fruits, accounting systems were required. Writing and numerology assisted in this process. But to record and transmit such information, the clay tablets and papyrus came into play. Roads and postal systems were built to facilitate market exchange and central government control. But agrarian societies could not possibly survive without a rudimentary science that made technological innovation possible, however slowly. Transmission of information through writing and libraries in such places as Alexandria in ancient Egypt and Gundishapur in ancient Iran, became the indispensable tools of knowledge storage and retrieval for successive generations. Despite the enormous diversity of agrarian societies, for the sake of simplicity, we may consider this long wave of human evolution as anticipatory modernization lasting some 8,500 years.

The development of the democratic ideas of freedom, equality and community during this long period has been somewhat haphazard, but the universalistic and egalitarian religions (notably Buddhism, Christianity and Islam) clearly paved the way. The rejection of the traditional tribal, caste or racial hierarchies has been at the heart of these religious traditions. In Buddhism, the possibility of spiritual enlightenment (*nirvana* or inner freedom from self-desire and its sufferings) is held up to all humanity without exception. In Christianity, Jesus offered his love and forgiveness to all but considered salvation a privilege especially available to those who have accepted his path and renounced the riches of this world. In Islam, all humanity stands as equal in the sight of God, but those professing Islam will be especially granted the peace of God.

The contributions of the secular creeds to democratization during this period is somewhat problematic. Athenian democracy in the Age of Pericles provided a form of direct democracy by allowing citizens to participate in the affairs of the state by discussing and voting on public issues, but citizenship was denied to women and slaves. The Roman Empire similarly limited its democratic privileges to the citizens of Rome, while women and slaves were excluded. Other imperial systems in China, India, Persia and Russia were largely based on the Divine Right of kings and absolute powers. Such famous legal documents as the Code of Hammurabi (1750 BC) and Magna Carta (AD 1215) may be considered as the precursors to America's contemporary Bill of Rights, but their rights and privileges were limited to a limited aristocracy. It took the civil rights movement of the 1960s for all Americans to finally arrive at universal suffrage.

The role of communication and communicators in the earliest processes of democratization is pivotal. The Agora in Greece, the Roman Senate and the Ka'aba in Mecca may be considered as the precursors of our own modern public sphere. In such forums, the shamans, soothsayers, poets, philosophers, orators and prophets could address a large audience publicly on matters of public importance. However, the transition from the oral to written traditions created a new cognitive and communication elite that replaced the orators. The rise of writing gave birth to the Holy Writ, and a new class of custodians who established their own religious institutions and priestly hierarchies. The emergence of religious institutions as distinct from the state institutions provided a basis for resistance against the arbitrary powers of rulers. To the extent that these institutions enjoyed autonomy in sources of financing, drawn from the guilds and merchants, they also exercised some check and balance *vis-à-vis* the state.

The seeds of commercialism and a kind of primitive capitalism were sown along the world's first global economy – the Silk and Spice Routes. Along these routes, in the ancient cities of Beijing, Xian, Kashqar, Samarkand, Bukhara, Neishapur, Rey, Isfahan, Baghdad, Mecca, Medina, Bombay, Damascus, Aleppo, Constantinople, Athens and Rome, urban civilizations developed that housed industrial arts and crafts, observatories, universities and libraries. Under the weight of rapacious agrarian empires, however, they constantly waxed and waned. The rise and fall of these multinational, agrarian imperial systems closely correlated with the rise or fall of the cities. The absence of autonomous municipalities and independent merchant classes to support their continuous prosperity often led to cycles of urban rise and ruin. Imperial systems provided for expanded security and trade, but their decline often caused political fragmentation and breakdown of trade routes.

Modernization II

The genius of modern Europe was in that it managed to break through this vicious cycle. A second tidal wave of modernization set in the Western European scene by the sixteenth century. The important historical watersheds in this tsunami were, in 1492, the final expulsion of the Muslims from Granada in Spain while Columbus was stumbling into a New World in the same year. Reformation and Renaissance followed shortly thereafter. Beginning with Martin Luther's posting of ninety-five theses on the church door at Wittenberg, in 1517, the Protestant revolt against the Catholic Church signalled a religious war that continued to the end of the Thirty Years War and the Peace of Westphalia in 1648. The Reformation took many different forms in Europe, but its Protestant ethics of frugality, hard work, savings and investment clearly ushered in a new spirit of capitalism (Weber, 1958; Tawney, 1984). Similarly, the Renaissance, lasting from the fourteenth to the mid-seventeenth century introduced a new spirit of humanism in arts and letters, scientific exploration and commerce.

The combined effects of Reformation and Renaissance were threefold – privatization, nationalization and secularization. First, through the Protestant challenge to papal authority and Catholic hierarchy, religious faith and morality in Christendom became increasingly privatized, that is, a matter between God and the individual's conscience rather than an issue in the hands of the intermediary, priestly class. Individual responsibility and freedom of conscience thus gave a further impetus to the processes of individuation that modernity entails. The distinction between the private and public spheres of discourse also was in part a consequence of this privatization. Secondly, as the Protestant revolution spread throughout Europe and the Americas, it branched into a complex variety of national and subnational churches that employed the vernacular languages instead of Latin, following particular national rather than the Catholic (i.e. universal) traditions. The Lutheran Church in Germany and the Church of England were the first national churches to declare their independence from Rome, but others soon followed. The national Protestant churches owed their growth in no small measure to the rise of the print technology, making the translation and publication of the Bible in the vernacular, European languages possible. Thirdly, the Renaissance, combined with the Scientific Revolution of the seventeenth century, led to the rise of a secular culture that, when combined with the privatization of faith and nationalization of religious institutions, provided a powerful ideological force towards modernization. That, in turn, rationalized the religious institutions away from their magical foundations (miracles, superstitions) towards more worldly concerns.

However, the second tsunami of modernization clearly owed its material force to the rise of the modern mercantile cities in which the seeds of modern capitalism were sown by the monetization and commercialization of the European economies. Urbanization during the Middle Ages was a very slow process but it created large cities such as Venice, Florence, Amsterdam, Lisbon, Barcelona, London and Paris, serving as the centres of a new urbanism. Although large cities were characteristic of the ancient Asian and African civilizations as well, the new European cities were markedly different in that they enjoyed some measure of municipal autonomy. Whereas Rome, Constantinople, Baghdad, Cairo, Isfahan, Delhi, Beijing and Timbuktu served as the urban centres of multinational, agrarian empires, the new European cities were breaking from the agrarian past into a new era of mercantile capitalism. The Crusades of the eleventh to thirteenth centuries, technological breakthroughs in ocean transportation, the discovery of the New World in the late fifteenth century, the flow of newly discovered gold from the New World to the Old World, the scientific revolution of the seventeenth century, the rise of manufacturing in the new towns, the Enlightenment Movement in the eighteenth century, and the political revolutions of the eighteenth and nineteenth centuries each contributed to a transfer of economic and political power from the feudal lords and manors to a new class of merchants in the new mercantile towns and cities under a new capitalist order. Heilbroner has aptly summarized the process:

> When the traveling merchants stopped, they naturally chose the protected site of a local castle or burg. And we find growing up around the walls of advantageously situated castles – in the *focus burgis*, whence *faubourg*, the French word

for 'suburb' – more or less permanent trading places, which in turn became the inner core of small towns. Nestled close to the castle wall for protection, the new burgs were still not 'of' the manor. The inhabitants of the burg – the burgesses, burghers, bourgeois – had at best an anomalous and insecure relation to the manorial world within. As we have seen, there was no way of applying the time-hallowed rule of 'ancient customs' in adjudicating their disputes, since there *were* no ancient customs in the commercial quarters. Neither were there clear-cut rules for their taxation or for the particular degrees of fealty they owed their local masters. Worse yet, some of the growing towns began to surround themselves with walls. By the twelfth century, the commercial burg of Bruges, for example, had already swallowed up the old fortress like a pearl around a grain of sand. (Heilbroner, 1962: 48)

The Commercial Revolution and its cultural orchestration by the Reformation, Renaissance and the Scientific Revolution of the seventeenth century thus contributed to the development of a modern, democratic cultural system that put the individual at the centre of social responsibility. The dual challenge to the authorities of the Church and monarchies on behalf of individual rights and responsibilities of citizenship received its ideological impetus from a new communication elite, the intellectuals, who were situated in the modern, secular universities while riding on the wave of the new technology of print. Print provided not only direct access to the Holy Writ, pluralizing its interpretations, but it also allowed the new secular, scientific and philosophical ideas to spread among an increasing number of the literate population (Eisenstein, 1979).

Modernization III

In the processes of anticipatory modernization, it was often the countryside that controlled the cities in the form of land-owning feudal aristocracies or tribal conquests. But the growth of modern cities signalled a reversal of that role. In fact, the new cities' superior technological and organizational abilities for accumulation of capital led, in turn, to a Third Modernization – the rise of the territorial nation-state system. It is customary to consider the Peace of Westphalia in 1648 as the beginning of the modern nation-state system. As an island 'nation', England led the way in this process, demonstrating, in effect, the advantages of the nation state as a new form of political and spatial organization. The ideology of the new political-spatial entity was Nationalism, its religion was embodied in a national church such as the Church of England and other Protestant churches declaring their independence from the Papacy; its language was no longer Latin, but instead the vernacular languages such as English, French, German and Italian; its ethos became the rationalized Protestant ethics which, as Max Weber (1958) has argued, emboldened 'the spirit of capitalism' towards hard work, frugality, saving and investment. Although the Catholic countries (France, Italy and Spain) did not break away from Rome, they too came increasingly under the impact of a nationalism that fostered the secular spirits of rationality, science and technology. In comparison to the imperial or city-states of the past, the nation-state system clearly supplied a far more homogeneous population, greater defensible natural boundaries, economies of scale, and superior social and political opportunities for mobilizing the population on national missions of consolidation and expansion.

The United States was the 'First Nation' (Lipset, 1963) to come about through a written constitution, demonstrating how the imaginary of nationhood could be realized more through solidarity of democratic ideas than ties of blood and race. Following the American example, the construction of the nation-state system reached its fruition in Europe during the nineteenth century by the unifications of the German and Italian states into two new nation-state systems. The system received further impetus following the First World War by the breakdown of the Ottoman, Austro-Hungarian and Russian Empires and the emergence of new nation states in the Balkans and the Arab world. The Second World War extended the system to Asia, Africa and Latin America through the breakdown of the European imperial systems. In 1991, the breakdown of the world's last empire, the Soviet Union, led to a further proliferation of the nation states.

The Third Democratization was mainly achieved through the liberal democratic revolutions of England (1688), the United States (1776) and France (1789). The ideas of liberalism and nationalism combined to provide the basis both for free trade and protectionism. The tension between the two imperatives of capitalist growth, at the domestic and international levels, became the main source of international conflict in the next century of imperialist rivalries. In the meantime, however, the Enlightenment *philosophes* in France, the liberal political economists in England, and the Federalist publicists in the United States had sown the seeds of a universal doctrine of liberty and equality that could and *did* later undermine the empires. Collectively known as the contractualist theorists (notably John Locke, Thomas Hobbes, Jean-Jacques Rousseau, and the American Federalists, Hamilton, Jay and Madison), they posited a doctrine of natural rights that viewed the individuals in the state of nature entering into a contract to form a government that would protect their life, liberty and property (or pursuit of happiness, in the Jeffersonian formulation). This was a radical departure from the Divine Rights of kings towards a doctrine of popular sovereignty that became the cornerstone of most democratic constitutions. The mass production of information (newspapers, magazines, books) and mass transportation (steam ships and trains) rapidly spread the new ideas around the world. Despite these democratic ideals, however, universal suffrage was not achieved in most countries until the twentieth century. The United States Constitution, for example, effectively limited voting rights to about only 10% of the US population in 1788. It was not until 1920 when that right was extended to women through the ratification of the 19th Amendment, and not until 1965 when the Voting Rights Act enabled the Afro-Americans to register and vote.

Modernization IV

As old empires were collapsing, however, a new, industrial imperialism was being born in the nineteenth century that may be considered as the Fourth Modernization. As Hobson (1902) and Lenin (1917) first recognized, the new imperialism was materially different from all empires of the past. It was built on the foundations of the new capitalist order, driven by the search for new sources of raw materials, cheap labour and consumer markets. Flag followed trade rather than the other way around. Military conquest served only as the last resort for opening up new territories for capitalist exploitation. The shifts from small-scale, entrepreneurial capitalism to large-scale, corporate capitalism, and from manufacturing domination to the supremacy of finance capital, all happening in the second half of the nineteenth century (Trachtenberg, 1982), made the growth of the new empires both possible and, from the capitalist point of view, desirable. Although *Pax Britannica* ruled the world between the end of Napoleonic Wars in 1815 and the outbreak of the First World War in 1914, the foundations for a multi-polar world were formed by the rise of the United States, Japan, Germany and Russia as rival superpowers. The two world wars of the twentieth century could be, in fact, viewed as the struggles in the imperialist game between the old players (England, France and Russia) and the new players (Japan, Germany, Italy and the United States).

Democratization took a new twist in this phase by developments against the centre of the political spectrum led by the leftist and rightist forces. The year 1848 was, ironically, both the year of liberal democratic revolutions in Western Europe as well as that of the publication of *The Communist Manifesto*. In that political tract, Marx and Engels predicted the rise of a proletarian revolution, first in Germany and subsequently elsewhere, while the logic of their own argument called for a global triumph of capitalism before socialism could be established. Their revolutionary enthusiasm had thus blinded them to their own more sober logic. Nevertheless, the class contradictions of liberal capitalism had already created two types of grave-diggers for liberal democracy, that is a revolutionary working class and a disenchanted lower middle class, both led by a new type of communication elite, *the ideologues*. Electrification of information through telegraphy and telephony had facilitated the communication systems of not only the empires but also those of the oppositions. Mass circulation newspapers, radio broadcasting, photography and film also added new arsenals to mass movements in Europe and Asia, challenging the authority of the imperial system. Lenin, as the chief ideologue of the left, revised the Marxist theories to argue that the socialist revolution need not wait for the world-wide triumph of capitalism; instead, it can strike at the weakest links of capitalist-imperialist chain in Russia and the colonial world. Hitler, as the chief ideologue of the right, revised the liberal theories to argue for the hegemony of capital within a national, rather than international, socialist framework. The populism of both ideologies drew millions of the working and lower middle classes within the vortex of movements that, despite their democratic appeals to egalitarianism, ultimately proved to be totalitarian in nature. In Germany, Italy, Japan and Spain, it united the capitalist class with the lower middle classes against the liberal and communist movements. In the Soviet Union, it led to the rise of a bureaucratic state capitalist *cum* communist regime.

The rise of totalitarian regimes of the right and the left proved that the transition to the modern, industrial world need not take place through a liberal democratic regime. In fact, the late-comers to industrialization have often been faced with a pathology of transition that calls for hyper-modernization by means of central planning and regimentation. The totalitarian temptation may be thus considered as inherent in the processes of modernization, particularly when class contradictions destroy or seriously threaten the ruling elites. In the former case, it often leads to a revolutionary movement, supported by the working class and peasantry, that has little regard for civil liberties. In the latter case, it usually brings about an alliance between the ruling elites and the mobilized lower middle classes, united in their struggles against liberalism and communism.

Modernization V

The Fifth Modernization may be considered to have begun, in 1945, with the rise of globalism at the conclusion of the Second World War. Two factors were paramount at this historical juncture – the collapse of the European empires and the pre-eminence of the United States. At the conclusion of the Second World War, the United States produced over 50% of the world gross product. However, assisted by the United States, Western Europe and Japan soon regained their lost economic power. But fortified by the establishment of the United Nations on the basis of the principle of national self-determination, the national liberation movements in the colonial world destroyed the old and exhausted European empires that could no longer endure as viable forms of political-spatial organization. As a former colony itself and a new superpower, the United States was well-poised to lead the way towards a new principle of globalism. The Bretton Woods Agreements (1944) provided the economic basis for such a global capitalist system by creating a World Bank to channel investments from the more to the less developed countries, an International Monetary Fund (IMF) to manage the international currency exchange convertibility, and the General Agreement on Tariffs and Trade (GATT) to encourage world trade by reducing the tariff and non-tariff barriers.

The United Nations also was to provide the political basis for a global collective security system guaranteed by the five permanent members of the Security Council. However, the unanimity needed for such a system broke down with the onset of the Cold War in 1947. The wars in Korea and Vietnam further undermined the UN collective security system by pitting the First World (i.e. the capitalist countries) against the Second World (i.e.

the communist countries), largely in alliance with the revolutionary parts of the Third World. Nevertheless, globalism continued its irresistible growth through 'the global reach' (Barnet and Muller, 1974) of the transnational corporations (TNCs). In their search for new sources of raw materials, consumer markets, investment opportunities, low taxes, low rents, low wages and low government control, the TNCs devised global strategies that ensured them centralized control but spatial and managerial dispersion. Globalism also has been further strengthened by the reach of global advertising and the culture of mass consumption that it fosters. The seductions of the 'soft power' (Nye, 1990) of cultural appeal have proved nearly as powerful as the 'hard power' of military might and economic gravity.

Globalism, however, appeared in two distinct versions – liberal capitalism and Soviet communism – each covertly or overtly opposing the nascent nationalism of the post-colonial world. During the Cold War, the Enlightenment Idea of Progress was presented to the world in the form of two options – development by the market rules or by central planning. The rivalries of the two superpowers for the hearts and minds of the rest of the world were a total war that employed both the cool methods of ideological struggle as well as the hot instruments of naked violence. In places such as Korea, Vietnam, Cambodia, Iran, Congo, Angola, Somalia, Chile, Nicaragua, Cuba and Afghanistan, it erupted into military confrontations or CIA subversions that assumed dramatic importance. Both camps employed all of the media arsenal at their disposal – print, film, radio, television, satellites and computers. Radio Free Europe, Radio Liberty, the United States Information Agency (USIA), and the American friendship societies were the government agents. They were supplemented by such commercial media as *Time* and *Life* magazines, Hollywood films, global advertising and direct broadcast satellites (DBS). Although less powerful and pervasive, the Soviet and the Chinese communist regimes also attempted to compete in all of these fields, by equal means or by jamming the enemy radio frequencies. In Eastern Europe and the Caribbean, radio wars sometimes assumed subversive proportions.

The 'big media' (BBC, Voice of America, CNN, MTV, Hollywood films, global newspapers such as *The Wall Street Journal* and *The International Herald Tribune*, and global news magazines such as *Time*, *Newsweek* and *The Economist*) have served as the ideological vehicles of the First World. Their equivalents in the Second World have been Radio Moscow, Radio Beijing, *New Times* and *Beijing Review*. On both sides of the ideological camp, however, a new and distinctly different communication elite was managing the huge technostructures of global communication. Standing apart from earlier print generations of *publicists* and *ideologues* and riding high on the technological wave of digitalization of information, the new communication elite may be called *technologues*. The convergence of voice, data and images into a single stream of electronic, digital signals known as ISDN, the Integrated System Digital Network, has been blurring the boundaries among media technologies, institutions and professions. For the technologues, knowledge of the emerging technologies has to combine with the managerial skills for running large and complex technocracies. In the advanced industrial societies, the locus of power seems to have decisively shifted from ideas and ideologues to techniques and technologues.

In the Third World, however, where the level of technological development has lagged behind, other types of communication elite have been in formation. The intellectuals and ideologues, associated with the print and broadcasting media, are situated in the emerging institutions of universities, mass media and mass political parties. However, the broadening and deepening of mass movements into the more traditional sectors of the population has led to the rise of a more recent communication elite that may be called *communologues*. In contrast to the intellectuals and ideologues who speak in the universal grammar of the Enlightenment project (namely liberalism and Marxism), the communologues converse in the vernacular of the indigenous religious, ethnic and nationalist discourses. In contrast to the intellectual-ideologues of an earlier generation of Third World leaders (such as Nehru, Mosaddeq, Nasser, Sukarno, Mao, Chou En-lai, Nkrumah and Nyerere), the communologue leaders such as Gandhi in India, Khomeini in Iran, Shaikh Fadlallah in Lebanon and the Theology of Liberation priests in Latin America, come from a religious perspective, rejecting the secular views of progress while reconstructing their own indigenous Hindu, Islamic or Christian traditions. When combined with mass movements, the small media of mimeographing and copying machines, audio and video-cassette recorders, transistor radios, and increasingly desktop publishing, have given the new communication elite a power to challenge the authority of the ruling elites and their big media.

The rise of political religion is not, however, limited to the Third World. The Electronic Church in the United States and its offshoots into Latin America, the re-emergence of the Russian Orthodox Church in the former Soviet Union, the rise of ethno-religious conflicts in the former Yugoslavia and the Republics of Armenia and Azerbaijan, all seem to suggest that religion is once again presenting a powerful source of political energy for a variety of social movements from the right as well as the left of the political spectrum. In fact, the terms 'right' and 'left', originating from the secular French revolutionary ideas and practices, have lost some of their analytical power in understanding neotraditionalist and postmodern politics.

The rejection of the grand metanarratives of evolutionary progress is a hallmark of postmodernism. The emergence of postmodern architecture and city planning in reaction to the preponderance of the rationalist, glass boxes of modernist architecture and urban design may be viewed as part of the transition from the Fifth to the Sixth Modernization (K. Tehranian, 1995). The universalism of the modernist, international style was challenged by the eclecticism and pastiche quality of postmodern architecture. The utopian cities of the modern world have been similarly giving their place to the 'collage cities' of the postmodern cities (Rowe and Koetler, 1992).

Rejecting the grand utopian visions of total planning and total design, the postmodernists are calling for an eclectic city of many faces and neighbourhoods that can accommodate a whole range of utopias in miniature.

Postmodernist cultural trends have similarly challenged the metanarratives of modernist culture. Exposure to the diversity of global cultures has, however, challenged the foundations of globalism as an ideology of modernity. It has decentred its universalistic claims of the Enlightenment project and created a new sense of cultural relativism. It also has juxtaposed localist cultures and practices alongside the global artifacts of skyscrapers, McDonald's, Coca-Cola and Hilton Hotels. Thus, the tension between the global and the local has been an incipient political and cultural feature of the Fifth Modernization. The unresolved contradictions have erupted into the open with greater gusto following the end of the Cold War and a balance of terror between the two superpowers. The military strategy of mutually assured destruction (whose appropriate acronym is MAD) ensured an international equilibrium that was disturbed only during crises and brinksmanships such as the Missile Crisis of 1962.

Modernization VI

The Sixth Modernization may be dated from 1989 when, at the meeting of Presidents Bush and Gorbachev in Malta, the Cold War came to an end. From Yalta (1945) to Malta (1989), the world witnessed an uneasy equilibrium between the two superpowers, each armed with weapons of mass destruction sufficient to annihilate the human race not once but several times. With the demise of the Soviet Union and the more gradual slippage of China into the vortex of world capitalism, the capitalist version of globalism seems more irresistible in the 1990s than ever before. The passage of GATT in the United States Congress, in late 1994, and its ratification by some 123 countries, signals another new and significant departure towards globalism. Known for years as the Global Agreement to Talk and Talk, the new GATT will be enforced by a newly established World Trade Organization (WTO), including panels of three judges from countries other than the disputants who would rule on trade disputes. WTO was part of the Bretton Woods Agreements in 1944, including the World Bank (IBRD) and the International Monetary Fund (IMF), all designed to manage the post-war world economic system. However, the US Congress rejected WTO as an infringement upon US national sovereignty. In its place, in seven successive rounds of talks, GATT became the channel for the negotiation of world trade issues. The passage of the 1994 GATT treaty was expected to lower tariffs by 38%, resulting in a gain of US$744 billion for the participating 123 countries, and hastening the processes of global modernization.

At the same time, however, the global forces unleashed by GATT are likely to undermine the social fabric of developed and developing countries.

The domestic cleavages resulting from rapid technological change, combined with huge transfers of capital and large-scale dislocations of labour, may prove too powerful for some regimes. The existence of some twenty-three million refugees around the world is already straining the capacity of some countries to sustain the burden of legal and illegal immigrants. In reaction, such measures as Proposition 187, passed in California in November 1994, are bound to fuel international ill feelings (in this case between the United States and Mexico). The phenomenon of 'ethnic cleansing' in Bosnia, Tajikistan, Rwanda, Somalia, Palestine, Kashmir, Muslim–Hindu conflicts in India, and Armenian–Azerbaijani conflicts in the Caucasus, suggests an alarming rise in tribal, ethnic and religious hatreds. Even more alarming is the fact that the Great Powers are not willing to intervene in such situations unless and until their vital economic or political interests are at stake. Compare the active and massive interventions in the Persian Gulf crises of 1990–91 and 1994 to the lukewarm and failed interventions in Somalia, Rwanda, Tajikistan and Bosnia. The rise of isolationism, appeasement of the aggressors and domestic indifference or hostility to the plight of the minorities are reminiscent of what happened in the inter-war period. Those developments led to the rise of fascism in Europe, resulting in the Holocaust. The failure of the international community to stop the aggressors has historically proved to be an open invitation to other expansionist aggressors.

Clearly, the post-Cold War world is not an orderly and peaceful place. The New World Order based on the rule of international law, promised by President Bush in 1990, was stillborn. The old world order of capitalist hegemony is continuing unabated but with a declining liberal inclination and a rising conservatism. However, several sources of resistance to the global hegemony of capital deserve notice. Nationalism is still a force to be reckoned with. It continues to provide the primary and irreducible principle of spatial-political organization in the world for nearly 200 recognized states, and holds the promise for some 4–5,000 stateless and linguistically defined nationalities in search of political and spatial recognition. Regionalism provides another source of resistance to globalism, with which it may or may not co-exist. Regional organizations such as the European Union (EU), the Association of Southeast Asian Nations (ASEAN) and the North American Free Trade Area (NAFTA) present actual and potential trading blocs which could turn into fortresses if and when the global system breaks down through economic or political crises. Localism within each large nation state such as the United States, Russia, India, China or Brazil also presents a source of resistance to the global hegemony of a capitalist order. Last but not least, religious revivalism, in the form of a variety of fundamentalist movements, could disrupt the rule of capital in important parts of the world. The fundamental problem is that while capitalism has unleashed immense productive possibilities in the modern world, it has also created great and growing disparities among and within nations. The rule of capital has therefore led to prosperity for the privileged sectors of the population, some trickling down, but not enough to guarantee social peace and solidarity. The global capitalist system, though ever growing and gaining, continues to be vulnerable – technologically, economically, politically.

The vulnerability of global capital is best demonstrated in the dual effects of its technologies in transportation and telecommunication. The new spaces of modernization are the airlanes of modern jet transportation and the deterritorialized cyberspace of modern telecommunication. International terrorism on the global airlanes and urban spaces, and international subversion through the cyberspaces of the global telecommunication networks provide some evidence of this vulnerability. Both of these technologies have increasingly blurred the conventional distinctions between the global and local. As the events in the Persian Gulf, Somalia and Bosnia have demonstrated in recent years, the global conflicts are often localized, and the local conflicts are as often globalized. Similarly, domination and resistance are simultaneously assuming global and local dimensions. The Iranian Revolution, the Iran–Iraq War, the Persian Gulf War, and the bomb explosion at the New York World Trade Center cannot be understood except by correlating the global with the local issues of the conflict.

The world system in this wave of modernization appears to be both unipolar and fragmented. With the decline of the Soviet Union, the inability of the European Union (EU) to speak in one voice, and the continuing reluctance of Japan and China to assume world responsibilities beyond their own region, the United States has assumed the role of the sole balancer of power. This is a role that Britain played during the nineteenth century. When the United States acts with determination, as in the Gulf War, others follow. When it vacillates, as in Bosnia, the rest also waver and jockey for positions. In the meantime, however, regional groupings such as the EU, CIS (the Commonwealth of Independent States), NAFTA and ASEAN are establishing powerful and competing economic and political blocs. At a summit meeting in December 1994, the heads of thirty-four states in the Americas decided to establish a Pan-American free-trade area by the year 2005. As NAFTA or its Pan-American successor enlarge into the whole of Latin America, it would become the largest free-trade zone in the world, encompassing some 850 million people and US$13 trillion in combined purchasing power.

The forces of globalization and regionalization are thus homogenizing the markets and styles of life at an accelerating rate. At the same time, however, the rapid diffusion and miniaturization of communication technologies are providing the vehicles for the expression of nationalist and localist voices that are threatened to be obliterated. As Robertson (1992) and others have argued, *glocalization* seems to be a dominant feature of the postmodern world. Indeed, the processes of globalization can be viewed at the same time as processes of localization. The global market is adapting to the local conditions while it employs them to gain competitive advantage. The global communication network is globalizing the local issues (e.g.

Bosnia, Tajikistan, Kurdistan) at the same pace that it localizes the global issues such as the environment, human rights and population control. Global forces valorize local traits and faces in the dissemination of such consumer items as food, tourism, modelling, arts and crafts. The top-down processes of globalization are thus working concurrently with the bottom-up processes of localization. Glocalization thus appears to be the wave of the future.

Democratization in the Sixth Modernization also is entering a new, broadening and deepening phase. In the absence of bipolar Cold War rivalries, the localist forces of ethnic, religious and tribal loyalties are resurfacing to challenge the authority of the existing state systems. Fred Riggs (1994) has argued that the forces of ethnonationalism have come through three tsunamis. The first wave came with the rise of European nationalism in the eighteenth and nineteenth centuries followed by a second wave of national liberation movements in Africa, Asia and Latin America in the twentieth century. The current, third wave of ethonationalism is witnessing the rise of those ethnic and racial minorities (and sometimes majorities, as in South Africa) who have been repressed by the nation states of the previous two waves.

In this respect, the example of the former Soviet Union is rather telling. Ethnonationalism is apparent in most of the post-Soviet republics because in the name of proletarian solidarity, the Soviet ideology had suppressed nationalist and religious expressions for some seventy years. The Soviets were rather successful in state building, that is the development of military, civilian and police structures as well as the educational, transportation and communication infrastructures of the state. However, by design, they failed in nation building. Although Stalin's doctrine of national self-determination for the fifteen Soviet republics was theoretically the state policy, in practice, the borders were drawn in such a way that each republic contained significant numbers of ethnic and religious minorities. As immigrants from the European parts of the Soviet Union moved into the Asian and Caucasian republics, the multi-ethnic nature of the republics was further reinforced. The imperial policies of divide and rule also kept the regions and ethnicities fairly separate and often at odds. For a combination of the foregoing reasons, the dissolution of the communist regimes in the former Soviet Union and its Eastern European satellites has been accompanied with a resurgence of ethnic and religious conflicts.

During the Sixth Modernization and Democratization, therefore, two distinctly different types of ideology and pathology are simultaneously at work. These may be characterized as globalism versus localism, and commodity fetishism versus identity fetishism. The global market-place clearly favours the secular ideologies of progress that encourage an acquisitive society and competitive individualism. Commodity fetishism, that is a desperate struggle to acquire the material symbols of modernity, seems to be therefore an intrinsic pathology of the modern world. Material poverty in the age of modernity is no longer a condition that can be borne with dignity. In this respect, modernized urban poverty fundamentally differs from the rural poverty of the premodern world. The urban poor in the modern centres of industrial and financial power live in constant company of the rich, spatially and symbolically. Through television signals they are exposed to the standards of living among the rich and the middle classes, while through their menial jobs, they occasionally come into contact with those whom they envy. Since the dominant culture holds up material success as a sign of superior moral standards, they also are incessantly reminded not only of their economic but also 'moral' failure. Modern poverty therefore induces ceaseless anxieties, feelings of shame and worthlessness, and frustrations that lead to regression and aggression. As the high rate of self-inflicted violence among the black youth in the United States shows, the aggression is often directed against one's own community. But when it finds a legitimate cause, it can be directed against the outside world as well. The regression to an earlier stage of dependency often leads to identity fetishism, a pathology that through collective identities, loyalties and actions breeds a sense of false security in an uncertain and threatening world. The mass hysteria and behaviour under the conditions of international, revolutionary, civil and gang warfare are symptomatic of such a pathology. Totalitarian ideologies such as fascism, communism and fundamentalism thrive under such conditions.

Totalitarianism may thus be viewed as a pathology of transition. By uprooting the social fabric and traditions of civility, rapid technological and social change provides the breeding ground for the ceaseless anxieties of commodity and identity fetishisms. The only recourse appears to be more, not less democracy. The homogenizing tendencies of totalitarianism can be checked only through an acknowledgement of social and cultural diversity and the development of civil societies that reflect that diversity by the formation of voluntary associations and free-speech communities. The newly emerging, interactive technologies of communication seem to have a bias for democracy (Tehranian, 1990). But they can be also used for surveillance in an information-perfect society. The dual potentialities of the communication and information technologies can be best seen in electronic eavesdropping as well as electronic town meetings, satellite remote sensing as well as direct satellite broadcasts, computerized surveillance as well as Internet's virtual communities.

The new cybermedia, characterized by interactivity and convertibility, are giving rise to several different and often contradictory types of communication elite, namely *technologues*, *communologues* and *jestologues*. The impact of computer technologies on every aspect of economic and social life has created a new class of *technologues*. But the diffusion of the small media of communication has boosted the power and influence of the traditional communication elites (the priests, mullahs, monks and community activists), that is the *communologues*, who can speak in the vernacular languages of common folks. The demystifying power of visual media (television, cable and video-cassette recorders) seems to have led to a new and sceptical generation of communication elite that sees through the pretensions of the ideologues, technologues and communologues. The new communication elite serves the same function as the jesters and clowns in the kings' courts. Hence, we may call them *jestologues*.

Jestologues mock the powers that be with a humour that is often tolerated, but they also risk their heads. As pioneers of a new culture of postmodernity, they are jestful, relativistic, anti-narrative, despairing, ecstatic, playful and self-mocking. The war between communologues and jestologues, between neo-traditional modernity and postmodern modernity, was officially declared by Ayatollah Khomeini's death warrant on Salman Rushdie. While the Ayatollah and his followers have been committed to the sacred mission of realizing the Kingdom of God on earth, Salman Rushdie poses as the postmodern jester who mocks all sanctities. Most interpretations of the confrontation between the two camps have portrayed the Ayatollah as the traditional, religious bigot and Salman Rushdie as the modern, free-thinking intellectual. But the two figures and what they stand for in the contemporary world can be perhaps better understood if we view each in terms of some of the distinctions made between premodern, modern and postmodern. The Ayatollah and his successors are a complex mix of premodernist and modernist Islamic leaders in their neo-traditional, totalizing strategy of fusing the state and the mosque into a single theocratic regime (Tehranian, 1992). By contrast, Salman Rushdie is a postmodern critic in his deconstructionist strategy of mocking the traditional and modern sanctities. The postmodern strategy is to shock, to startle and to decentre in order to dethrone the sacred and the naturalized. Its paramount medium is the musical video, which has developed a nearly universal and irresistible language in the global MTV channel. Its heroes are the deconstructionist anti-heroes (e.g. Beavis and Butthead), the new self-mocking shamans of rock music (e.g. Sting or Bono), or the glittering stars of multiple identities and sexualities (e.g. Madonna and Michael Jackson). The conflict between the premodern, modern and postmodern is thus part of the cultural landscape of an economically uneven, politically tribalized and culturally schizoid, contemporary world.

Modernization VII

The contradictions of the Sixth Modernization and Democratization will be, no doubt, carried into the Seventh. The film *Blade Runner* has given us a cinematic glimpse of what the Seventh Modernization might look like in Los Angeles in the year 2019. As we are writing this chapter, the Hubble Telescope is scanning the universe for other planets and life forms. Michio Kaku (1994), a leading theoretical physicist, argues that string theory has mathematically deduced the existence of ten dimensions of reality. As in *Flatlands*, the two dimensional beings cannot conceive of the three-dimensionals except as fleeting sensations. As four-dimensional beings (three of space and one of time), the humans also cannot perceive the higher dimensional beings except as fleeting sensations. The spaces of the future to be conquered and understood are therefore the ten-dimensional *hyperspaces* of theoretical physics. By then, cyborgs will be an important part of the systems of production, distribution and information. Democratization VII, therefore, will be characterized by a struggle between the economic-political-scientific elites of the future allied with their cyborgs against the masses of humanity whose numbers will swell into billions, threatening them with periodic revolts. If we are to believe the current crop of science fictions, genetic engineering, time-travel and space voyages will be part of the routines of life sometime in the twenty-first century. But the struggle between good and evil, democracy and tyranny, shamans and jesters, communologues and jestologues will not cease.

Balanced versus unbalanced modernization

Modernization and democratization may be thus viewed as dialectical processes in which the requirements of economic accumulation and political participation are competing for resources (Tehranian, 1990: ch. 9). In the early stages of primitive accumulation, the need for high levels of national savings and investment tends to lead to monopoly capitalism or centralized state planning. This is even more true of the late-comers to industrialization such as Japan, Soviet Union, China or the two Koreas. In order to catch up, they all have pursued strategies of unbalanced development and forced savings. Levels of national savings have reached as high as 30% in these countries as compared to the 5–10% of GDP in the more leisurely and balanced pace of economic growth of Western European and North American countries. Sooner or later, however, modernization leads to demands for political participation by those sectors of the population which have been denied increases in their wages. At this stage, the state can choose to democratize and raise wages or repress. Following long periods of keeping wages down by repressive regimes, the Soviet Union, China, Singapore, Taiwan and South Korea have been undergoing such processes of democratization. Conversely, in the face of a mobilized population, democratization can take place without modernization. Many of the LDCs in their post-independence phase of development faced such a dilemma. When resources are meagre, the state can be both regressive and repressive, resulting in failure of both modernization and democratization. A more balanced approach to modernization can accommodate the progressive needs for democratization with the requirements of modernization by lowering expectations and levelling incomes, while increasing national savings and investment. Freedoms of speech, assembly and organization, to the extent that they exist, provide a public sphere of discourse in which the conflicting demands for resources are negotiated and mediated democratically. Table 6.3 provides a few historical examples of modernization with or without democratization.

Table 6.3   *Modernization and democratization: trade-offs and stand-offs*

Modernization with democratization	Modernization without democratization	No modernization, no democratization
North America	South Africa (Apartheid period)	Much of Africa, south of
Western Europe	Soviet Union	the Sahara
Japan (post-war period)	China	Burma
Australia	Cuba	Afghanistan
New Zealand	Vietnam	
India (post-independence)	North Korea	
South Korea	Iran	
Costa Rica	Iraq	
	Egypt	
	Algeria	
	Libya	
	Indonesia	

Source: Adapted from Tehranian, 1990.

Typically, however, the course of modernization is characterized by historical cycles from high accumulation to high mobilization. The development of democratic institutions reduces the severity of the cycles by allowing feedback mechanisms to correct the excesses of income inequalities that inevitably occur in the course of capital accumulation. In other words, communicative rationality and public discourse integrate society along more consensual patterns of progress. Figure 6.3 presents a schematic view of these historical cycles of high accumulation versus high mobilization versus high integration strategies.

A greater problem facing the LDCs is that the more developed world does not stop for them to catch up. Through global communication and advertising, it exposes them to rising political and economic expectations while introducing them to opportunities for production (technological) as well as consumption leapfrogging. As Table 6.4 shows, the modern industrial system has evolved into a succession of different types of capitalism, including the variety known as 'communism' or 'state capitalism'. Communism or state capitalism has been probably an appropriate social and economic formation in the early stages of primitive accumulation when a lack of infrastructural facilities, heavy capital requirements and imperfections of the market often called for state planning and investment. However, as economic development reaches higher levels of accumulation and consumption, the complexity of the decisions that need to be made calls for a market orientation. The interplay of the forces of supply and demand in the market is far more effective in making the increasingly complex investment and consumption decisions. Moreover, the post-war rise of transnational corporations has facilitated the transfer of science, technology, capital and management techniques to the less developed areas of the world. No Planning Commission or Gosplan can take the place of the numerous investors, producers and consumers that run a modern,

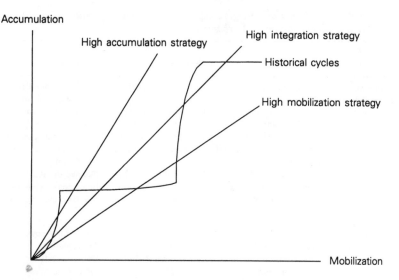

Figure 6.3   *Modernization and democratization: historical cycles*
Source: Adapted from Tehranian, 1990

complex, industrial economy. As demonstrated by the rise of market economies in the communist (read state-capitalist) countries, there is reason to believe that capitalism will continue its evolution and adaptation to new economic, socio-cultural and environmental circumstances. As the latest purchase of a majority share by the United Airlines employers suggests, capitalism may even gradually evolve into a workers' or communitarian capitalism.

The demise of the Soviet Union and the growth of market economies in China, Vietnam and Cuba may be viewed as continuing efforts in modernization, but democratization is not a necessary outcome. The excesses of primitive accumulation by new market economies in Eastern Europe also is bringing former communists to power (witness Poland in 1995). Similarly, the rise of religious ideologies has demonstrated that the processes of modernization are replete with many twists and turns, including the possibility of theocracies that may become themselves carriers of modernization (Marty and Appleby, 1991, 1992, 1993; Juergensmeyer, 1993; Tehranian, 1993b). Contrary to the prevailing interpretations of 'fundamentalism' that see it as a reaction against modernization, the current religious resurgence may alternatively be considered as disguised forms of modernization movements to mobilize deeply dislocated, traditional societies. After all, that was what the Reformation and its Protestant off-shoots accomplished for the Christian West. What form will modernization take in the future perhaps depends less on the inherent, cosmological features of conflicting civilizations and more on the economic, political and cultural relations among the world centres and peripheries of power.

Table 6.4 *A typology of emerging capitalisms: modes of production, regulation, communication and urbanization*

Types of capitalism:	Fordist	Technocratic	Communitarian
Modes of production (economy)	Fixed accumulation	Flexible accumulation	Familial accumulation
	Goods	Services	Knowledge/information/signs
	Economies of scale	Economies of scope	Economies of status
	Assembly line	Batch production	Communal work
	Mass:homogeneity	Tailored:heterogeneity	Custom-made production
	Operational management	Strategic management	Community management
	Big firms	Medium firms	Small firms
	Planned obsolescence	Planned disposability	Planned durability
	Mechanical technology	Electronic technology	Indigenous technology
	Long-term employment	Short-term employment	Life-term employment
Regulation (polity)	Class politics	Status politics	Charismatic politics
	State power	Financial power	Community power
	Monetary and fiscal	Deregulation	Re-regulation
	Centralization	Partial decentralization	Decentralization
	Universal rules	Technical rules	Indigenous rules
Communication (culture)	Print	Electronic	Multimedia, virtual
	Ideologues	Technologues	Communologues and jestologues
	Broadcasting	Narrowcasting	Interactive-casting
	Clock, map	Computer	MTV, Disney World
	Nationalism	Cosmopolitanism	Localism
	Practical rationality	Instrumental rationality	Communicative rationality
	Public vs private	Network	Connection
	Partial surveillance	Total surveillance	Community surveillance
	Reality-orientation	Image-orientation	Community-orientation
Spatialization (city)	Urbanization	Suburbanization	Urban dispersion
	Public housing	Homelessness	Community housing
	Urban renewal	Urban ghettoization	Urban revitalization
	Form is function	Form is fiction	Form is meaning
	Internationalism	Eclecticism	Vernacular localism
	Space	Place	Community

Sources: K. Tehranian, 1995; Harvey, 1989.

The prevailing patterns are full of contradictions. Globalization of the world economy is connecting the major urban centres of the world into a deterritorialized Core of technocratic capitalism with corporate and financial headquarters. The semi-peripheries (the emerging middle classes) are clamouring for political democracy (in China, South Korea, Taiwan, Latin America). The peripheries are resorting to the primordial, tribal identities of language (India), religion (fundamentalism), race (Africa, the United States), ethnicity (old and new imaginaries), and gender (women) to regain the lost grounds and press for human rights. The neo-tribalist politics can be, and often are, intolerant and totalitarian in orientation, but to blame the symptoms without considering the root causes is neither theoretically correct nor practically wise.

The ideological choices of the Sixth and Seventh Modernizations are therefore between dialogue versus clash of cultures, ecumenicalism versus fundamentalism, communitarian versus totalitarian capitalism, viewing the Plant Earth as a single unified organic system (the Gaia Hypothesis) *or* as a set of clashing civilizations, religions, regional blocs or warring nations seeking domination. Table 6.4 provides a schematic view of a possible evolutionary process from Fordist to Technocratic and Communitarian forms of capitalism. The table focuses on the main features of production in the economic sphere, regulation in the political sphere, communication in the cultural sphere and urbanization in the patterns of spatial settlement. Two caveats are in order. First, the distinctions proposed here are of the Weberian 'ideal type' variety and for heuristic purposes only. Moreover, they do not represent any stage theory. As a result, some of the features outlined are more potential than actual, particularly in the case of communitarian capitalism, which might be struggling to be born in some parts of the world by the creation of employee-owned stock companies competing in the national and international markets. Secondly, the associations suggested are *not* proof of historical causation. In a typical postmodernist fashion, any system could coopt the features of the others and juxtapose them with its own. Thus, the homogenization and Coca-Colonization of the world is taking place side by side with the rise of religious fundamentalisms. Tribalization of politics in the peripheries is taking place partly in reaction to the transnationalization of the economy at the centres (Tehranian, 1990: ch. 1). In the meantime, the material and cultural trappings of modernity, such as Holiday Inns, McDonald's, Madonna, Michael Jackson, MTV, CNN and the Internet, are paving the way for a global economy and culture side by side the indigenous economies and cultures.

In its current post-Cold War phase, however, global capitalism is facing severe challenges in the rise of religious revivalisms, regionalisms (EU, NAFTA, ASEAN, ECO, APEC)[1], nationalisms and localisms (Tehranian, 1993a). These reactions to modernization have historically expressed themselves in a variety of ideological and political movements that may be called hyper-modernization, counter-modernization, de-modernization, and post-modernization. Table 6.5 provides a schematic view of the main features of each reaction, focusing on the stage in the developmental process, the main ideological manifestations and the best-known examples of each in modern history.

The lesson of Table 6.5 is clear without much elaboration. We live in a very uneven world that promises to become ever more uneven in the twenty-first century (Attali, 1991). The bitter fruits of the growing gaps in the world seem to promise less peace and more violence, less tranquillity and more tension. One of the emerging forms of conflict might be what Huntington has called 'the clash of civilizations'. However, as noted earlier, his ideological casting of the problem is also a recipe for a self-fulfilling prophecy. The encounter of the materially uneven worlds can lead to clashes of cultures and civilizations unless new strategies of modernization

Table 6.5 *The peripheries' reactions to modernization*

	Development Stage	Ideological Manifestations	Historical Examples
Hyper-Modernization	Post-independence; Post-revolution; Crash programmes of industrialization to catch up	Nationalism, Communism, Fascism	Russia's Gosplans; China's Great Leap Forward; Iran's White Revolution; Hitler's Third Reich
Counter-Modernization	Early stages of industrialization; Critiques of Industrialism	Romanticism (Rousseau Effect) Transcendentalism (Thoreau Effect) Pacifism-Ruralism (Gandhi Effect)	Russian Narodniks Jeffersonian Democracy Gandhian Philosophy
De-Modernization	Late-Industrial Stage: De-industrialization; Dismantling of the industrial apparatus; Weakening of work ethics; Return to nature	Naturalism Pacifism New Ageism	The Flower Revolution of the Sixties
Post-Modernization	Post-Industrial Stage: Robotics, CAD-CAM, shift from manufacturing to services and knowledge industries	Post-Modernism Relativism Nihilism	Post-Modern Angst of the First World vs. Hyper-Modernism of the Third World

are adopted to reduce the gaps and provide bridges of trade, cooperation, dialogue and understanding. Civilizations are epistemological and knowledge systems. When two civilizations interact, they often develop a third civilization, culture, epistemology and knowledge system. Out of the worldwide confluence of civilizations, we are developing a global civilization side by side the old regional civilizations as well as national and local cultures. Dialogue is therefore the key to a successful development of a universal, human civilization in whose idiom we all need to speak in order to understand the national and local in the rich variety of human sub-cultures.

National and global policies can therefore mitigate or exacerbate, regulate or unleash, prolong or resolve conflicts. In this light, modernization and democratization may usefully be viewed as contradictory top-down and bottom-up processes mediated through communication channels. Since all three processes have been significantly transnationalized, Table 6.6 provides a schematic view of the global policy formations with respect to each. The table is based on the following premises: that power is ubiquitous; that even the most powerless have the power to resist; that hegemonic power is never absolute; and that it always has to negotiate with, adjust to, and incorporate the interests of the effective oppositions. The table presents the public communication channels as the arena for such mediation and policy negotiations. Broadening the base of global governance and democratization of communication thus go hand in hand.

Reforming global governance may usefully focus on the structures and processes of international relations. The structures of the international system consist of the states, inter-governmental organizations (IGOs) and at least four increasingly powerful non-state actors, including the transnational corporations (TNCs), the non-governmental organizations (NGOs), the unrepresented nations and peoples organizations (UNPOs) and the transnational media organizations (TMCs). The processes of international relations may be viewed in terms of the problems of conflict regulation, conflict management and conflict resolution. These involve such processes as exchange (trade agreements), negotiation (diplomacy), adjudication, arbitration, mediation, public mis/communication, violent and non-violent struggles.

Globalizing the local, localizing the global

A dual process of globalization of the local, and localization of the global has thus made isolationism and dissociation virtually impossible for any nation – even those that devoutly attempted it for a while such as China, Saudi Arabia, Burma and Iran. While globalization is fundamentally a top-down process, localization is bottom-up. The agents of transnationalization consist of the global hard and soft networks primarily facilitated by the non-state actors. The hard networks consist of transportation, telecommunication and tourism (TTT) facilities spun around the globe connecting the Core

Table 6.6 *The global policy formation process: a schematic view*

Resources	Problem Definition	Policy Formulation	Policy Legislation	Policy Legitimation	Policy Implementation, Regulation, Adjudication, & Evaluation
Top-Down Process: Generated by the interests and policies of the Great Powers and transnational corporations					
Natural, Technological, and Human Resources	Think tanks, foundations & commissions, e.g. Rand, Rockefeller, & Trilateral Commission	Great Powers & Transnational Corps, e.g. G7 + Russia & China, Esso, AT&T, British Telecom, Mitsubishi	National Legislatures & Intergovernmental Organizations (IGOs)	Politicians, publicists, press, & broadcasting	TNCs, IGOs, national government agencies, regulatory commissions & the courts
Mediation Process: Generated by the media constructions of reality and discourses in response to governments & oppositions					
Global Telecom Networks	Global elite press, e.g. *International Herald Tribune*, *Wall Street Journal*, *The Economist*	Media owners & editors	National media laws, & international covenants on copyright, spectrum & orbit allocation, technical standards	Global media networks, e.g. elite press, CNN, news agencies	Media Associations, e.g. International Press Inst. International Publishers Association
Bottom-Up Process: Generated by the small & medium powers, revolutionary & opposition parties & associations					
Human, Natural, & Technological Resources	Revolutionary movts, NGOs, and related foundations, think tanks, & civil and religious networks, e.g. Amnesty International, World Council of Churches, etc.	Small-medium powers & global lobby groups, e.g. G77, Physicians for Social Responsibility, American Friends Service Committee, Greenpeace, etc.	States in exile, revolutionary movts, e.g. PLO, Tibet government-in-exile Unrepresented Peoples Organization (UNPO), etc.	The alternative & underground media; the informal networks of gossip, rumour, civic, religious associations	Voluntary associations, labour unions, religious institutions, out of power political parties

in networks of communication. The soft networks provide the programmes that negotiate and integrate the competing interests and values of the global players. These include global broadcasting, advertising, education and exchanges of information. In the meantime, the localization processes are working through their own hard and soft networks, at times employing the Core networks and at other times developing their own independent periphery systems. The agents of localization and tribalization consist of the nationalist, religious and culturalist movements and leaders voicing the peripheries' interests and views. In contrast to the 'big media' of the Core, they often employ the low-cost, accessible and elusive 'small media' such as low-powered radios, audio-cassettes, portaback videos, copying and fax machines, and personal computer networking. Their software consists of the rich heritage of primordial myths and identities embedded in the traditional religious, nationalist, tribal and localist ideologies.

However, the infrastructure of a global consciousness is fast growing by the media events and a pop culture orchestrated by such transnational networks as CNN, BBC, World TV, Star TV, MTV, the Internet and non-governmental organizations (NGOs). While the first five are largely one-way, top-down channels, the last two provide interactive, bottom-up, international communication channels. The media events (Dayan and Katz, 1992) of the last few decades (the landing on the moon, the Sadat visit to Jerusalem, the Tiananmen Square incident, the Gulf War, and the signing of the peace accords between Yitzhak Rabin and Yasser Arafat) have brought about a new global consciousness of the common human destiny.

Since 1985, the steady growth of CNN into the world's first global news network has provided the elites in most parts of the world with a stream of live broadcasts in English, Spanish, Japanese, Polish, and soon French and German. In 1987, to counter the Western bias of its news, CNN started airing the CNN World Report, providing uncensored and unedited news reports from local broadcasters all over the world. 'By 1992, 10,000 local news items had been aired on the World Report, originating from a total of 185 news organizations representing 130 countries. CNN's internationally-distributed satellite signal is within reach of 98% of the world's population' (Pai, 1993; see also McPhail, 1993; Flourney, 1992). CNN has thus become more than a news medium. It is also serving as a channel for public diplomacy, working often faster than the private channels of traditional diplomacy. Many heads of state and responsible officials watch the CNN during crises in order to assess directly the events abroad while gauging the impact of those events on the domestic and international public opinion. Fidel Castro is reported to have been one of the first world leaders regularly to watch the CNN service. During the Gulf Crisis, President Bush indicated at a press conference that he would call up President Ozal of Turkey while the latter was watching the CNN's live coverage; the telephone call came through a few minutes later while President Ozal was waiting for it. Peter Arnett's reporting from Baghdad during the Gulf War filled some of the communication gaps between Saddam Hussein and the rest of the world.

CNN, however, provides a global picture primarily through an American prism. Britain is trying to emulate the CNN success story through the BBC World Service Television, while Japan has considered the establishment of an NHK-led Global News Network (GNN) (Lee, 1993). Star Television, acquired by Rupert Murdoch's News Corporation in 1993, covers most of Asia through direct broadcast satellite (DBS).

Similarly, MTV is exporting youthful, whimsical, irreverent, postmodernist, American cultural values into Europe, Asia, Africa and Latin America. Although possessing universal appeal, MTV is following a localization strategy wherever it goes. Stimulated by the example of a popular programme that is promotional in selling the music it plays, local record companies have been quick to take up the challenge. India's Megasound spent only US$5,000 to produce a video featuring India's first Hindi rap tune by the local artist Baba Segal.

> The album ended up selling 500,000 copies. Darren Childs, MTV Asia's head of programming, said that the Asian content of its programming has risen from 5% when the channel first aired, to as high as 50% at certain times of the day. The station has 'broken' formerly unknown acts and turned them into regional stars. In addition to the regional stars, the VJ's (Video Jockeys) of MTV Asia are another important reason why viewers tune in. They are all Asian or part Asian and provide Western wackiness while toning down the grungy, street-smart image of MTV VJ's elsewhere to ensure that local audiences can still identify them. (Lee, 1993)

MTV is thus contributing to the creation of an intended or unintended global, postmodernist sub-culture with far-reaching consequences.

INTERNET is another fast-growing transnational network that connects an estimated thirty million people around the world via over one million mainframe computers in a global network of networks. One million new users are estimated to be joining the network each month. At that rate, the network will have about 100 million users by the year 2000. If we count the members of such major commercial, on-line services as Prodigy, America Online, Delphi, Dialogue and Compuserve logging into the Internet, that figure will be probably soon surpassed. In 1992, *The Whole Internet Users' Guide and Catalogue* sold 125,000 copies. A dozen other guides currently compete for the market, including *Zen and the Art of Internet* (Anon., 1994). It is no wonder that marketers are viewing the network as a potential electronic gold mine. However, attempts at commercializing the network have faced resistance by the current users. As Stecklow notes,

> residents of 'cyberspace,' as the on-line computer galaxy is known, are a world apart. They do not take kindly to sales pitches or electronic cold calling. Many view themselves as pioneers of a new and better vehicle for free speech. Unlike television viewers, radio listeners or newspaper readers, they are hooked up to the message sender and other Internet parties interactively – meaning that an offense to their sensibilities can result in quick, embarrassing reports viewed by countless of the network's estimated 15 million users. (Stecklow, 1993: A1)

This new Network Nation consists of computer-literate professionals from all continents and all fields, united in the fine arts of chatting, gossiping, exchanging information and collaborating in a variety of projects from scientific research to lifestyle preferences, dating, financial transactions and social movements. The National Science Foundation (NSF), which subsidizes the network, has no control over a number of other data lines that are also part of the web. The NSF started phasing out its US$11.5 million annual subsidy in 1994. However, the US government and businesses are stepping in. Rupert Murdoch's News Corporation has announced it will acquire Delphi Internet Services Inc., an on-line service that provides Internet access to consumers; Continental Cablevision, the third-largest cable-television company in the United States, is offering Internet access to its cable subscribers; and American Telephone and Telegraph Co. has made Internet available to some data communication customers via a nationwide, toll-free telephone number (Stecklow, 1993: A1).

The Clinton Administration has promised that by the year 2000, every school and public facility will have the capability of logging into this vast network. On 15 September 1993, Vice-President Al Gore unveiled a plan to coordinate the public and private sector efforts in building a national 'electronic superhighway'. This has raised the perennial question of the trade-offs between efficiency and equity in telecommunication. While the US National Information Infrastructure plans still remain ambiguous, they aim at creating a more efficient flow of communication and information through Integrated System Digital Networks (ISDN). Similar to an earlier drive for the construction of transcontinental, inter-state, superhighways under the Eisenhower Administration, the metaphor of 'electronic super-highways' under the Clinton Administration promises greater mobility and productivity. However, it cannot necessarily guarantee greater equity. Just as the transportation superhighways facilitated the transfer of population and resources from the US Northeast to the South and the West, the new electronic superhighways are also going to redistribute wealth, income and information access. The transportation superhighways facilitated the industrialization of the South and the West, de-industrialization of the Northeast, the migration of the Afro-Americans to the northern cities, the out-migration of upper and middle income white groups from the cities into the suburbs, the consequent erosion of the urban tax base and urban decay, and the creation of an urban underclass. Unless public policy vigorously pursues the achievement of equity and universal access, an unintended consequence of the new electronic superhighways could be the creation of a permanent information underclass. Similar information superhighways are under construction by the European Union, Japan and other major economies. They will also probably by-pass the poorer regions of the world and create a global information underclass.

Without telephones, the less developed countries and regions of the world would not be able to log into the global electronic superhighways. Telephones are the linchpin of the new integrated telecommunication systems.

Without them it would be impossible to log-in the new data-bases and networks. Yet, the global distribution of telephony is more lopsided than any other modern media. In 1992, some fifty countries, accounting for over half the world's population, had a teledensity of less than one, that is less than one telephone line per 100 inhabitants. While the high-income countries have 71% of the world's 575 million phone main lines, upper middle-income countries control 15%, lower middle-income 10%, and low-income only 4% (Tarjanne, 1994). Some newly industrializing countries in East Asia are, however, closing the gap, but many other LDCs are falling behind. On the whole, world telephone distribution patterns have remained relatively unchanged in the last 100 years. In the light of this fact, is information hegemony to replace military domination and repression? Or will the two be mutually reinforcing as in the past?

The new global information market-place includes four major components: (1) the owners of the highways, the common carriers, paid for by the private or public sectors; (2) the producers of information hardware such as telephones, televisions, and computers; (3) the producers of information software such as the press, broadcasters, libraries and infopreneurs; and (4) information consumers who demand efficiency, equity, privacy, affordability and choice. In response to the convergence of information and communication technologies, the US government aims at the removal of all barriers to entry into any particular sector of the market. This will eventually lead to the full technological and economic integration of the print, film, broadcasting, cable, telephone, cellular phone, computer and data-base industries – a process that has already begun by the emergence of giant, multi-media conglomerates.

In another speech on 11 January 1994, Vice-President Gore outlined the following five principles that will guide any future US legislation and regulation concerning communication industries. The Administration will: (1) encourage private investment; (2) provide and protect competition; (3) provide open access to the Network; (4) take action to avoid creating a society of information 'haves' and 'have nots'; and (5) encourage flexible and responsive governmental action (CRTNET, no. 915, 12 January 1994). Given these policy principles, will the coming information superhighway be accessible to everyone regardless of their income? The Vice-President had been reassuring on that question:

The principle of universal service has been interpreted in the case of telephone service to mean that what we now have is about 93, 94 percent of all American families have telephone service and it is regarded as affordable to virtually – by virtually everyone. Our definition of universal service, once the cluster of services that are encompassed is agreed upon is that approximately the same percentage should have access to the richer information products as well, so that a school child in my hometown of Carthage, Tennessee, population 2,000, could come home after class and sit down and instead of playing a video game with a cartridge, plug into the Library of Congress and learn at his or her own pace according to the curiosity that seizes that child at the moment – not just in the form of words, but color, moving graphics and pictures. (CRTNET, no. 900, 22 December 1993)

The same concerns for information access and equity have been expressed by an international movement for a New World Information and Communication Order (NWICO) (Galtung and Vincent, 1992; Lee, 1985; Traber and Nordenstreng, 1992). As the advanced industrial world has moved ahead, the gap between the information 'haves' and 'have nots' has demonstrably grown on a global scale. Except for a handful of East Asian countries (Japan, South Korea, Singapore, Hong Kong and Taiwan), and low population, high-income oil exporting countries (Saudi Arabia, Kuwait, United Arab Emirates), other LDCs have been so far unable to catch up. One relatively hopeful sign in this bleak picture is the role that non-governmental organizations (NGOs) are playing (Boulding, 1988). The convergence of NGO computer networks and low-cost information technologies is offering opportunities for social movements to develop their own news services and information dissemination systems. In the late 1980s, the Association for Progressive Communication (APC) was established as a non-profit network to facilitate global communication among the NGOs (see Frederick, 1993; 98). As Frederick notes:

> Comprising more than 20,000 subscribers in 95 countries, the APC Networks constitute a veritable honor role of organizations working in these fields, including Amnesty International, Friends of the Earth, Oxfam, Greenpeace, labor unions and peace organizations. There are APC partner networks in the United States, Nicaragua, Brazil, Russia, Australia, the United Kingdom, Canada, Sweden and Germany and affiliated systems in Uruguay, Costa Rica, Czechoslovakia, Bolivia, Kenya and other countries. The APC even has an affiliate network in Cuba providing the first free flow of information between the United States and Cuba in thirty years. Dozens of FidoNet systems connect with the APC through 'gateways' located at the main nodes. (Frederick, 1993: 97)

APC affiliates now broadcast more than twenty alternative news agencies, twenty newsletters and magazines, four radio station news scripts, and a wide variety of specialist files to which non-conventional voices contribute news and opinion. There are also over 10,000 NGOs, enlisting millions of people around the world, working for a vast variety of civic goals, from protection of the global environment to the defence of human rights and endangered species. These social and technological networks together constitute a global civil society that provides, to some degree, a countervailing power to those of national states and transnational corporations.

Conclusion

This chapter has: (1) critiqued the current discourses on the New World Order; (2) presented a historically grounded view of the current global continuities and discontinuities; and (3) drawn out the implications of those changes for modernization, communication and democratization.

As the absence of a consensus on the shape of the New World Order demonstrates, we are in an age of paradigm shifts. Our political and economic institutions are clearly lagging behind the accelerating pace of scientific, technological and cultural changes. That, in turn, has led to the dramatic breakdown of some political and economic systems such as those in Central and Eastern Europe. As the bombing of the World Trade Center in New York, and the Federal Building in Oklahoma City, as well as the nerve gas attack in Tokyo's subway have demonstrated in the last few years, the 'zones of peace' in MDCs are not as immune from violence as some observers would have us believe. Terrorism as the weapon of the weak will continue to operate against a technologically and socially vulnerable global system that has created huge economic and cultural chasms in the world. The 'zones of turmoil' are spilling over from the peripheries of the peripheries (the rural areas in the LDCs) to the centres of the peripheries (Cairo, Tehran, Bombay, Manila, Mexico City), and into the centres of the centres (New York, Los Angeles, Berlin, Frankfurt, London, Tokyo). Complacency (read undue optimism) or alarmism (read undue pessimism) are not warranted in the current transition to a New World Order, whatever that turns out to be. In fact, the very fluidity of the situation allows us more room for greater human agency. If wars represent the failures of human imagination, the price of peace is human vision and action.

The future of the world depends, in large measure, on how modernity can be tamed to ensure a continuing production of wealth without disastrous consequences for the global natural, social and cultural environments. That, in turn, vitally depends on how humanity can balance its competing and complementary interests in the search for more common norms, laws and sanctions. The emerging world order is caught up in the contradictions of uneven and combined economic, political and cultural modernizations. Economically, modernization has achieved stunning feats in the establishment of a world market of trade and development that is threatened by increasing environmental pollution, international and intranational inequalities, exclusionary regional blocs, and the political upheavals that may result from those. Politically, modernization has created a multipolar world in which no single Great Power can rule the world with impunity. It has also unleashed democratic forces that in societies with sizable middle classes have led to the institutionalizations of freedoms of speech, assembly and organization. Culturally, however, modernization has produced contradictory effects. The history of modernization has been so far a history of the dominance of instrumental reason as reflected in modern science and technology. The diverse spiritual and cultural traditions of the world provide countervailing perspectives on how to both universalize and localize knowledge. The antagonisms between the global and local, however, have led too frequently to the tyranny of one against the other rather than creative tensions and interactions.

As for international relations, the most significant change of the last few decades appears to be in the stunning expansion of channels of global communication. This has proved to be a mixed blessing. On the one hand, it has led to the hearing of new voices – the Kurds, the Shiites, the Palestinians, the Tatars, the Tibetans, the Abkhazians, the Uighurs, the Chechens, and hundreds more. On the other hand, it may be producing a communication fatigue leading to a 'dialogue of the deaf in international communication' (Tehranian, 1982: 21). Marshall McLuhan's 'global village' is looking more and more like a neo-feudal manor with a highly fortified and opulent castle (centres of industrial, financial and media power) surrounded by a vast hinterland of working peasants clamouring for survival and recognition.

The debate on NWICO has been largely polarized between those who wish to give new means of self-expression to the peasants and those who consider the media monopoly of the lords to be a greater guarantee of order and growth (Singer and Wildavsky, 1993). As in any debate, the two sides may have over-simplified a more complex reality. The new media, as the old, tend to have dual effects, dispersing and centralizing power, democratizing and controlling. While the state and corporate institutions use them largely for surveillance, legitimation and persuasion, the NGOs and UNPOs (Unrepresented Nations and Peoples Organizations) are employing them to resist, organize and mobilize. As raconteurs of international relations, the media mediate in the top-down and bottom-up processes of global governance and communication (see Table 6.6). They construct the global realities that frame the global events, feeding the media constructions of global realities. The emergence of Somalia and Bosnia to the top of the international agenda may be, in part, considered as the work of Cable News Network International (CNNI). By focusing on the tragedies of famine and ethnic cleansing, the world media forced the governments into taking action. However, the media could not lead them to *appropriate* actions. In fact, aid and communication fatigue are leading them away from those trouble spots. Setting agendas is a powerful media function, but it does not necessarily lead to resolving agendas.

NWICO can be best constructed by developing communication competence for the voiceless. Pluralism in voices, however, requires pluralism in structures of media access. No single system of media control (governmental, commercial, public or community) can alone guarantee that plurality of voices. A balance among them might use the expanding channels of communication for an expanding plurality of voices more reflective of the international community. Diverse and autonomous centres of media control are a better guarantee of freedom of speech than the pious wishes of legislatures. However, increasing media monopoly in the hands of a dozen global media conglomerates does not augur well either for free or balanced flow of information. The project of a New World Order calls for a free and balanced flow of communication among the 5.5 billion inhabitants of this planet who are caught up between the imperatives of the premodern, modern and postmodern worlds to which they belong (see Table 6.7). It calls for a beginning rather than an end of history for the two-thirds of

Table 6.7 *Premodern, modern and postmodern worldviews: a schematic perspective*

	Premodern	Modern	Postmodern
Time	Circular	Linear	Multilinear
	Eternal	Material	Ephemeral
	Past-oriented	Future-oriented	Present-oriented
Space	Hierarchical	Functional	Anarchical/playful
	Organic	Designed	Vernacular
	Closed	Enclosed	Open
	Home/office	Home vs. office	Home + office
	Fixed	Fluid	Modular
Being	God the Father	Man/Son	The Holy Ghost
	Supernatural	Natural	Ecological
	Heaven	Society	Community
	Sacred	Secular	Self
	Transcendent	Material	Immanent
Power	Feudalism	Fordism	Flexible accumulation
	Land	Capital	Knowledge/information
	Gold	Paper money	Electronic money
	Authoritarian	Representative	Participatory
	Matriarchal	Patriarchal	Androgyny
	Mother church	Fatherland	The community
Science,	Practical reason	Instrumental reason	Communicative reason
Technology	Exegesis	Interpretation	Deconstruction
& Aesthetics	Fate	Determinacy	Indeterminacy
	Fusionism	Universalism	Particularism
	Mystification	Rationalization	De-mystification
	Metaphysics	Paradigm	Syntagm
	The wheel	The steam engine	Telematics
	Form	Multi-form	Antiform
	The Holy Book	Genre/boundary	Text/intertext
	Holy Relic	Art object	Performance/happening
	The Creation	Narrative	Anti-narrative
	Trans-history	*Grande Histoire*	*Petite Histoire*
	Classicism	Design	Chance
	Sanctification	Centring	Dispersal
	Divinity	Totalization	Deconstruction
	Logos	Purpose	Play
	Traditional	Modern	Eclectic

Source: Adapted from K. Tehranian, 1995.

humankind who have been hitherto primarily objects rather than subjects of history. It calls for dialogue rather than a clash of civilizations, in order to redefine modernity in consonance with the traditions of civility embedded in most world religions and civilizations. The challenge lies in how to tame the forces of modernity for the fulfilment of human needs *in* rather than *against* nature, for the celebration of democratic diversity and discussion rather than against it, for cultural pluralism rather than cognitive tyranny.

NWICO may be conceived of as a network of networks, among the NGOs, to mobilize the global civil society, to empower the deterritorialized peripheries in the urban centres and rural hinterlands, to enhance their communication competence and media capabilities, to negotiate with the state and non-state actors, the IGOs, TNCs and TMCs in order to redress the conditions of dehumanizing poverty and violence, manifest and latent, so characteristic of our world.

Notes

This is a revised and expanded version of an article published under the title of 'Where is the New World Order: at the end of history or clash of civilizations?', *The Journal of International Communication* 1 (2), December 1994, and under the title of 'That certain suspicion: democratization in a global perspective', in Philip Lee (ed.) (1995), *The Democratization of Communication*. Cardiff: University of Wales Press. Thanks are due to John Tehranian's sharp eyes for catching our errors of omission.

1   The alphabet soup stands for European Union, North American Free Trade Agreement, Association of South East Asian Nations, Economic Cooperation Organization, and Asia-Pacific Economic Cooperation.

Further questions

1   Tehranian and Tehranian provide us with a coherent deconstruction of the idea of a New World Order. Summarize their argument.
2   The authors suggest that the future of the world depends, in large measure, on how modernity can be tamed. How do they understand 'modernity'? Why is taming modernity so important in their view? Do you agree with this analysis?

Part IV

GLOBALIZATION, CULTURE AND THE CONTROL OF DIFFERENCE

This part of the book is concerned with the more cultural aspects of globalization, and especially with the question of theory, of culture, power and identity.

Tomlinson's chapter is concerned especially with the way in which contemporary globalization – the concept and the process itself – forces critical theorists to re-think their existing understanding of cultural power and hegemony, world-wide. In particular, it shows the limits of older understandings of Western power as 'cultural imperialism'. Perhaps globalization is both more ambiguous and less ominous than cultural imperialism? He argues that conceptualizing cultural processes in more dialectical terms (which does not ascribe all the power to one side) offers a more complex picture of cultural globalization. Cultural influence may not follow the sort of linear paths that cultural imperialism predicts. He argues that the globalization process is essentially a 'decentred' one, producing new patterns of advantage and disadvantage that we are only just beginning to recognize.

In the second chapter of the final section of this book, Maxwell offers a detailed analysis of the work of market researchers, drawing on his own research into their dilemmas and practices. He explores the ways in which market researchers get to know us by employing various techniques. He is especially concerned with questions of desire and identity – two crucial aspects of the value of commodities to consumers.

Maxwell suggests that market research is a globalized industry which influences thousands of localities around the world with techniques of information extraction that are both quantitative and qualitative. Local value assessments provide information for enhancing a commodity's value. Market researchers are situated between popular and dominant interpretations of value. They expropriate local information about personal values for the benefit of multinationals, who are merchandisers operating around the world.

Both of these chapters draw not only upon the study of international communication – in its more critical tradition – but also on sociological theory and on cultural studies. Tomlinson, for example, draws on the work of the British sociologist Anthony Giddens. Maxwell draws on the work of one of the founders of British cultural studies, Raymond Williams, and on well-established debates about the complexities of consumption among students of culture more generally. Because they are more concerned with cultural processes, these chapters often differ in emphasis from those of Parts I, II and III. They show the diversity and capacity for development of 'critical' work in the area.

7

Cultural Globalization and Cultural Imperialism

John Tomlinson

In this chapter Tomlinson focuses on debates around the cultural aspects of globalization. In order to clarify the complexity of the globalization process, he invites us to compare the contemporary theories of cultural globalization with older understandings of globalization in terms of 'cultural imperialism'. In this, he draws heavily on the debates about globalization and cultural identity, not only in the field of international communication, but also in sociology and in cultural studies. He invites us to think about such questions as:

- *Is contemporary globalization something entirely new?*
- *Does it take new, more complex forms compared with earlier phases?*
- *What are the specifically cultural aspects of the process?*
- *Are our existing theories adequate to grasp contemporary global–local relations?*
- *What, above all, does contemporary globalization imply for our existing critical theories of power and culture in the world?*
- *How can we appreciate the novelties, while still retaining a critical perspective on global inequalities?*

From these points of view Tomlinson is interested in theories of globalization and transnational cultural processes for their 'iconoclasm', that is their power in forcing us to rethink critical frameworks. His essay is, therefore, a good example of the critical differences and dialogues that exist within what we have called the 'critical tradition'.

The iconoclasm of globalization

Globalization in its most general and uncontroversial sense – and as I shall understand it in this chapter – refers to the rapidly developing process of complex interconnections between societies, cultures, institutions and individuals world-wide. It is a process which involves a compression of time and space (Harvey, 1989), shrinking distances through a dramatic reduction in the time taken – either physically or representationally – to cross them, so making the world seem smaller and in a certain sense bringing human beings 'closer' to one another. But it is also a process which 'stretches' social relations, removing the relationships which govern our everyday lives from local contexts to global ones. Thus, at its highest level of generality, globalization can be understood, in Anthony Giddens's most recent formulations as simply 'action at distance' (Giddens, 1994).

But no matter how general a description is given to it, globalization remains a difficult process to get to grips with, either theoretically or empirically. While many have seen it as central to any description and analysis of the contemporary (social, cultural, political) condition (Featherstone, 1990; Giddens, 1990, 1991; King, 1991; Lash and Urry, 1994; Robertson, 1992; Waters, 1995), others have approached the idea in a much more sceptical way, dubious of the term's associations – for example, its use not only in academic discourse but in the rhetoric of corporate marketing – and its accompanying 'mythology' (Ferguson, 1992).

Even if we do – as I think we should – accept the term as significant, there are many problems in deciding what, precisely, it refers to. Is globalization something entirely new – a phenomenon of the late twentieth century? Or is it a process having deep roots in human civilization? Is it essentially a political-economic term or a cultural description? How is it connected to modernity or 'postmodernity'? How is it connected to the nature of contemporary capitalism or the idea of a capitalist 'world system'? What is the relation between the 'global' and the 'international' and what implications does globalization have for the system of nation states? Does globalization have the utopian aspect of unification and the emergence of a world community or even a world society? Or, on the contrary, does it threaten various fragmentations – the disintegration of the nation-state system, the dissolution of stable national identities, the emergence of new ethnic rivalries? Finally, what critical theories can we bring to bear on the process? How, for example, does globalization yield to the familiar critical vocabularies of class, race and gender? What are its implications for the critique of neo-imperialism, of the post-colonial cultural order, of core-periphery power relations, of development and dependency?

Anyone who has tried to follow debates about globalization will have found a perplexingly wide range of positions on all these issues and this is unsurprising, given the huge analytic scope that the concept of globalization (either implicitly or explicitly) claims for itself. I do not propose to elaborate directly on these problems here but to focus instead on the more general issue of the iconoclastic implications of the concept of globalization. By this I mean the implicit fundamental challenge that the idea – if taken at all seriously – must pose to other, more familiar ways of describing the social world. It is because the concept of globalization is both so general and so radical in its implications that it threatens to destroy the images of the world cherished in so many intellectual and critical traditions.

To be clear about the nature of this challenge, and the character of globalization's iconoclasm, it might be useful to fix its limits at the outset, by way of a brief comparison. There is a form of what might be called epistemological iconoclasm to be found somewhere in every contemporary discipline in the humanities and social sciences. This sort of position – most readily identified with the discourse of postmodernism – is one in which the rug is, apparently, pulled from under entire intellectual/political/critical traditions (for example, The Enlightenment, Marxism, empirical science, the ideal of emancipation, the standpoint of human subjectivity) by attacking the basic epistemological assumptions that make such traditions of thought and critique possible. This is done by invoking the general unreliability of any epistemological foundations, or, slightly more subtly, by pointing to the incommensurability between criteria of truth and judgement in competing discourses or 'language games', and thus to the inevitably dominating, even 'terroristic' (Lyotard and Thébaud, 1985), character of any 'metanarrative' which claims for itself superior purchase on reality. Epistemological iconoclasm has a certain positive function in disturbing the complacency of established theoretical positions. However, as has often been pointed out, it is ultimately self-defeating, sharing 'the fate of all sceptical theories which deny the sense or even the possibility of truth: either they claim it for themselves, thus running into a flagrant contradiction, or they end up condemning their own validity claims, in which case they cease to be credible' (Larrain, 1994: 117).

Now the concept of globalization is iconoclastic in an entirely different way to this. Its challenge comes not at an epistemological level, but arises from the inevitable implications that such a general theory of the social world will, if at all plausible, have for other established theories and perspectives. Where postmodernism was deliberately and provocatively iconoclastic, globalization theory threatens cherished beliefs simply in its potential for displacing or forcing re-examination of certain givens of social/cultural analysis. So, globalization's iconoclasm might be described as both 'substantive' rather than 'epistemological' and 'positive' rather than 'deconstructive'. Regardless of whether globalization turns out to be a new process, its recognition in theory is new and this, taken together with the breadth of its implications and at least the prima-facie persuasiveness of its tenets, has radical consequences for other theories and positions.

Here are some very brief examples. In social theory the very idea of a 'society' as a fundamental analytic category becomes problematized once the complex interconnections of globalization, cross-cutting assumed societal boundaries are recognized. Why is this? Because it then becomes clear that the (generally received) concept of a society is not a social-ontological fundamental, but is merely modelled on the historically contingent social formation of the nation state (Giddens, 1990; Mann, 1986). It is the boundaries of the nation state which are traversed by the interconnections of globalization – by the global capitalist market, by global media flows and cultural identifications. And this reveals social reality as comprised, in Mann's terms, of 'structuring networks' of state, culture and economy, rather than on the basis of 'one master concept or basic unit of "society"' (Mann, 1986: 2).

In a rather different way, the permeable and structurally fragile nature of the nation state itself, as disclosed by globalization theory, poses obvious challenges to the discipline of international relations, in so far as this discipline places the nation state at the centre of its conceptual world. For, as McGrew argues, the process of globalization compromises 'four critical aspects of the nation-state: its competence; its form; its autonomy; and, ultimately, its authority or legitimacy' (McGrew, 1992: 87; see also Held, 1991). Thus such phenomena as the increasing inability of nation states to regulate their internal economies in the context of global market forces (marked, for example, by economic crises resulting from attacks on national currencies in the foreign exchange markets) suggest a diminishing competence of the nation state. This connects with the other aspects McGrew discusses to 'reduce the effectiveness of government which, in turn, undermines the legitimacy and authority of the state' (McGrew, 1992: 91). Simply put, if the nation state cannot deliver the goods of political, economic or environmental security, it begins to lose its credibility and hence its authority. Without pursuing these arguments – and without subscribing to the view that globalization signals the demise of the nation state – it will be clear that this compromising of the key agent in the discourse of international relations is a significant challenge to the whole enterprise.

Similar sorts of challenges can be seen in the area of cultural theory – what, for example, against the background of globalization, can be made of the relationship between culture and locality? What, in this context, are we to understand by national identity? And in the field of development studies, do any of the critical categories used to mark relations of domination and dependence – First World/Third World, core/periphery, North/South – describe the situation of global power and resource distribution with enough precision anymore?

The point about all these challenges is that, though it poses radical questions, globalization, unlike epistemological iconoclasm, does not undermine either the aspiration to establish reliable knowledge and understanding, nor the critical and emancipatory inspiration behind traditions of thought and enquiry. The iconoclasm of globalization lies simply in the implicit demand to re-envisage the world that arises once the nature of complex global interconnectedness and the processes of time–space compression and action at distance are recognized. Re-envisioning is disturbing and inevitably involves the destruction of shibboleths, many of which may be linked to political and moral commitments. But re-envisioning is not the same as revisionism, where the latter carries the implication of a weakening of critical resolve or a retreat from fundamental moral and political commitments. There is nothing, so far as I can see, that prevents globalization theory being a critical theory, but this may involve the rethinking of some of the assumptions of existing critical theories.

What are the options for a tradition of thought when faced with such a challenge? It seems to me that there are at least four. First, it may dismiss the premises on which the challenge is made as so implausible as to be unworthy of serious consideration. But I think we can discount this option since there is too much evidence of the impact of global compression (for example, in the operations of world capitalist economy) for it to be rationally discounted. Secondly, it can simply ignore the challenge and carry on business as usual, within the security of its Kuhnian paradigm. This is probably the most common response and enormous amounts of work in all areas obviously go on without any reference to globalization theory. But this is also clearly the least interesting response. Thirdly, it can take the challenge on board and rethink its own premises in light of it. There is now quite a considerable body of work across a range of disciplines in which this is occurring. And fourthly, it can try to absorb or assimilate the conceptualization of globalization within the terms of its own discourse, thus disarming it. This response can be seen, for example, in the recuperation of globalization within international or 'global sociology' (Albrow and King, 1990; Sklair, 1991) or in Immanuel Wallerstein's contributions to debates on global culture, framed firmly in the perspective of world-system theory (Wallerstein, 1990, 1991).

Now, it is the last of these responses that I want to focus on here. For there ought to be some value in assessing the success with which globalization can be absorbed into existing discourses. This should not only tell us how truly challenging the globalization process is to existing theories and perspectives, but also, perhaps, provide insights into new critical responses. Since my specific interest in globalization is broadly in its cultural aspect, the discourse I will consider is that of 'cultural imperialism'. In what follows I will first discuss the case for viewing the cultural aspect of globalization from the critical standpoint of cultural imperialism theory and then I will try to show how 'cultural globalization' resists this incorporation.

Cultural globalization or cultural imperialism?

The argument that links cultural globalization to cultural imperialism goes roughly like this: globalization is either just the latest term for, or the latest stage in, a process with a long history, a history more or less co-extensive with the history of Western imperialism. It is simply the global working through of a process of domination in which the West (or America, or transnational capitalism) draws all cultures into its ambit. As Jonathan Friedman says, the discourse of cultural imperialism tended to set the scene for the initial reception of globalization, casting the process as, 'an aspect of the hierarchical nature of imperialism, that is the increasing hegemony of particular central cultures, the diffusion of American values, consumer goods and lifestyles' (Friedman, 1994: 195; see also McQuail, 1994: 113).

What the cultural imperialism argument does is to bring the globalization process into an immediate critical focus – one which I shall argue is, in fact, premature and misses the proper object of critique. But it is easy to see why this perspective is so attractive – cultural imperialism is itself a very general and elastic concept, gathering in notions of domination in terms of both general hegemonic cultural formations (the West, Western modernity, consumer culture) and of particular national cultures (America) and accommodating this critique alongside a critique of political economy (transnational capitalism). Moreover, the discourse of cultural imperialism has a particular (though not exclusive) reference to the situation of the Third World, providing, in Ulf Hannerz's terms (1991), a dramatic, pessimistic 'master scenario' for the absorption of peripheral cultures into an homogenized, commodified, 'globalized' future. The immediate plausibility of this scenario lies in the way it extrapolates from very widely accepted models of centre–periphery flows and relationships, and from equally compelling evidence of historical patterns of domination – for example European colonialism.

Now, despite these attractions, the perspective of cultural imperialism has, in fact, come in for sustained criticism on a number of fronts (Boyd-Barrett, 1982; McQuail, 1994; Schlesinger, 1991; Sinclair, 1992; Tomlinson, 1991), so much so that McGuigan (1992; 229) scarcely exaggerates in calling it 'a deeply unfashionable problematic' in the late 1980s and early 1990s. However this may be, there are still reasons why cultural imperialism has to be taken seriously as a perspective through which cultural globalization may be viewed. First, because certain of the assumptions of cultural imperialism continue to find voice in the work of some major, and sophisticated, cultural critics (see, for example, Hall, 1991; Said, 1993: 352–3). Secondly, because real cultural policy issues (for instance, the famous stalling of the final GATT round in 1993 over disputes about film and television imports) demonstrate how seriously some national governments continue to take the threat of cultural imperialism.[1] And thirdly, because there are issues posed within this perspective which command the attention of anyone viewing the globalization process with a critical eye. Although, as I have argued elsewhere (Tomlinson, 1991), the discourse of cultural imperialism is a highly contradictory one, it does give voice to genuine and important concerns over cultural value and cultural autonomy in the context of global modernity. But it is precisely the critical focus of these concerns that globalization problematizes: here lies its iconoclastic potential. So the question of whether cultural imperialism can absorb the globalization process within its own critical terms is important for both discourses. Let us now consider the arguments in favour of such an assimilation.

There are three good reasons to assimilate cultural globalization to cultural imperialism.

The ubiquity of Western cultural goods

The first and most obvious reason is that there is a wealth of evidence that Western cultural tastes and practices are becoming global ones. Take any index, from clothes to food to music to film and television to architecture (the list is only limited by what one wants to include as 'culture'), and there is no ignoring the sheer massive presence of Western (meaning here North American, Western European, possibly Australian) cultural goods, practices and styles in every inhabited area of the world. And one could be more specific. Isn't global mass culture, as Stuart Hall argues (1991: 27; see also Lash and Urry, 1994: 127), actually predominantly American culture? Certainly,if the process has to be tied to one national culture, there really isn't much competition. And if we agree with Hall in seeing the global cultural sphere as 'dominated by the visual and graphic arts . . . dominated by television and by film, and by the image, imagery, and styles of mass advertising' (Hall, 1991: 27), then the case for seeing cultural globalization as 'Americanization' is a persuasive one, endorsed as each new Hollywood blockbuster outgrosses the previous one in world box office receipts, or every time the CNN logo appears on our screens superimposed over the latest, most 'immediate' global news footage.

Notice that at this point the argument is simply a broad empirical one. Once we start to ask more pointed questions – even at the empirical level – the issues, as we shall later see, become more complex. However there is, without doubt, at least a prima-facie case to be answered here. Doesn't the sheer material ubiquity of Western – and indeed American – cultural products world-wide support casting cultural globalization as in some sense the extension of at least 'Western' – if not American – cultural empire? Granted, this is a 'soft' imperialism, quite different from the bloody coercive cultural impositions of, for example, nineteenth-century European colonial expansion. But is it not still, in some more general sense, inescapably 'domination', the wilful displacement of 'weaker' cultures by a more powerful one?

When viewed from this perspective, the complex web of interconnections of globalization takes on more specific features: it appears to have specific points of origin and concentrations of power – to grow denser towards the centres of cultural production (which coincide, of course, with concentrations of power and wealth). And the complex cross-cutting and overlay of communication paths and flows now takes on a less benign aspect: now it is a 'web' which enmeshes and binds in all cultures. Or, to take the other image of globalization, action at distance. As Giddens describes this, it refers to the extent to which 'locales are thoroughly penetrated by and shaped in terms of social influences quite distant from them' (Giddens, 1990: 19). The perspective of cultural imperialism invites us to construct this idea around the issue of the locus of control of lived experience. Thus, the distanciated influences which order our everyday lives can easily appear as those of the culturally dominant other: from the McDonald's restaurant that replaces the local café, to the multiplex cinema 'vertically integrated' into the Hollywood distribution system and thus showing almost exclusively American films. If you happen to live in the Third World, the sense of distanciated influences must seem almost total: from the Western brand marks which carry the most social cachet, to the transnational that owns the plant where you work, to the World Bank that provides the development loans but also dictates the pattern of that development, and, *in extremis*, to the foreign-aid workers who try to keep you alive at feeding centres and in refugee camps. And with this thought, we can move to the second reason in support of the cultural imperialism perspective on globalization.

The long history of Western imperialism

This is because what we (nowadays rather uncertainly) call 'Third World' countries stand in a historical relation of political and economic subordination to those of the developed West, ineluctably bound up with a colonial past. This is a history which provides a very strong context in which cultural as well as political-economic globalization can be grasped. Nearly all descriptions of the globalization process admit of its 'uneven' character – of the fact that its effects and consequences are not uniformly experienced everywhere in the world. As Doreen Massey puts it, there is a 'power geometry' of globalization in which 'some people are more in charge of it than others; some initiate flows and movement, others don't; some are more on the receiving-end of it than others; some are effectively imprisoned by it' (Massey, 1994: 149). There are, then, clear 'winners and losers' (Lash and Urry, 1994) in the process of globalization. And given this, it seems almost perverse not to see the historically established patterns of neo-colonialism repeating themselves here.

More than this, it seems almost a betrayal. If we recognize the discursive struggle which established the critical terms – neo-imperialism, dependency theory, world-system theory – through which the 'real foundations' of the history of the Third World were disclosed, then any theory which fails to engage with this context – to take it as a firm, hard-won and enduring point of reference – is liable to some suspicion. The suspicion must be that globalization theory might be just another theory through which the West formulates world history in terms of its own experience – 'a predominantly white/First World take on things' (Massey, 1994: 165). For there have surely been plenty of these, from the long-established and pervasive cultural discourse described by Edward Said, through which Europe constructed its identity by 'relegating and confining the non-European to a secondary racial, cultural, ontological status' (Said, 1993: 70) to the 'modernization theory' and 'developmentalism' which not only placed Western culture as the telos of human development, but at the same time, ignoring the entire history of imperialism/colonialism, tried to account for Third World 'underdevelopment' via various intrinsic deficit models.[2] And as for more recent cultural-critical fashions – postmodernism for example – what sort of a world do these describe? Seen from the perspective of the Third World, which we must remember is where most people in the world live, the experience postmodernism narrates might seem simply irrelevant: its ironic stance and fascination with aporias and ambiguities are cultural luxuries they cannot afford. Or else it might seem – in respect of the epistemological iconoclasm we discussed earlier – a bitterly ironic abandonment of the emancipatory moment of enlightenment thought by Western intellectuals just at the point at which the excluded 'other' was gaining access to discourse and beginning to re-write this history.[3]

Given this long history of Western-dominated global discourse, is it not entirely reasonable to suspect globalization theory if it fails to place the history of Western imperialism squarely in the centre of its world picture? And isn't the corollary to this, that a truly global analysis of cultural globalization needs to begin with a critique of the capacity and the tendency the West has to impose its versions of reality on the rest of the world – precisely the issue of cultural imperialism?

The centrality of capitalism as a cultural influence

The third reason in favour of the cultural imperialism approach concerns its critique of the cultural implications of transnational capitalism. 'Globalization is really advanced capitalist globalization' write Lash and Urry (1994: 280) and, if we do not take this to mean it is solely and exclusively a phenomenon of capitalist expansion, it is hard to disagree. For few would not place the dynamics of capitalism near the centre of the analysis of globalization.[4] Indeed, the use of the term 'globalization' itself is common among corporate managers to describe their strategies (Robins, 1991: 36).

Many of the complex interconnections of globalization both derive from and facilitate an expanding capitalist production system and market. And some of the most striking images of the shrinking world of globalization have to do with the immense power of global markets opened up by information technology: foreign exchange markets, for example, trading hundreds of millions of dollars per minute, dwarfing the trading power of even the largest nation states. It is this gigantic 'decentred' order of capitalist transnational practices that not only threatens the economic and political autonomy of nation states (Lash and Urry, 1994: 280; McGrew, 1992: 91), but also provides some of the most dramatic imagery of cultural globalization. For example, Fredric Jameson argues that the 'high tech paranoia' of some contemporary popular-cultural representations of the apocalyptic power of information technology systems – 'labyrinthine conspiracies of autonomous but deadly interlocking and competing information agencies' – are really 'a distorted figuration of something even deeper, namely the whole world system of a present-day multinational capitalism' (Jameson, 1991: 37–8).

There is a sense here that global capitalism is significant not only in terms of its economic power, and thus its bearing on the material well-being of everyone on the planet, but also on our cultural experience – the very way in which we understand our day-to-day lives. This is the point at which the cultural imperialism argument engages, urging us to understand globalization as the process whereby all global cultures are inexorably drawn into the sphere of influence of one single 'capitalist culture'. This is a position consistently argued by Herbert Schiller (1976, 1985) and broadly supported by others directly associated with the cultural imperialism position (e.g. Dorfman and Mattelart, 1975; Hamelink, 1983) as well as in some more recent neo-Marxist accounts (e.g. Sklair, 1991). And even a theorist like David Harvey, who combines a Marxist political-economy analysis with a 'postmodernist' cultural perspective, argues in this vein: 'Precisely because capitalism is expansionary and imperialistic, cultural life in more and more areas gets brought within the grasp of the cash nexus and the logic of capital circulation' (Harvey, 1989: 344).

Now within this broad perspective there are clearly more and less sophisticated and discriminating positions. Some, like Schiller, tend to elide the capitalist culture argument with the 'Americanization' thesis – the diffusion of 'homogenized North Atlantic cultural slop' (Schiller, 1985: 19), while others make a point of distinguishing the two. For example, Lesley Sklair claims, with some justification, that:

> to identify cultural and media imperialism with the United States or even with US capitalism is a profound and profoundly mystifying error. It implies that if American influence could be excluded, then cultural and media imperialism would end. . . . Americanization itself is a contingent form of a process that is necessary to global capitalism, the culture-ideology of consumerism. (Sklair, 1991: 135)

The actual cultural implications read off from the logic of capitalism argument also vary, from the straightforward idea of incorporation into consumer culture (Sklair; Schiller) to the corollary (though, in fact, more controversial) claim about cultural homogenization. But, despite such differences, the critical thrust of all these positions for globalization theory remains the same: that, in order to avoid idealism in the analysis of cultural globalization, one must start with a grasp of the 'real foundations' of global culture – the expansionary imperatives of the capitalist production process and market.

Taken together, then, these seem to me to make a plausible case for viewing cultural globalization as cultural imperialism. It is not difficult to make this case since it is based on a number of undeniable general empirical observations which dovetail well with what we know about the distribution of power in the world in recent history. So, to borrow an American idiom that only adds to the case: if it walks like a duck and it squawks like a duck, why not call it a duck? Well I hope I haven't made the case for the prosecution too convincing, because now I want to offer three reasons for resisting this 'obviousness'.

Each of the points made in the previous section have some merit and it is not my intention here to try to refute them one by one. What I think needs to be shown is that, important though the issues and concerns that lie behind the cultural imperialism perspective are, the insights of globalization theory require that we frame these – and our critical responses – rather differently. So what I offer here is three reasons – perhaps, better, three invitations – to take a fresh look at these issues.

Look beyond the self-evidence of global cultural goods

My first reason is that the sheer presence of Western, or even specifically American, cultural goods distributed around the world is not a self-evident cultural fact, but something which always needs interpreting. This is a point I have made elsewhere (Tomlinson, 1991) and I do not want to labour it here. However, I do think it is one of the fundamental conceptual mistakes of the cultural imperialism argument to make unwarranted leaps of inference from the simple presence of cultural goods to the attribution of deeper cultural or ideological effects.

In the first place, the 'evidence' itself often turns out to be more ambiguous. Take the obvious example of US television exports. There is, first of all, a common assumption that American television enjoys a virtually unchallenged position of dominance in the global market, particularly in the 'Third World'. Certainly, it enjoys a very strong position, but, as Sinclair (1992) points out, it is certainly not entirely without competition. Companies such as TV Globo in Brazil and Televisa in Mexico have not only managed to dominate their own domestic markets, but to become exporters of products to other Latin American countries, to European countries such as Spain, Portugal and Italy, and even to the United States itself, which contains, of course, an important market for Spanish-language programming in its large and growing Hispanic population. Indeed, these companies now represent 'the biggest television networks in the world outside the US' (Sinclair, 1992: 108). The point Sinclair wants to make is not that the rise of such companies in 'Third World' countries suggests they will overtake the United States in a position of global dominance in a sort of 'reverse cultural imperialism'. Rather, he argues that we have to take a more nuanced view of the global market in communications, recognizing the pluralization of cultural production centres around the world and the significance of geo-linguistic factors influencing market share. These are both points that the rhetoric of cultural imperialism tends to ignore, and which the 'undialectical centre–periphery model' (Sinclair, 1992: 114) it employs tends to obscure.

But, it might still be argued that an undeniable case can be made for US cultural imperialism simply from scanning the number of US television shows on, for example, European national channels. No one denies that there is a lot of US product around. But if we look closer, it almost always turns out that: (a) it is home-produced programmes which top the ratings (Silj, 1988); and (b) that foreign imports generally operate at a 'cultural discount' in terms of their popularity with audiences (Hoskins and Mirus, 1988). Morley and Robins summarize the implications for the reception of American television in Europe:

US imports tend to do well when domestic television is not producing comparable entertainment programming – and whenever viewers have the alternative of comparable entertainment programming in their own language, the American programmes tend to come off second best. (Morley and Robins, 1989: 28)

Neither is it simply a question of language. As McGuigan (1992: 149–50) argues (following Geraghty, 1991), the cultural specificity of British soap operas like *Coronation Street, Eastenders* and *Brookside* – tuned to the everyday experience of a British audience – is what makes these shows consistently more popular than American imports like *Dallas* whose broad 'global' appeal depends precisely on their lack of specific cultural reference. Thus the sheer presence of US televisual texts does not necessarily signal a swamping of national cultural tastes and a threat to national cultural identity.

Careful scrutiny of the schedules shows that US imports frequently fill in the spaces in the day outside peak viewing hours. This might make us interpret the significance of the alien presence quite differently. It might have much more to do with simply the economics of providing a full daily schedule of television programmes. Now I am not denying that there are issues of power involved here – in what US television executives call the American 'subsidy' of world television and what critics call the manipulation of the market by 'programme dumping'. These are important issues, particularly for the 'less developed countries'. But they are primarily economic issues which do not translate directly into cultural ones – certainly not into the 'obvious' issue of cultural influence – without raising other, perhaps more interesting, questions such as why should we want/ expect continuous television 'flow' anyway?

But it is not just a question of interpreting evidence. The preoccupation with the presence of cultural goods can also lead to that other familiar set of theoretical problems with the cultural imperialism argument: its misrepresentation of the cultural agent as a cultural dope – as passive, unreflexive recipient of alien cultural goods – and to the associated fundamental misinterpretation of cultural processes as a uni-directional flow of power. Now, again, these are fairly familiar criticisms which I do not intend to harp on about. But it is perhaps worth summarizing the issues in a single maxim which will serve as my second theoretical invitation.

Always approach global culture as a dialectic

If we follow this maxim, we should not only avoid the rather patronizing attitude towards cultural agents that sees them as the passive terminus of a flow of cultural influence, we should also be able to see that there is in fact never a simple 'delivery' of cultural influence. Movement between cultural/ geographical areas always involves translation, mutation, adaptation and the creation of hybridity.

Now the key advantage of globalization theory in this respect is its insistence on the centrality of the 'global–local dialectic' – in Anthony

Giddens's formulation: 'the oppositional interplay between local involvements and globalizing tendencies' (Giddens, 1991: 242). Giddens applies this idea of the inherent 'push and pull' of countervailing tendencies across the whole range of globalizing processes but it has, perhaps, particular force in the sphere of culture.

Within this dialectical conception we can locate the rise of centres of cultural production and 'indigenous' media entrepreneurship in 'Third World' countries that Sinclair refers to. But the idea can also grasp some of the broader complexities of interaction between cultures generally, and particularly those between the 'hegemonic' cultures of the core and the 'dependent' ones of the periphery. A major point to recognize here is how the sheer vocabulary of the discourse of cultural imperialism – hegemony, dependency, core–periphery – inflects the description of these relations towards simplistic linear uni-directional conceptions. In contrast with this, there is a tradition of cultural analysis coming from the Third World itself – from Latin America – which insists on the dynamic interaction between external cultural influence and local cultural practice. This tradition is now becoming known in the Anglophone world in the work of Nestor Garcia Canclini (1992) and Jesus Martin-Barbero (1993), and can be traced back through the work of Angel Rama on 'transculturation' (1982) and beyond.

At the risk of oversimplifying what is a complex and subtle cultural debate within the Latin American context (Yudice et al., 1992), we can identify a key aspect of this tradition in the concern with the nature of cultural mixing and hybridization rather than with direct cultural imposition from the developed world. In Martin-Barbero's words, what is central to the experience of cultural modernity in Latin America is the way in which, 'the steady, predictable tempo of homogenizing development [is] upset by the counter-tempo of profound differences and cultural discontinuities' (Martin-Barbero, 1993: 149). Now, though this stress on 'transculturation, hybridity and indigenization' (Lull, 1995: 153) is important in understanding the dialectic involved in the reception of hegemonic cultural influence, it also has a wider significance. For, if we always approach the cultural process as a dialectic, it becomes clear that the idea of the emergence of a monolithic global culture, universally reproducing one hegemonic national culture, is rather implausible. This is because, in James Lull's apposite phrase, global culture is always 'meaning in motion' (Lull, 1995: 115f), thus its space is between rather than within cultures and its 'essential' nature is that of the hybrid.

We have only to think of the complex mutations involved in popular music culture – in something like 'hip hop' culture which is often taken as the essential expression of Black American urban poor, born in the South Bronx – and now something like a global youth movement. But in fact 'hip hop' is not quintessential Black American music but a complex hybrid mix of Afro-American and Caribbean musical cultures. This is a form which, in Paul Gilroy's words, 'flaunts and glories in its malleability as well as its transnational character' (Gilroy, 1993: 33). So what sort of grasp of the significance of 'hip hop', as it crosses and re-crosses what Gilroy calls the Black Atlantic, can we have if we treat it merely as an American cultural export? There is, I think, the world of difference between recognizing the global popularity of such essentially hybrid forms – forms which perhaps belong to no particular locality – and the rather grotesque universalism of the late Ithiel de Sola Pool's assumption that the popularity of American mass culture was really 'the discovery of what world cultural tastes actually are' (Pool, 1979: 145).

There is one final way in which I want to consider the dialectical conception of the globalization process and that is in terms of the actual movement of populations and the cultural implications of this. One of the consequences of capitalist modernity as a process of uneven development has been to displace huge numbers of people from their homes in Asia, Africa or Latin America and to bring them to the West as either refugees or, most significantly, as labour migrants. Stuart Hall puts these movements in the context of globalization:

> Driven by poverty, drought, famine, economic underdevelopment and crop failure, civil war and political unrest, regional conflict and arbitrary changes of political regime, the accumulating foreign indebtedness of their governments to Western banks, very large numbers of the poorer peoples of the globe have taken the 'message' of global consumerism at face value, and moved towards the places where 'the goodies' come from and where chances of survival are higher. In the era of global communications, the West is only a one-way airline charter ticket away. (Hall, 1992: 306–7)

The political-economic impact of such migrations is ambiguous for Western nation states, at the same time offering cheap exploitable labour and representing a threat of demographic invasion. The growing anxiety in the developed world over these population movements can be seen, for example, in the notoriously heavy policing of the US–Mexican border, and in the current debate about 'Fortress Europe'. However, the cultural implications of this 'deterritorialization' (Appadurai, 1990; Canclini, 1992) are likely to be more complex and, eventually, perhaps more significant.

Nestor Garcia Canclini, discussing the case of migration from Mexico to the United States cites the demographic trends in California: 'In downtown Los Angeles, for example, 75 percent of the real estate belongs to foreign capital and 40 percent of the population of the greater metropolitan area is composed of Asians and Latinos. By the year 2010, this percentage is expected to rise to 60 percent' (Canclini: 1992: 41). He goes on to quote Renato Rosaldo's claim that the 'Third World is imploding into the First' making 'the idea of an authentic culture as an internally cohesive and autonomous space . . . untenable' (Rosaldo, 1989: 217). This claim raises a number of crucial issues of cultural identity: in the first place, of course, for the migrants themselves. There is a sense in which migrants inevitably live their identities in the interstices between their culture of origin and their 'host' culture. Where this migration becomes permanent, as in the post-colonial 'diasporas' of Asian, African and Caribbean people, the question of cultural identity attaching to an authentic 'homeland' becomes entirely problematic and such people 'have had to renounce the dream or ambition of recovering any kind of "lost" cultural purity, or ethnic absolutism' (Hall, 1992: 310). One then has to ask how the discourse of cultural imperialism works for these diasporic cultures – and the answer is probably not very well. For it is difficult to see how its generalized rhetoric of 'cultural authenticity under attack' can possibly account for the lived experience of hybridity – of precisely not belonging to one culture. Furthermore, it is easy to see how the rhetoric of cultural authenticity may lend spurious support to the enemies of multiculturalism (Tomlinson, 1991: 73).

But another question we can pose here is of the implications of migration for the construction of cultural identity in the countries of the West themselves. And here we can connect Rosaldo's observations with those of Kevin Robins, who argues that the post-colonial diaspora represents a sense in which the 'Other has installed itself within the very heart of the western metropolis, . . . [t]hrough a kind of reverse invasion, the periphery has now infiltrated the colonial core' (Robins, 1991: 32). Now talk of globalization often draws attention to the more obvious cultural consequences of this process – the commodification of the exotic and the ethnic in Western culture – in food, fashion and so on. But Robins draws what I think is a deeper implication, that the self-confident, stable cultural identity of the West is becoming threatened: 'Through this irruption of empire, the certain and centred perspective of the old colonial order is confronted and confused' (Robins, 1991: 33).

What is at stake here is a shift in the cultural relations between the West and its post-colonial Others, a shift in the balance of what might be called 'cultural power', as distinct from political-economic power. The 'certain and centred perspective of the old colonial order' was established in some ways on the basis of unquestioned cultural assumptions, identities and self-images which could only be maintained in binary oppositions preserved by the insulating power of distance. So long as the colonized Other stayed firmly in their place, both literally and metaphorically, the imaginary geographies (Said, 1979) generated in the West could, by mapping cultural and racial stereotypes on to place, maintain a sense of confidence in a universal order which both justified the colonial project, and fed back into confirmation of Western self-identities. But as global communications collapse physical distance – in this context bringing the subordinate culture into direct proximity with the dominant one – so collapses the cultural distance necessary to sustain the myths of identity. It is as though the cultural pluralism which Western modernity exported to the rest of the world, and which destroyed the certainties of tradition, now returns to undermine its own certainties.

But what, we might ask, does this imply for the post-colonial world itself? Well, in terms of a simple and direct shift of cultural influence, perhaps not much. Despite the turn to non-Western cultural forms, religions and philosophies that is now a common feature of Western counter-cultural movements, no one could seriously claim that these are about to supplant Western secular consumerism, however unstable its cultural-existential deep-structures are becoming. It is not as though the Eastern religions or African folk cultures are about to become dominant global forms. But what we can say confidently is that increasing 'multi-culturalism' in the West, combined with the long-term (and, seemingly, accelerating) decline in Western cultural confidence, coherence and certainty from its high water mark in nineteenth-century imperialism does represent a significant decline in its cultural power. And this means that one of the central informing images of the cultural imperialism thesis – the image of the imposition of a 'strong' coherent culture (the West) on to 'weaker' more vulnerable ones – no longer applies. And though the long-term implications of this historically extended dialectic are by no means clear, it is obvious that we shall have to think them through in a more complex framework of analysis – one that recognizes all these dimensions of the push and pull of globalizing tendencies – than that offered in the discourse of cultural imperialism. My final invitation, then, is to consider a more complex model of the operation of global cultural power.

Recognize globalization as a complex decentred process

If we return to our original image of the globalization process as a complex set of interconnections, and add to this the dialectical conception of cultural processes, we get a very different image of the world from that implicit in the cultural imperialism thesis. Instead of the idea of settled, well-established and confident centres of economic and cultural power exercising global hegemony, we end up with an image of a decentred network, in which the patterns of distribution of power are unstable and shifting and, indeed, in which power is in some ways diffused rather than concentrated.

Now the iconoclastic potential of globalization theory really comes to the fore here in the implicit critique of the 'core–periphery' model that not only informs the discourse of cultural imperialism but, of course, a great deal of critical analysis of the global distribution of political and economic power. Indeed, theorists like Giddens are quite explicit in their criticisms:

> [The global economy] is much more thoroughly infused with reflexive mechanisms than once it was; and it is increasingly decentred, no matter what power Western states and agencies continue to hold over what was 'the periphery'. . . . However critical one might still want to be of the unfettered processes of capitalist enterprise, the target has now become much more elusive. Conspiracy-style theories of Global disparities don't have the purchase they once seemed, to some observers at least, to have. (Giddens, 1994: 87)

And this is by no means simply a view from the First World. Garcia Canclini argues in much the same vein when he criticizes the inadequacy of the centre–periphery model as 'the abstract expression of an idealized imperial system' (1992: 40) and calls for a more nuanced view of cultural power 'within a transnational system that is diffuse with a complex form of global interrelations and interpretations' (Garcia Canclini, quoted in Martin-Barbero, 1993: 207).

The general point here is not, it needs to be stressed, to suggest that global economic, political and cultural disparities are somehow being smoothed out. All available indices of quality of life continue to show the highest levels in the 'core' countries of North America, Europe, Japan and Australasia[5] and the levels of poverty and immiseration in large areas of Africa, Latin America and Asia scarcely need pointing out. No, the point, rather, is to suggest that the core–periphery model does not adequately grasp either the complexities of the operation of global capitalism, the way this cuts across and refigures relations between nation states and regions within nation states, and resulting shifts in the balance of global power. This is not to under-estimate the obvious weight of disadvantage suffered by the 'less developed countries', but it is to argue that they cannot be understood in the rather monolithic terms that the core–periphery dualism encourages. The so-called 'Asian Tigers' (South Korea, Taiwan, Singapore, Hong Kong, Malaysia and Indonesia) are the most obvious cases of Third World economies that have rapidly and 'successfully' developed within the framework of global capitalism. And though, of course, we have to recognize all the social and cultural costs and contradictions of such 'success', they do represent evidence of shifting patterns of economic power which cannot be ignored.

Of course, this raises a whole range of controversial issues which cannot be properly addressed here. But it does seem to me that such developments in global capitalism, viewed in the long term, leave the West – and any particular nation state in the West – without any guarantees as to its continuing position of dominance. As Anthony Giddens argues, globaliza-tion links the fates of localities in complex ways which do not necessarily reproduce the familiar historical patterns of Western dominance: 'The increasing prosperity of an urban area in Singapore might be causally related, via a complicated network of global economic ties, to the impoverishment of a neighbourhood in Pittsburgh whose local products are uncompetitive in world markets' (Giddens, 1990: 65).

So what globalization theory calls attention to here is emerging patterns of the distribution of advantage and disadvantage which cut across the North–South, First–Third, core–periphery divides. These new patterns – the result of the dense web of connections which characterize globalization – disengage the economic fates of regions, cities, even, as Giddens suggests, neighbourhoods and yet smaller localities from their generalized core or periphery locations, and connect them with globalizing systems which may, in another sense, bring the First World into the Third World and vice versa: 'Two areas that exist directly alongside one another, or groups living in close proximity, may be caught up in quite different globalizing systems, producing bizarre physical juxtapositions. The sweatshop worker may be just across the street from a wealthy financial centre' (Giddens, 1994: 81).

Recognizing such emergent patterns clearly places a question mark over one of the grounding assumptions of the cultural imperialism argument: the assumption of the continuing concerted dominance of the West, seen as a coherent cultural–economic–geographical totality at the centre of global processes, over the rest – the peripheral, the marginalized. But should such changes surprise us? No, of course not, if we think historically, and particularly if we emphasize the imperatives of capitalist expansion: for it is clear that capitalism has no 'loyalty' to its birthplace, and so provides no guarantees that the geographical patterns of dominance established in early modernity will continue. Globalization theory requires us to take seriously the much-used term 'global capitalism' and to pay attention to its long-term implications. These seem likely to include an eventual dismantling of the sort of elective affinity between the interests of capitalism and of the West that might have obtained hitherto. We can see signs of this, for example, in the increasingly uneasy relation between the capitalist money markets and the governments of Western nation states – the periodic currency crises besetting the Western industrial nations.

In this connection, and having mentioned Singapore and decentred capitalism in one breath, the obvious example that suggests itself (as I write in February 1995) is the fate of the British merchant bank, Barings. This is, of course, a spectacular illustration both of the sort of instability I have been pointing to, and of the dramatic possibilities of electronically mediated local–global interconnections – the local in this case being represented as a single individual, the trader Nick Leeson who apparently lost over 700 million pounds and bankrupted his employers. Now it is tempting to dwell on the ironies here: 'old European capitalism' in the shape of Baring Brothers – Britain's oldest merchant bank, dating back to 1762, Bankers to the Queen and so on – being destroyed in a few days by the actions of a twenty-eight-year-old dealing in the most refined, abstract of market trading – derivatives – on the youngest of markets – that of South East Asia. There are tempting images here, I think, of the old, confident world of global imperial control being overtaken by the new decentred world of globalized capitalism, in which effects can be instantaneous, catastrophic and completely without regard to established traditions of influence. But there is perhaps a larger point to be made. As the British newspaper *The Guardian* pointed out: 'It is significant that the incident came to light while the group of seven leading countries – the G7 nations – were thrashing out a common policy on information superhighways in Brussels *because they are part of the same problem*' (*The Guardian*, 27 February 1995: 19; my emphasis). Why should these two events be linked? Well, according to *The Guardian* leader writer, because the development of the technology of globalization – electronically mediated instantaneous transmission systems – coincided with the globalization of world financial markets. The article went on: 'Governments ceded their sovereignty over capital flows leaving no international body to do the necessary global surveillance. Then the new global highway spawned a new generation of financial products – of which trading in derivatives is the most spectacular – to utilise its almost unlimited capacity' (ibid.).

So, in short, the situation that could produce such dramatic financial débâcles is one indicative of the nature of globalization itself – the combination of the phenomenally powerful communicative capacity of globalizing technology with totally inadequate levels of global political-economic control. For who is to provide the 'necessary global surveillance' that *The Guardian* talks of? Not, apparently the G7 countries. For what they decided to do about regulating the information superhighway was, in effect, virtually nothing. The decision was that market forces – 'dynamic competition' – should be allowed to determine developments. And this is by no means surprising, for in the essentially competitive context of international capitalism, regulation is not only anathema, it is actually difficult to imagine other than in terms of policies of economic and cultural protectionism deployed by individual nation states, policies which can easily be shown to be unworkable. What global regulation requires, rather (and this applies not just to the spheres of communications technology or of the global political economy, but to vital issues like global environmental protection) is something like a global polity – some sort of mutually binding political structure or some community of interest above the level of the nation-state system. And there is no sign at the present that globalization is about to produce this.

Recognizing globalization as a decentred process, then, obviously does not imply the imminent equalization of global power. And, clearly, those countries who have enjoyed dominance in the past will strive, with all the considerable resources at their disposal, to hang on to it. The point is that the complexities of globalized networks and their unpredictable consequences may well prevent them from doing so.

Conclusion: CNN comes to St Helena

Let me now try to pull some of these thoughts together. I have tried to suggest that globalization, including its cultural aspects, is indeed a new and perplexing phenomenon and, tempting though it is, is not something that can be made sense of in the critical terms of cultural imperialism. And I have suggested three sets of reasons for this.

First, because the immediate evidence of the global distribution and impact of Western/American cultural goods is both more ambiguous and less ominous than the cultural imperialism thesis tends to represent it. Secondly, that conceptualizing cultural processes in dialectical terms offers a more complex picture of cultural globalization which suggests that cultural influence is unlikely ever to follow the sort of linear paths that cultural imperialism predicts. And finally, because the globalization process is essentially a 'decentred' one, producing new patterns of advantage and disadvantage that we are only just beginning to recognize and which do not map neatly on to the familiar geographies of domination that the discourse of cultural imperialism assumes.

The implications of this last thought are that the West should not be seen as possessing either the economic or the cultural guarantees that can keep it securely in the driving seat of global modernity. To use one final image from Giddens, we need to think of globalizing modernity not as a finely engineered, effortlessly controllable machine, but as a 'juggernaut', something which no one – not the West, America, nor multinational capitalism – can fully control. It is this which definitively separates it from the idea of cultural imperialism.

To conclude, I want to consider an event which might be used to speculate about the long-term implications of cultural globalization. The account of this event, as reported by the journalist Dina Rabinovitch (1994), was of globalizing media technology reaching the last place on earth. Or at least one of the last thoroughly remote places: the island of St Helena in the South Atlantic. This island – the one to which Napoleon was exiled – is a British protectorate, English-speaking, but truly remote. It has no airfield and can only be reached by sea – two weeks from Britain, five days from Cape Town and two days from its nearest neighbour, Ascension Island. Post takes months to arrive and newspapers are always out of date. But in November 1994 the islanders finally received their first satellite television, courtesy of Cable and Wireless. The only channel they can receive so far is CNN.

What will be the implications for the islanders of becoming hooked into the global media network? The cultural imperialism thesis obviously suggests a sort of 'closure', a final triumph of cultural incorporation. CNN, seeing itself in the role, as expressed by one of its senior executives Ed (not Ted) Turner, of 'town crier to the global village', will bring in its images and messages about the way the world out there is. And these will no doubt contain representations of the 'American way', of consumer capitalism and so forth. The fear is already being expressed that television will begin to erode the special characteristics of St Helenian culture and social structure – for example its particular patterns of child care in the extended family system.

But on the other hand, as Rabinovitch's story points out, the very isolation which the global media are now beginning to penetrate has been one which has sustained all sorts of injustices and unfreedoms. St Helenians have not enjoyed autonomy in their isolation, but rather this isolation has helped to preserve old patterns of British imperial rule and paternalism – what Stuart Hall has referred to as 'the globalization of an earlier phase' (Hall, 1991: 25). The British Governor of the island still maintains wide colonial-style powers, including powers of censorship; living standards are poor and jobs are few, all the best jobs have routinely been reserved for British ex-patriates. This has created a situation in which the St Helenians have been used as reserves of cheap labour for the garrisons of Ascension Island and the Falklands. So one has to ask, what is the cultural and social experience which needs to be preserved here – and in whose interests?

Now, it is Rabinovitch's hope that access to global television will bring some beginnings of emancipation from this old pattern of political-economic – and yes – cultural domination. 'If television brings nothing else to the island', she writes, 'let it bring them the knowledge – as infinite as the ocean surrounding – of what is possible' (Rabinovitch, 1994: 13). Without exaggerating and romanticizing the emancipatory potential of globalizing media technology, I think she has a point. None of us can say how globalization will precisely change the pattern of life on St Helena, but what seems almost certain is that it will not simply reproduce the old systems of domination. Pretty obviously, globalization does not promise the techno-utopia of McLuhan's global village, but neither does it look likely to produce the homogenized dystopia, dominated by the same old power players, predicted in the cultural imperialism thesis. Perhaps all we can predict at present is an uncertain, uneven, but radically open cultural future.

Notes

1   For a summary of this issue see Annenoon van Hemmel's paper 'European culture versus GATT trade' in the collection assembled to accompany the conference 'GATT, the Arts and cultural exchange between the United States and Europe', Tilburg University, The Netherlands, 20–21 October 1994.

2   The most trenchant critique of 'modernization theory' can be found in the work of 'dependency theorists' such as Andre Gunder Frank (e.g. Frank, 1969), but see also Cornelius Castoriadis's highly original and subtle critique of the ideology of developmentalism: 'Reflections on "Rationality" and "Development"' (Castoriadis, 1991).

3   See, for example, Garnham (1992: 369) who also seems to have in mind the enlistment of post-structuralist thought in 'post-colonial theory'.

4   A notable exception here being Roland Robertson who explicitly relegates capitalism to a subsidiary position (Robertson, 1992: 100).

5   For example, the United Nations Development Programme's 'Human development index' reported in 1992. For details of this and other relevant indices, see Thomas et al.'s excellent *Third World Atlas* (1995).

Further questions

1   How far can globalization be viewed as an extension or deepening of the cultural imperialism of the West? Concentrate on the cultural aspects of the process.
2   Which of these descriptions of cultural globalization do you prefer and why:
   (a)   The extension of US culture across the globe?
   (b)   The hybridization of cultures on a world-wide scale?
   (c)   A new dialectic of the local and global.
3   What are the relationships between cultural globalization and the changes in the capitalist production system (including technology) that are discussed in this chapter and in other parts of this book?

8

International Communication: The Control of Difference and the Global Market

Richard Maxwell

As we are getting near the end of the twentieth century, international media systems are, as we have seen throughout this book, becoming increasingly global or transnational in their reach. But the mega corporations require knowledge of local needs and new trends in taste and consumption. As Richard Maxwell puts it, 'knowledge of local value assessments and how they differ inside and outside national territories is a geo-strategic asset'. In other words, modern global consumption depends on certain cultural conditions; these concern people's desires and identities, which are formed and experienced in particular localities.

Market research is one way in which this dependence on the local is handled. Maxwell suggests that market research is continuously in the process of extracting information and meaning from popular culture and everyday life in order to promote new ways of consumption. Understanding people's cultural taste means better control over people's consumption habits. Without a knowledge of localities and identities, marketers can, as Maxwell shows, make major blunders. An important aspect of this intervention is the presentation of globally produced commodities as corresponding to particular lifestyles and having a local use and character.

At one level, Maxwell calls our attention to marketers' problems and intentions. At another, deeper level, he raises the very complex and important questions of 'what makes us desire' and how we define ourselves by fulfilling our desire. In understanding contemporary communication industries it is crucial to recognize how eager the cultural industries are to know and to cultivate our desires and identities for their further production of cultural objects and texts. It is this, rather than some simple imposition, that is the basis of their power. It is important, therefore, to question the seemingly innocent practices of market research and the ways in which they may curtail freedoms.

It's yourself you should scrutinize to see
Whether you're center or periphery. (Goethe, 1820/1958)

'What makes us desire?' (Hennion and Meadel, 1993: 169–92, 192). This little question stirs million-dollar giants into knowing all there is to know about people's desires and values. Market research gets to know us by telephone, in door-to-door surveys, in focus groups, or on the street; it is unobtrusive too, secretly videotaping us in offices, shops and malls. Market researchers want information about our tastes for everything, from soap and cigarettes to advertisements and bank accounts, to figure out how desire works differently for different people. They have learned to reject the idea that there are inherent use-values in things, presuming and documenting instead a range of interpretative variations of use-values. They have orders from their clients to organize these diverse values into emotions that can be purchased along with commodities, putting the use-values to work as exchange values of goods and services. After years of facilitating product design and exchange in this way, marketers and advertisers have understandably come to see desire as the quest for self-identification in commodities.

The purchase of self-definition occurs locally but perpetuates a global exchange within an economy dominated by transnational corporations. The decision to buy goods or services is always, in a key sense, about feeling safe or 'close to home', whether it's done by telephone or at the corner market. Market research is therefore in the business of suppressing an object's foreignness, literally when the client is a global merchandiser, and expressing a commodity's familiarity as a local good. Localization benefits the seller, of course; but it also demonstrates a commodity's respect for what is near to the buyer. Localization reduces both risks for the seller and threats to the buyer while it socializes commodities for local sales. Commodities habituate us to (supra local) exchange by appealing to our local presence in the world, for without a stable sense of a boundary identity, exchange is unsettling, threatening (Shapiro, 1993: 36, Ch. 3 *passim*). Marketing capitalizes on this inherent mutuality of sovereignty and exchange by securing our presence in the world and turning self-identification into a desire for commercial exchange.

Market research is a globalized industry penetrating thousands of localities around the world with techniques of information extraction that are both quantitative and qualitative. Interviewers and survey technicians do not preserve the integrity of the stories they retrieve, but they cannot always translate them into their client's objectives either. People tend to value objects in a manner merchandisers cannot predict or control. In order to solve this problem, the range of possible meanings ascribed to commodities must be narrowed; this is the function of advertising and packaging. Through market research, local value assessments provide the raw material for creating a narrower, exchange-driven interpretation of a commodity's value.

This process inverts the old imagery of dominant ideology being injected like cultural dope into an unsuspecting public, showing the hypodermic extracts meaning instead (cf. Fiske, 1987: 39). It also disturbs the category of resistance to dominant ideology that became an imperative of cultural studies in the last two decades. The extractive practice of market research thrives on resistance to dominant ideology, renewing itself by proving that commodities have no inherent, and hence no predictable, use-value. At the same time it confirms the success of hegemonic culture by absorbing local differences of value and taste into the global sales effort.

How merchants operate around the world

If desire is not outside domination, then, as Raymond Williams says: the 'true condition of hegemony is effective self-identification with hegemonic forms' (Williams, 1977: 118). Market research appears to act on this Gramscian assumption too, only in its case there is profit in answering the question about what makes us desire (Schiller, 1989: 153).

Once established as accepted practice, both legally and socially, market research firms can expropriate local information about personal values for the benefit of merchants operating around the world. The empathy shared between the interviewer and the interview subject is the main technique for linking local populations to global operations. A brief encounter between two strangers, based on a sense of solidarity, and often kindness, not only makes surveillance less obtrusive, it marks the first step in organizing local value assessments according to the needs of global capitalist enterprises.

This chapter begins with the encounter of interviewer and public, treating it as a secular confessional where people receive a sympathetic hearing from global merchants' proxies. Business imperatives to eliminate cultural blunders of mass marketing motivate this close scrutiny of consumers' concerns, leading marketers to improve localized surveillance techniques. As we will see, enhanced surveillance of local cultures runs into public resistance in a number of forms and phases, renewing and improving market research. 'Non-response' to surveys is still the most effective, though unorganized, means of defence against the intrusions of globalized market research, public policy not yet establishing effective supranational protections. The economics of extracting personal information simultaneously generates two aesthetic dimensions which socialize the marketing perspective. One is a popular aesthetic of composing 'lifestyles' out of forms of advertising, packaging, and design of goods and services. The other is a labelling aesthetic derived from invented identities and their labels as clusters, audiences, quotas and targets; these generic figures furnish marketers' clients with a way of seeing and acting in a world of cultural difference.

Space reorganized is power reorganized: cultural imperialism has been reconstituted in places and forms made familiar by localized marketing, less obviously imperious but no less inclined to annex desire and value to transnational capital expansion. Calculating the probability of people's whereabouts, actions and sentiments has become big business. The 'primary sector' of this extractive information business is personal data collection, where an admixture of profit, prophesy and frustration drives innovation.

To put it in industry terms, 'know them all. . . . What they read, what they watch, what they buy, what they like, what they do' (Mediamark Research, Inc. 1992).

A secular confessional

Market researchers listen to stories about people's relation to every imaginable kind of product, from household cleaners to perfumes and flight attendants. Market researchers interpret these stories as local assessments about the value people ascribe to goods and services, reporting what they find to corporate clients wishing to improve merchandising techniques in as many different local markets as possible. The clients with the most influence on market research are transnational firms with sales networks that reach around the globe. Market researchers are employed to think about people within a narrow framework of social categories (targets, audiences, quotas, and so on); however, their actual work takes them into a quotidian world rich with diverse views about a commodity's value. And though billboards, cars and computers contain something of marketing's categorical imagination, these products also contain the diversity of local values. The market researcher furnishes a place for people to report their beliefs and opinions, doubts and successes, gossip on the streets, and rumours from the neighbours. This secular confessional is the first station supplying the human face to global products.

Perla Haimovich, an Argentine sociologist in her mid-forties, has worked as an independent marketing researcher in Spain for almost fifteen years. She is an expert in qualitative studies and conducts focus group analysis for transnational commercial broadcasters and consumer goods manufacturers. She studied sociology, dreaming it would help her make social change, a dream interrupted by the military Junta in Argentina. Like many in her generation of Argentine immigrants, she found Spain's transition to democracy demanded the work of social scientists and psychologists, and within ten days of arriving she found a research job in marketing. Today she owns her own market research and consulting firm with an exclusive contract to conduct qualitative studies for Silvio Berlusconi's Spanish TV network Tele-5.

Perla candidly explains how interviewers extract information from people. 'Most of us who do the actual interviews for marketing are really more like frustrated concierges than social scientists.' This is not an eccentric view, but one that captures the sociological reality of many field researchers in the marketing business. Perla uses a number of different popular figures to describe the technique of the interviewer: concierge, confessor, bartender, hair-stylist, gossip, confidant. She regards people's desire to confess as natural: 'Ask someone to tell you how they feel about something, give them a chance to speak freely, and they begin to open up' (Interview, 19 February 1995).

On-the-ground research, from the technical directors to the people con-
ducting door-to-door interviews and focus group sessions, consists of one
decisive attribute: the ability to get people to open up and tell their stories.
Manuel Almeijeiras is technical director of survey research at the Spanish
market research company, Alef. He began his career at Alef when it was a
progressive institute devoted to investigating the living conditions of Spain's
working class. Alef is now a subsidiary of the British multinational market
research firm, Millward Brown International, which is part of the Kantar
Group of the mega-conglomerate, WPP. Manuel Almeijeiras is an energetic
man in his forties, quick to tell you he is from Galicia in the north of Spain,
where the cheese is good and the small-farm economy limits the advances of
consumer marketing. 'The work of an interviewer', he said, 'is about
opening doors and extracting information from a citizen who initially does
not want to give an answer about anything.' Interviewers must be insistent
but not pushy; they have orders 'to get an answer and make sure the person
interviewed sees that their answers are important' (Interview, 26 January
1995). To succeed, the interviewers must demonstrate that they are good
listeners. They must also show that they hold in high regard the personal
accounts of those willing to speak. 'One of the conclusions I would make
about interviewing', says Valle Rodriguez, an interviewer at Alef, 'is that
there are people with a need to explain their lives; above all, older women
who may keep you there three hours telling you everything: economic
problems, relations with their kids, maybe how good it would be to get one
of their kids a job as an interviewer.' (Interview, 27 January 1995).

Interviewers and supervisors

Interviewers and their supervisors are unique among cultural workers. They
are charged with carrying people's life stories across the divide separating
two structurally differentiated groups: manufacturers and consumers. Given
this context, we might expect the researcher and the interview subject to
share a sense of purpose in making manufacturers aware of what consumers want; in return, consumers expect their wishes will be met and their
lives improved if they answer the survey questions. However, what
motivates the field researcher is not this higher purpose, of course; it is a
very good salary for a psychologically and physically draining job. There is,
nevertheless, a crucial emotional exchange at the heart of the job. Valle
Rodriguez is in her mid-twenties and has conducted door-to-door surveys
at Alef for four years. In an accent softened by family ties to Latin
America, she spoke sympathetically of the people she has met: 'There I am
and this person has given up some of their time to answer the questionnaire
and if they want to chat about other stuff, well I get into it a bit. That's the
nice part of the work, really, since without it the job would be too sour. I
don't want to be like a robot, a little machine taking down their answers.'
(Interview, 27 January 1995). This emotional exchange underlies the

interview subject's desire to speak as well, as the reason most people give for opening up to the interview situation is the sense of empathy they feel with the interviewer. Surveys on the public rejection of interviews conducted by the Centro de Investigaciones Sociológicas (Centre for Sociological Research) in Madrid between 1976 and 1985 confirm that a feeling of solidarity between interviewer and interview subject is essential for carrying out a successful interview (unpublished surveys 1379 and 1799; REIS 1978: 229–63; REOP 1976: 266–92).

Meanwhile, not far from the friendly exchanges described here, Alef–Millward Brown is readying the statistical machinery that will process these data collection interviews and transform them into information it can sell to its clients. Millward Brown International has survey networks in France, Germany, Britain, Italy and Spain. As part of WPP's Kantar Group it also has ties to other market research firms and interlocks with WPP's Hill & Knowlton, J. Walter Thompson, and Ogilvy & Mather Worldwide. Milagros Benito heads the research department at Alef, where she takes the international job orders and coordinates their technical design with field research in Spain. She explained Millward Brown's global network this way: 'The data bases are divided, but the one in London is where the processing takes place – it's very large and all the multi-country data are stored there. We send them the raw data and they send back the processed information with all the tables we want and the comparative data with past studies or similar studies in other places' (Interview, 25 January 1995). Interviewers at Alef take the British-designed survey to the Spanish streets where they collect simple bits of data such as the time people spend watching television, brand names people recall, products used to tidy up homes or bodies, or how people rank a new perfume or detergent. Milagros Benito adds the caution: 'If the information weren't centralized in London, then we'd all be working in an isolated way on a local level.' Such isolation would not be good business, since multi-country data processing can reveal profit potentials of distinct national taste cultures, either by raising the spectre of local distaste for global merchandise or by finding cosmetic solutions for the sales effort. For this reason 'it's very common that a client will be doing the same study in a number of different countries', Benito said. She described one such study in which Millward Brown examined various geographical points in Spain and Germany to compare tastes in perfume, revealing distinct smell cultures in each country. Selling odour seems to be one job in which tabulating local interpretations of value requires a soft touch. As Benito put it, 'smell is a very personal thing' (Interview, 25 January 1995).

Information production

In the end, information produced from personal data collected in Spain by Alef will be incorporated into a number of the products sold in Spain. The irony is that these questions about perfume preferences, or other taste issues, are designed for the greater benefit of a transnational firm hawking a local sale to Spanish consumers. Alef sells information about cultural differences in Spain so that a foreign client's products appear as local goods, a double exploitation of the interview subjects. Stories they tell about themselves are taken from them in the same way mineral deposits are mined for export – raw data as raw material in the information economy. Another kind of expropriation is also initiated here. In talking about themselves interview subjects produce a legitimate claim on an enhanced life, with greater choices and fewer annoyances. But in doing this they submit intimate information, like a surplus of labour, for the benefit of the multinational firm. In short, life-enhancements are exchanged for forms of surveillance.

Reduced to sociological cogs in this system, interviewers like Valle and Perla function as proxies for the multinational firms for which they work. Perla does qualitative analysis for Silvio Berlusconi's Tele-5 in Spain (among other clients). Valle's work for Alef has put her on the front-line of a number of studies about Spanish consumers for manufacturers like Johnson and Johnson and Unilever. Valle and Perla work as extractors of local information to help multinational firms ensure that the ways Spanish shoppers value goods and services does not run counter to exchange values in global sales. This is part of a bureaucratic rationality of global firms who must compete for dominance over diverse taste cultures around the world. Knowledge of local value assessments and how they differ inside and outside national territories is a geo-strategic asset, making the occupation of personal data collection, and those who work in it, indispensable in a globalized market-economy.

Interviewers never admit to being proxies for a global client while they are on their rounds. In fact, they are instructed against discussing clients with the interview subject, although a researched brand can be mentioned if the survey theme is about brand recognition. The 'foreignness' of a client is a distasteful feature of a brand, and mentioning a client is like having one there, pushing the product. Most brands are already known locally as local products – the sense 'it is from here' – and interviewers know that staying local makes their job easier, especially after they cross the threshold into an interview subject's life. Being 'from here' also helps the interviewer hide the main contradiction activating market research: global merchants and local values come into collision as part of the domination effect of competition for global markets. Interviewers avert collisions of values as best they can, using empathy to humanize personal data extraction (softening the conflict for them and the interview subject). Valle Rodriguez speaks of this contradiction as her embarrassment for the interview subject: 'I really feel sorry for the people who are trying to answer the questions when the theme doesn't interest them at all', she said. 'Really, they only do it as a favour to me, so sometimes you find yourself forced to ask a question like "how often do you comb your hair?" and the person your quota instructs you to interview happens to be going bald' (Interview, 27 January 1995).

Local blunders in the global market

As Valle's comment suggests with cruel irony, global merchants face a popular competition over how a commodity's value gets interpreted in local cultures. Hence, they are understandably interested in market research's promise of improving the commercial message by eliminating local blunders. Since the early 1970s, product sales and distribution in marketing campaigns world-wide have been trying with greater intensity to get the transnational message into local idioms. Much has been written about the re-appropriations of top-down culture from a cultural studies perspective, from work inspired by Frantz Fanon, to recent studies on 'Third World' audiences re-interpreting meanings of metropolitan television programmes. Along with cultural studies professors, marketers share an interest in the popular rejection and playful re-interpretations of the transnational message.

Research on blunders concerns the overall effectiveness of standard advertising campaigns, motivating innovations like localization and direct marketing techniques. Standardization still dominates product design and marketing in most sectors, especially in producer goods manufactures and high-technology products (marketers tellingly call the latter 'non-cultural goods'). Standardization reduces costs of 'non-price' competition through lower overall advertising expenditures, uniform packaging, simplified distribution, minimal management and bureaucracy (Shamoon, 1985: 52). While standardized campaigns generally reduce costs for the transnational merchant, there are no guarantees that the people conceptualized as mass markets, with homogeneous tastes and purchasing habits, will think and shop alike around the globe (Levitt, 1983a, 1983b).

Localization strategies of marketers turn to ideas of cultural-demographic difference rather than homogeneity in order to reduce risks of misfired mass marketing strategies. This shift began in response to problems of cultural translation and ignorance of local tradition that caused many advertisements to fail. For instance, consumers in Thailand rejected a standardized campaign for Listerine mouthwash – developed in the United States – because it portrayed heterosexual affection in advertisements. On the advice of the South Asian manager of the company, the advertisements were replaced with a more acceptable image of two young Thai women in conversation (Ricks, Fu and Arpan, 1974). To overcome these self-described blunders, marketers have improved on-site field research methods in the last decade. Some methods employed to eradicate blunders include work study programmes sponsored by US Business Schools. Management and marketing departments send groups of students around the globe to function as small armies of field researchers, collecting data on cultural distinctions and consulting about marketing campaigns (Gabor, 1991: 66). 'Copy testing' of an advertising campaign in a Ghanaian village revealed that the advertising images mistakenly showed hairstyles unfamiliar to the women of the village. As a result, the villagers identified the product with the Nigerian expatriate community (Farley, 1986: 17–20). In Spain, a country only partially outside the core of the European image market, a Japanese-made off-road vehicle was renamed because the standard brand name being used throughout the rest of Europe would have translated roughly as 'The Masterbator' (Alonso, 1995).

At Alef–Millward Brown, methods include pre-tests, tracking and post-test evaluation of advertising spots, helping Millward Brown clients to avoid blunders and recognize major differences between European countries. One test charts a curve of interest in real time while viewers watch a TV advertisement. Multi-country results for a household cleaner showed the Italian curve and Spanish curve are more alike than Britain's curve. 'It's funny, but it's true that there are differences', says Milagros Benito. 'We can't really know why this happens, just that it does. Of course, it does make sense', she concluded, 'after all the English sense of humour is completely different from the Spanish.' In another study of a TV advertising spot, Alef showed that viewers' interest nose-dived just as the brand name appeared on the screen. Milagros Benito laughed as she described the finding: 'It was as if people were saying, "get that thing out of here, I was watching and I want to see what happens next".' Findings like this provoke enmity between market research firms and the people who create the advertising spots. 'I understand that for the ad agency the creative product is like their child', said Benito, 'but in this case something went wrong and the ad had to be changed' (Interview, 25 January 1995). Benito's remarks reflect a kind of *schadenfreude* typical among market researchers: they often enjoy finding failure in multi-million dollar merchandising campaigns (a feeling shared by many cultural studies professors); though, of course, marketers do not usually convey this sentiment in reports to their clients.

When market research runs into these kinds of blunders, it reveals its similarity to social science. To paraphrase Anthony Giddens, people are always 'one jump ahead' of institutions that research them, a problem that forces marketers to contend with what Giddens calls, in the context of sociological research, a 'double hermeneutic' (Giddens, 1989: 289). When marketers invent their version of a Generation X, for example, there is a good chance that people will embrace the label and associated products in unpredictable ways – in terms that betray the commercialized name of Generation X. In order to give the consumers what they want, market researchers must think of ways to account for this unruly engagement with labels and products. It is a process in which people and labels, or people and commodities, conspire in an uneasy partnership, that can quickly foul the merchant's plan.

In short, the blunders, and the reflexive process that overcoming them engenders, have the added effect of constantly renewing the demand for market research. The accompanying interface between researcher and research subject supports one claim consumers have to being active subjects in commercial culture. As Nick Browne argues, consumers can only indirectly participate in commercial culture through the figure of what is wanted of them (Browne, 1984: 178). That figure is composed out of the data market researchers generate from the stories people tell them. It is a composite figure to which the interview subjects contribute twice: in the initial, personal exchange with the information extractor, and then in their identification with the figure during the (always local) sales pitch. That composite figure adorns the product and invites us to recognize our desire in the commodity. The cycle does not end here, however, as savvy local publics muddy this institutional vision of commodities, and new market research is produced to clean up the mess. This 'problem of knowing', as Todd Gitlin called it, creates a permanent crisis in the cultural industries where certainty about the degree and kind of public desire for commercial goods and services cannot be guaranteed (Gitlin, 1983).

Phases of resistance

The question of social antagonisms to the practice of market research is a pressing one for privacy advocates. While information extraction has become a transnational affair, efforts to protect consumers are largely restrained within national legal frameworks. The most effective form of regulating flows of global market data still comes from street-level resistance to the field research. While public rejection of merchandising and advertising keeps the market researcher in business, perhaps the greatest public resistance faced by market researchers does not concern messages at all, but the outright refusal to be interviewed.

'Non-response' is part of the daily trial of the interviewer's skills as confessor, and comprises the central maths problem for the statistical technicians. People do not have time, they are not home, they cross streets to avoid surveyors with clip boards, they are annoyed by the interruption at their door, they do not know the performative rules of being interviewed, they have a visceral hatred for soliciting, they are the wrong person for the quota, or they fear for the sanctity of their privacy. Surveys on privacy fear in the United States, for instance, show the magnitude of this resistance when they conclude that 'nearly four in five Americans (79%) express general concern about threats to personal privacy' (Schwartz and Edmondson, 1991: 10). We can speculate that, in fact, there was more intense rejection than demonstrated by this and other surveys, since obviously the sample can only count those people who actually agree to answer questionnaires. Moreover, this sentiment is expressed in the country with the longest tradition of consumer surveys and the most sophisticated market research techniques, raising a number of questions about the meaning of resistance to marketing.

Comparisons of the United States to newer sites of market research, like Spain or the former East Berlin, suggest that resistance to survey techniques develops in three general phases. For people confronted with the novelty of market research, unspecific fear is very high and so is unspecific resistance.

People are on the defensive for a mix of reasons, including the fear of state authority, the lack of confidence to make judgements and distrust of strangers. This encourages more educational content in the interview process, marked by a number of key disavowals (e.g. the information is not personalized, it is not used for selling and it cannot be used to punish you). This produces increased, though half-hearted, response rates. Finally, a regular population of interview subjects is settled, both mathematically and geographically (accompanied by use of the quota system, national panels and itinerant focus groups). In sum, interviewers must establish a social presence, and their methods must be taken for granted as a feature of a modern capitalist democracy. As the interview process becomes a more common one, the content of resistance, when it arises, changes. The once unspecific resistance to survey techniques turns into explicit opposition to the economic function of market research: the 'non-respondent' becomes a conscious agent who knows what the interview will be used for. In the event of unobtrusive data extraction, of course, the marketing function can remain beyond question. After all, if it is not bothersome, why be bothered to resist it?

Twenty years ago there were no regular polls or surveys carried out in Spain; and up until the early 1980s, only scattered and very unreliable studies were conducted. 'People were not used to being asked what they thought', says Perla Haimovich, 'but after the transition to democracy [1975] people began slowly to realize that nothing would happen to them if they spoke up' (Interview, 19 February 1995). Similarly, in the former East Berlin, people were reluctant to answer marketing questions – partly because no one knew what a market researcher was, and partly because it recalled the activities of the secret police in the former GDR.

According to Edith Spielhagen, media researcher at Ostdeutscher Rundfunk Brandenburg, marketers assumed the two Germanys were alike, leading to difficult encounters in the field research and to failed campaigns directed at eastern shoppers (Interview, 16 February 1995). In both the former East Germany and in Spain, two very different cultures, responses to the arrival of marketing research were very similar during their respective transitions to democracy and the opening of markets: general distrust, a rash of blunders, followed by a more stable system of interviewing accompanied by greater public awareness of what a market researcher does.

Because the public image of the market researcher is important, each interviewer is, as it were, their own public relations campaign. According to Alef's Manuel Almeijeiras, 'there's no doubt that when the interviewer arrives at the door, being a stranger, bad things can happen'. There is always the rumour or published report of a robbery committed by someone impersonating a survey-taker; or conversely, news that an interviewer was assaulted while on their rounds. If a negative event is widely publicized, 'then people don't want to open their doors'. For this reason, it is very clear to Manuel Almeijeiras that success hinges on 'the charisma of the interviewer. The most professional interviewer uses the truth; the one who fails the most is the one who says deceptive things like "the interview only takes a minute, don't worry"' (Interview, 26 January 1995).

Class attitudes towards surveys

As the idea that interviewers perform a necessary function spreads through a society, there is still no guarantee that potential interview subjects will share the kind of social competence that sees marketing as an ordinary part of everyday life. Enrique Rodriguez, an interviewer for Alef, put it this way: 'A lot depends on the neighbourhood where you do the survey, where differences of class are important. Some people tend to know what a survey is and others don't have a clue, which makes your job difficult' (Interview, 27 January 1995). Teresa Ortega, who also works at Alef, explained in more detail some of the complexities of resistance met by the interviewer: 'It's easier to work in the popular neighbourhoods, with working-class people, because they're more open.' She added that while they are open to talking, 'these same people are the most distrustful of the actual interview – you have to explain more, how nothing will happen, and that it's not a bad thing. With data collection you have to explain that you aren't going to try to sell them something.' Though market research is, in fact, an important part of the sales effort, Teresa uses the immediate absence of selling in the interview process to elicit trust. 'In contrast', Teresa said, 'middle-class people, especially the ones who aspire to be upper-class types', think they understand how a survey works and how it is used for selling things. 'They're the worst', she concludes, because 'they're less trusting and more full of themselves when they do answer' (Interview, 27 January 1995).

City and country also present distinct work zones for data collectors. Interviewers at both Alef and ECO, the two largest market research firms in Spain, agreed that working the small villages was usually a pleasure – even though they were forced to spend hours instructing the interview subjects on the nature of the survey (often this took place over a generous meal). This crucial distinction about openness to the interviewer is confirmed by studies from two US firms, Backer Spielvogel Bates and Mediamark Research Inc., which found that responsiveness to surveys increases as median home values decrease. Blue-collar workers and farmers from small towns pay the most attention to the interviewers, while middle-class urban dwellers pay the least (Kraft, 1991: 14). The interviewers in Spain concur: for them 'middle-middle to upper-middle class' urbanites as a group were not only the least agreeable bunch – grumpy and know-it-all – they also shunned the door-to-door surveys with more regularity than workers and farmers.

In short, socializing people to the idea of data collection interviews is a task distinct from that of getting people to open up to the interviewer. Knowing this is one of the skills interviewers take to the streets with them. As Enrique says, 'with some people you can tell almost immediately when they open the door that they will answer the questionnaire; then there are those others whose faces tell you that you're going to have a hard day ahead of you' (Interview, 27 January 1995).

A popular aesthetic

In the survey stage of market research, all kinds of people are asked to reflect and make a judgement about the goods and services under review. This is a moment of cognitive reflection about taste. For the most part, people are asked opinions that are tabulated on surveys; they are asked to judge how they feel and to say what they think in such a way that the data can be fitted to a statistical model. Because most of us cannot express judgements without telling stories, and most stories are told with emotion, interviewers find themselves constantly translating narratives and eliminating emotion to fit boxed answers on surveys. Though qualitative testing for affective responses to a product or service is an important, and often decisive, factor in marketing research, it is not the dominant technique. What is sought by the market researcher is a cognitive interpretation, one that in the survey, or focus group analysis, demonstrates what interview subjects would say if they were able to stand back and assess their thoughts and feelings in a detached way.

This situation is reversed in the selling stage, when people are not only expected to relate to commodities on an emotional level without thinking, but are also diverted as much as possible from making any detached interpretation about the value of the product. This aspect of marketing is best captured by advertising slogans like 'We sell the sizzle, not the steak'. After all, the engineers of desire would have nothing to do if they thought of us as rational choosers – for them, even a vegetarian enjoys the sizzle (see Strasser, 1989: 158). In the selling stage of the life of a commodity or service, we are returned to a pre-cognitive state; we are invited by the commodity to desire it or assign it emotional energy (Lash and Urry, 1994: 5). What a commodity does for us is measured by its fit into the sum of all of the goods and services composing our lives. That is, we value a commodity for how it enhances the composition of a 'lifestyle'. In this popular aesthetic, what a commodity says about us is more important than what it says about itself. Herein lies the attraction: we desire the expressive components, not the rational use (Lash and Urry, 1994: 131–3). The process that puts those expressive components into a commodity is, paradoxically, bureaucratic and rational. By hiring the services of market researchers, merchants plan on putting information about 'lifestyles' and tastes into the very design of goods and services.

A labelling aesthetic

The decline of the nation state and the extension of global 'information and communication structures', say Lash and Urry, are processes that have reterritorialized our sense of common cause (Lash and Urry, 1994: 6). The nation state and institutions supporting it can no longer be understood as autonomous, self-determining, and self-regulating social structures. As a consequence, collective identity – a sense of common cause – is freed from the traditional social bases of citizenship: organized class affiliations, the nuclear family, the Cold War, and so on. Instead, networks of information and communication, where market research holds a strategic position, unite the world into lifestyle categories of clusters, quotas, targets and audiences. Market research invents identities according to the needs of the client firm, harnessing sales efforts to the divergence of individual 'psychical configurations' (Elias, 1991: 60). Marketers and their clients live by this labelling aesthetic, which they have composed in bit-streams of interview data and organized into metaphorical figures who stand in for citizens (Schiller, 1982).

A labelling aesthetic invents identities through a process Lash and Urry call appropriately 'niche-marketed individuation' (Lash and Urry, 1994: 142–3). When the interviewer asks for an individual assessment of a commodity or service, they are evoking a person's presence in the world, and this presence is validated throughout the interview with remarks like 'that's good', 'your answer is very important', 'this will help a lot.' The notion that one is giving an individual response is a curious one – as Voloshinov says: 'Every sign, even the sign of individuality, is social' (Voloshinov, 1986: 34). Nevertheless, the interview appeals to a typical longing, as Norbert Elias points out: one 'thinks, feels and to an extent wishes that the individuality of a person, the distinctive structure of his or her self-regulation in relation to other people and things, exists in the same independent way, isolated from all relations, as one feels one's own body to exist in space' (Elias, 1991: 58).

Inventing identity clusters

Individuated value assessments diminish in stages under the pressure of the labelling aesthetic, turned into expressive base material, as it were, for the composition of lifestyles. Each question on the survey forces the raw material into a static frame by following the simple guideline of 'getting to the point', which is to make diversity fit into the framework of the client's values and needs. The labelling aesthetic segments interview subjects into invented identities through figures organized in clusters, quotas, targets and audiences. Claritas Corporation, the most successful manufacturer of identities in the market research business, represents every American with at least one of forty identity clusters. They see them as part of a Bohemian Mix or the Urban Renewal, living in Dixie Style Tenements or Norma Rae-ville. They are part of the Pools and Patio crowd or maybe one of the Hard Scrabble. If their family lives in a row house or a five-unit building in an ethnically diverse working-class neighbourhood, they are stamped as Bunker's Neighbours, Old Melting Pot, or Heavy Industry. Americans' features are commensurable with those of their neighbours, and their label stands in for them in an aesthetic circulating among advertisers, market researchers, ratings firms, manufacturers and other cultural industries (Larson, 1994).

Techniques of identity invention have historically followed two paths: on the one hand, there are objects whose natural affinities persist despite the label we use to conceptualize them, things like planets, stars, trees, etc.; on the other hand, there are objects which we make up at the same time that we invent a name for them, things like gloves and the name 'glove', both invented at more or less the same time (Hacking, 1986: 228–9, 1990: 1–10, 1991a, 1991b, 1995). Factory workers are in the first group, since they only came to 'fit their categories' after factory inspectors sorted out functions in the nineteenth century, whereas in the suicidal person the label and the object were invented simultaneously (Hacking, 1991b, 1995). As Ian Hacking argues, adjectives like suicidal are not mere descriptions of 'a kind of person who came increasingly to be recognized by bureaucrats or by students of human nature', but rather was a person who 'came into being at the same time as the kind itself was being invented' (Hacking, 1986: 228).

Like suicidal persons, in the consumer we have also invented a group and label that came into being at the same time (Ewen, 1976). These techniques of the labelling aesthetic are derived from a complex of surveillance techniques that Oscar Gandy calls 'the panoptic sort' (Gandy, 1993). In the case of market research, the panoptic sort performs a kind of triage that segments and stratifies consumers according to their usefulness for merchandisers (Gandy, 1993: 15).

In the words of a senior vice-president at Claritas: 'By nature segmentation is discrimination; I'm discriminating against people I don't think are willing to buy my product' (Quoted in Larson, 1994: 56). The labelling aesthetic reproduces this salesperson's perspective in landscapes where Gold Coasts and Blue Blood Estates eclipse the zones of Public Assistance and Tobacco Roads (Larson, 1994: 47; see also Gandy, 1995).

If these marketing labels were generalized to public discourses, they would end up caught between two vectors of competing uses. One issues 'from above, from a community of experts who create a "reality" that some people make their own'. The other comes from 'the autonomous behavior of the person so labeled, which presses from below, creating a reality every expert must face' (Hacking, 1986: 234). From above, the cultural industries do invite people to live under certain of their labels and identify with them, for example, the consumers in the Generation X and the audiences for US cable channels like Discovery, Arts & Entertainment, Lifetime, Nickelodeon, and so on. As Mary Douglas cautions: 'The responsiveness to new labels suggests extraordinary readiness to fall into new slots and to let selfhood be redefined' (Douglas, 1986: 100). Yet from below, people resist, misrecognize themselves in the objects, or reinterpret the labels or commodities on their own terms. Marketers and other experts react by confronting resistance, absorbing the differences and adjusting labels and commercial messages.

The imperious measures

Recent advances in computerized telecommunications networks have made tracking actions, preferences, assets and habits of people easier and less obtrusive than earlier techniques. As a consequence, new problems concerning cultural domination have surfaced. The introduction of microchip computer technology forged a common link of management and control techniques across economic sectors. The same technology now supports workplace surveillance, credit checks, cash machines and transborder data flows of market surveys. Businesses everywhere are acting on the assumption that the integration of once fragmented operations into telematics networks will lead to greater efficiencies of speed, control and design (Beniger, 1986). As these techniques become socialized through cultural and consumer goods industries, the 'panoptic schema' that Foucault imagined as 'polyvalent in its applications' becomes a practical reality; its globalizing potential to survey all human bodies is realized most clearly by transnational market research (Foucault, 1979: 205). The multi-country data processing described in this chapter could not function with speed and across space without the telematics network in place.

Any reorganization of space and time is also a reorganization of the way power is expressed. The growing collections of survey data, increased file storage capacity, faster processing technology and sophisticated software – all have aided the surge of information flows from local contexts to global markets. A new geography helps coordinate these instantaneous flows of local differences across space. Market research sets parameters around spatial heterogeneity by extracting and mapping diversity in space, but they do not eliminate difference. Instead, they reproduce a rational system of control in a new cartography of difference and identity.

Market research recharts the world's boundaries, replacing the logic of proximity with the logic of demographic identity. There are six market zones in Spain, for example, created by A.C. Nielsen but used by all marketers – only a few correspond to official political regions. These zones break down further until the streets of neighbourhoods, like Madrid's poor Vallecas and chic Chamberi, are uprooted and targeted individually by Alef, ECO and Nielsen. A similar re-mapping uproots districts like 'easty' Weissensee and 'westy' Tiergarten out of Berlin or toney Islington and poor Southall out of London. Neighbourhoods, postal zones and census blocks splinter into a demographic mosaic, reorganized by a logic that joins places together as spaces of exchange. As the Saatchis used to say, 'there are more social differences between mid-town Manhattan and the Bronx than between Manhattan and the 7th arrondissement of Paris' (Robins, 1989: 21).

A new geo-politics has emerged with the extension of transnational market research. Impositions, invasions and imperialisms are less perceptible when global powers present themselves as local phenomena. In the experience of the interviewers for the market research firms, the job was all-consuming; for the interview subjects, what mattered most was what confronted them at their doorstep. Just as a professor's job of educating well-heeled undergraduates often appears to extend no further than the classroom, the market researchers work in conditions that disencumber them of the knowledge of their place in the political economy. What is nearest to interviewers is the fact that they do not sell, though theirs is a selling business; they do not punish, though the information is used to segment and stratify; they do not harm privacy, though the heightened presence of market researchers makes surveillance something we come to live with. The political economy of the business is not as much an experiential reality as the daily routine of the work. We do our job without knowing what job is being done on us.

Cultural imperialism

Cultural imperialism today appears as merely 'the pressures and limits of simple experience and common sense', which is how Raymond Williams defined living in hegemony two decades ago (Williams, 1977: 110). The most vexing problem for those who wrote about cultural-informational imperialism was to find the points of contact between the global culture industries and people. This problem was usually conceptualized as a matter of injection of ideology and mind management, which has always been a difficult process to document or, for that matter, to debunk. The critical work on global cultural industries since the 1960s used to see cultural imperialism for the most part as a reflection of interstate/international relations. The practice of market research shows the extent to which transnationalism has, as it were, deterritorialized national economies and markets around the world; international relations, in turn, are increasingly internalized into the global operations of transnational businesses.

If we think of informational imperialism as the extraction of popular interpretations of value rather than as injections of dominant values, we come to a difficult conclusion. The techniques of imperious measurement spread out across the globe in an innocuous network that is built often upon the kindness of strangers. The process can take place in an interview when two hard-working women discuss how to make the tasks of living easier in a world that denies respect for domestic labour. It may be activated by discount and check-cashing cards that your local supermarket has generously provided for your 'convenience'; the information stored in a Citibank computer. It may be embodied by a sympathetic researcher who immerses herself in the culture of chocoholics at the behest of Nestlé (in another actual case) to discover that, like wine lovers, the chocolate lovers shelve the expensive stuff in the cellar and leave the Snickers lying around for unexpected guests. The immediate encounters between proxies of the popular and commercial cultures possess no apparent violence or violation that can be construed as imperialistic. Rather, they present a Foucauldian paradox (on one hand we have freedom of choice, on the other hand we lose our personal independence): they offer life enhancements at the same time as they diminish our personal autonomy to decide for ourselves the fate of personal information.

Communications scholars are familiar with the bureaucratic rationalizations for this structural inequality in informational imperialism: product improvements do return to the consumer for their contribution of intimate details; free flows of information do in fact help smooth out functions in international industry, especially in sectors that still make things, but also in finance; research of this kind does add greater efficiency to decision-making units in large organizations, and so on. At the same time, it is surveillance, it proscribes individual freedom; it invades privacy and intrudes into the intimate spheres of everyday life. The focus here is on consumer behaviour, but surveillance relations of this kind have been widespread within modern bureaucratic societies for some time. They include organizational monitoring, credit checks, workplace snooping, state intrusions and the like (Dandecker, 1990; Webster and Robins, 1986). The counter-argument developed above suggests that audiences are rather more unpredictable when confronted with cultural goods and services than the merchants of these things would like. The discursive frame of the commodity form minimizes the conditions of possibility for interpretive outcomes, but it does not do away with competition over the interpretation of value. There are blunders, misfired campaigns and all sorts of non-response. The goal of market research, however, is to know more about popular taste and responses – no matter what they are – and to classify and operationalize that knowledge in order to complete the circuit of 'buy-and-sell' as efficiently as possible. Terry Curtis argues that 'no current technology would allow for cost-effective collection, storage, and processing of information about every individual' (Curtis, 1988: 103). But as we have seen, it is possible to construct a bestiary of composite creatures created by methods like psychographics, geo-demographics, and matching and modelling techniques. We may or may not live under these labels, but what matters here is that key divisions within the bureaucracies of media and marketing firms act as if we did live this way. The institutional belief in these imagined communities of consumers determines a great deal of what we see and hear in public culture. Television producers will tell you they think ratings are bogus, but find one who is not under the spell of daily tabulations.

Interviewers, survey technicians and other market researchers are stationed in between the popular and the dominant interpretations of value. Market research is a social practice that thrives on the fact that a commodity has no inherent or predictable use-value, no definition, and no intrinsic meaning. Market research collects stories about how we value things, mostly in their commodity form, and organizes these stories within a frame of reference maintained by million-dollar clients. In the fight over social definitions of value, as Marx argued, the big money is always on exchange-value. Even market research knows exchange is merely capital's preferred interpretation of value; everyday they go out and find further evidence that the value of things is actually rich with interpretive variation and struggle. This discovery entails imperious measures to extract and transform diverse value assessments into a commodity form as a narrow feature inviting exchange. From turns of solidarity, empathy, kindness and regard for local difference to lifestyle compositions and life under labels, the process begins and ends with a disavowal of the stranger facing us.

Note

This chapter is a revised version of an article which appeared in *Media, Culture and Society* 18 (1) 1996: 105–26.

Further questions

1 Why do blunders in marketing and advertising happen?
2 Why is market research so important for the operation of international communication industries?
3 How would you describe the job and the function of a market researcher, and what are the typical difficulties of the practice?
4 'The extraction of popular interpretations of value rather than the injection of dominant values.' What do you understand by this phrase? Give examples of the process of 'extraction'.

Bibliography

Abler, R. (1991) 'Hardware, software, and brainware: mapping and understanding telecommunications technologies', in S. Brunn and T. Leinbach (eds), *Collapsing Space & Time. Geographic Aspects of Communication and Information*. London: HarperCollins Academic.

Adams, W.C. (1986) 'Whose lives count? TV coverage of natural disasters', *Journal of Communication*, 36 (2) (Spring): 113–22.

Adonis, A. and Hill, A. (1993) 'Lifting the lid on liberalisation', *Financial Times*, 10 May 1993: 15.

Ajami, Fuad, et al. (1993) 'Commentaries on the clash of civilizations', *Foreign Affairs*, September/October:

Albrow, M. and King, E. (1990) *Globalization, Knowledge and Society*. London: Sage.

Alleyne, D.M. (1995) *International Power and International Communication*. Oxford: St Antony's College/Macmillan.

Alonso, V.M. (1995) Head of Research of Eco.

Anderson, B. (1983) *Imagined Community: Reflection on the Origin and Spread of Nationalism*. London: Verso.

Anon. (1994) 'America's Information Highway', *The Economist*, 25 December 1993–7 January 1994: 35–8.

Appadurai, A. (1990) 'Disjuncture and difference in the global cultural economy', in M. Featherstone (ed.), *Global Culture*. London: Sage. pp. 295–310.

Appadurai, A. (1993) 'Patriotism and its future', *Public Culture*, 5: 411–29.

Atkin, C. (1996) 'Designing effective media campaigns', Unit 47, MA in Mass Communications, Centre For Mass Communication Research, University of Leicester, Leicester.

Attali, J. (1991) *Millennium: Winners and Losers in the Coming World Order*. New York: Times Books.

Bagdikian, B. (1989) 'The lords of the global village', *The Nation* (special issue), 12 June.

Bannister, N. (1993) 'Free phone call offer stirs up competitors', *The Guardian*, 8 September: 11.

Barnet, R.J. and Muller, R.E. (1974) *Global Reach: The Power and the Multinational Corporations*. New York: Simon and Schuster.

Bell, D. (1960) *The End of Ideology: On the Exhaustion of Political Ideas in the Fifties*. Glencoe, Ill.: The Free Press.

Bell, D. (1973) *The Coming of the Post-Industrial Society: A Venture in Social Forecasting*. New York: Basic Books.

Beniger, J.R. (1986) *The Control Revolution: Technological and Economic Origins of the Information Society*. Cambridge, MA: Harvard University Press.

Berger, John (1995a) *Aids to the Wedding*. London: Bloomsbury.

Berger, John (1995b) 'The Observer essay', *The Observer Review*, 17 December: 4.

Best, S. and Kellner, D. (1991) *Postmodern Theory, Critical Interrogations*. New York: The Guilford Press.

Boafo, S.T. Kwame (1991) 'Communication technology and dependent development in sub-Saharan Africa', in G. Sussman and J.A. Lent (eds), *Transnational Communications*. London: Sage. pp. 103–25.

Boulding, E. (1988) *Building a Global Civic Culture: Education for an Interdependent World*. New York: Teachers' College Press.

Boyd-Barrett, O. (1980) *The International News Agencies*. London: Constable.

Boyd-Barrett, O. (1982) 'Cultural dependency and the mass media', in M. Gurevitch et al. (eds), *Culture, Society and the Media*. London: Methuen. pp. 174–95.

Brandt, W. (1980) *North–South: A Programme for Survival*. London: Pan Books.

Brandt, W. (1985) *Common Crisis: North–South Cooperation for World Recovery*. Cambridge, Mass.: The MIT Press.

British Telecom (1993) Private communication with author.

Bronowski, J. (1973) *The Ascent of Man*. Boston, Mass.: Little, Brown & Co.

Brown, L. (1994) 'The seven deadly sins of the digital age', *Intermedia*, 22: 33.

Browne, N. (1984) 'The Political Economy of the Television (Super) Text', *Quarterly Review of Film Studies*, 9 (3): 174–82.

Brunn, S. and Leinbach, T. (eds) (1991) *Collapsing Space & Time. Geographic Aspects of Communication and Information*. London: HarperCollins Academic.

Business Week (1994) 14 November.

Calabrese, A. and Redea, W. (1994) 'Is there a US foreign policy in the telecommunications? Transatlantic trade policy as a case study', IAMCR, Seoul, Korea, July 1994.

Canclini, Garcia N. (1992) 'Cultural reconversion', in G. Yudice et al. (eds), *On Edge: The Crisis of Contemporary Latin American Culture*. Minneapolis: University of Minnesota Press. pp. 29–44.

Carnoy, M., Castells, M., Cohen, S., Cardoso, F. (eds) (1993) *The New Global Economy in the Information Age*. Pennsylvania: Pennsylvania State University.

Castoriadis, C. (1991) 'Reflections on "rationality" and "development"', in *Philosophy, Politics, Autonomy*. Oxford: Oxford University Press. pp. 176–218.

Centro de Investigaciones Sociológicas (n.d.) unpublished surveys 1379 and 1799, Madrid.

Chomsky, N. (1992) *Deterring Democracy*. New York: Vintage Books.

Chomsky, N. (1994) *World Orders, Old*. London: Pluto Press.

Collins, R. (1983) 'Broadband black death cuts queues', *Media, Culture and Society*, 5 (3/4) (July/October).

Commercial Satellite Report (1988) Washington, DC.

Communications Steering Group (CSG) Report (1988) *The Infrastructure for Tomorrow*. Department of Trade and Industry, London: HMSO.

CRTNET (Communication research and Theory Network) (1993) no. 900, 22 December.

CRTNET (Communication Research and Theory Network) (1994) no. 915, 12 January.

Curtis, T. (1988) 'The information society: a computer-generated caste system?', in Vincent Mosco and Janet Wasko (eds), *The Political Economy of Information*. Madison: University of Wisconsin Press.

Dahrendorf, R. (1990) *Reflections on the Revolution in Europe*. London: Chatto & Windus.

Dandecker, C. (1990) *Surveillance, Power and Modernity*. New York: St Martin's Press.

Dayan, D. and Katz, E. (1992) *Media Event: The Live Broadcasting of History*. Cambridge, Mass.: Harvard University Press.

Demac, A. (1986) *Tracing New Orbits: Cooperation and Competition in International Satellite Development*. New York: Columbia.

Dizard, W. (1985) *The Coming Information Age*. New York: Longman.

Docherty, T. (1993) *Post Modernism: A Reader*. New York: Columbia University Press.

Donnelly, J. (1993) *International Human Rights*. Boulder, Col.: Westview Press.

Donovan, L. (1993) 'Wired for trade in Singapore', *Financial Times*, 20 July: 9.

Dorfman, A. and Mattelart, A. (1975) *How To Read Donald Duck: Imperialist Ideology in the Disney Comic*. New York: International General Editions.

Dowler, R. (1992) 'Rebuilding telecoms in Eastern Europe', *Intermedia*, 20 (4/5): 43–5.

Downing, John, Mohammadi, Ali and Sreberny-Mohammadi, Annabelle (eds) (1995) *Questioning the Media: A Critical Introduction*. London: Sage.

Drucker, Peter F. (1957) *Landmark of Tomorrow*. New York: Harper & Row.

During, Simon (1987) 'Postmodernism or post-colonialism today', *Textual Practice*, 1.

During, Simon (1995) 'The cultural studies tradition of media research', Unit 5, MA in Mass Communications, Centre for Mass Communication Research, University of Leicester, Leicester.

Edgerton, R.B. (1992) *Sick Societies: Challenging the Myth of Primitive Harmony.* New York: Macmillan.

Eisenstein, E.L. (1979) *The Printing Press as an Agent of Change* (Vols 1–2). Cambridge: Cambridge University Press.

Elias, N. (1991) *The Society of Individuals.* Oxford: Basil Blackwell.

Erlichman, J. (1993) 'Consumers pay for profits', *The Guardian*, 13 September: 5.

Ewen, Stuart (1976) *Captain of Consciousness.* New York: McGraw-Hill.

Ewen, S. and Ewen, E. (1982) *Channels of Desire: Mass Images and the Shaping of American Consciousness.* New York: McGraw-Hill.

Farley, J.V. (1986) 'Are there truly international products and prime prospects for them?', *Journal of Advertising Research*, 26: 17–20.

Featherstone, M. (ed.) (1990) *Global Culture.* London: Sage.

Ferguson, M. (1992) 'The mythology about globalization', *European Journal of Communication.* 7: 69–93.

Fisher, Heinz Dietrich and Merril, C. John (eds) (1976) *International and Intercultural Communication.* New York: Hastings House.

Fiske, John (1987) *Television Culture.* London: Methuen.

Flourney, D. (1992) CNN World Report. London: John Libbey & Co.

Fortner, S. Robert (1993) *International Communication.* Belmont, Cal.: Wadsworth.

Foucault, M. (1979) *Discipline and Punish: The Birth of the Prison.* Trans. Alan Sheridan. New York: Vintage Books.

Foucault, M. (1980) *Power/Knowledge: Selected Interviews and Other Writings, 1972–1977.* Brighton: Harvester.

Frank, A.G. (1969) *Latin America: Underdevelopment or Revolution.* New York: Monthly Review Press.

Frankfort, H., et al. (1963) *Before Philosophy: The Intellectual Adventure of Ancient Man.* Baltimore, MD: Penguin Books.

Frederick, H.H. (1993) *Global Communication and International Relations.* Belmont, Ca.: Wadsworth.

Freire, P. (1972) *Pedagogy of the Oppressed.* Harmondsworth: Penguin.

Friedman, J. (1994) *Cultural Identity and Global Process.* London: Sage.

Fukuyama, F. (1989) 'The end of history?', *The National Interest*, 16 (Summer): 3–18.

Fukuyama, F. (1992) *The End of History and the Last Man.* New York: The Free Press.

Gabor, A. (1991) 'Training for global markets', *US News & World Report*, 29 April.

Gaddy, G.D. and Tanjong, E. (1986) 'Earthquake coverage by the western media', *Journal of Communication*, 36 (2) (Spring): 105–12.

Galbraith, J.K. (1989) 'Assault: an overview', *The Guardian*, 16 December: 15–17.

Galbraith, J.K. (1990) 'The price of world peace', *The Guardian*, 8 September: 23.

Galtung, Johan and Vincent, Richard (1992) *Global Glasnost: Toward a New Information and Communication Order.* Cresskill, NJ: Hampton Press.

Gandy, O. (1993) *The Panoptic Sort: A Political Economy of Personal Information.* Boulder, CO: Westview Press.

Gandy, O. (1995) 'It's discrimination, stupid!', in J. Brook and I. Boal (eds), *Resisting the Virtual Life: The Culture and Politics of Information.* San Francisco: City Lights Books.

Gardner, Katy and Lewis, David (1996) *Anthropology, Development and the Post-Modern Challenge.* London: Pluto Press.

Garnham, N. (1991) *Telecommunications in the UK.* Fabian Society Discussion Paper No. 1. London: The Fabian Society.

Garnham, N. (1992) 'The media and the public sphere', in C. Calhoun (ed.), *Habermas and the Public Sphere.* Cambridge, Mass.: The MIT Press. pp. 359–76.

Geraghty, C. (1991) *Women and Soap Opera.* Cambridge: Polity Press.

George, S. (1989) *A Fate Worse than Debt.* London: Penguin.

Gerbner, G. (1992) 'Testimony for the House Judiciary Committee's Subcommittee on Crime and Criminal Justice: oversight field hearing on violence on television', 15 December, New York.

Giddens, A. (1989) 'A reply to my critics', in D. Held and J. Thompson (eds), *Social Theory of Modern Societies: Anthony Giddens and His Critics*. Cambridge: Cambridge University Press.

Giddens, A. (1990) *The Consequences of Modernity*. Cambridge: Polity Press.

Giddens, A. (1991) *Modernity and Self-identity: Self and Society in the Late Modern Age*. Cambridge: Polity Press.

Giddens, A. (1994) *Beyond Left and Right*. Cambridge: Polity Press.

Gilroy, P. (1993) *The Black Atlantic*. London: Verso.

Gitlin, T. (1983) *Inside Prime Time*. New York: Pantheon.

Goethe, J.W. (1820/1958) 'True enough: To the Physicist'. Trans. Michael Hamburger, in S. Spender (ed.), *Great Writings of Goethe*. New York: Mentor Books/New American Library.

Golding, P. (1974) 'Media role in national development: a critique of a theoretical orthodoxy', *Journal of Communication*, 24 (3): 39–53.

Golding, P. and Elliott, P. (1979) *Making the News*. London: Longman.

Gordon, David (1988) 'The global corporation', in *Airport Magazine*, August, 13.

Guehenno, Jean-Marie (1995), *The End of The Nation State* (trans. V. Elliott). Minneapolis: University of Minnesota Press.

Habermas, J. (1984) *The Theory of Communicative Action, vol. 1: Reason and the Rationalization of Society*. Boston, Mass.: Beacon Press.

Habermas, J. (1987) *The Theory of Communicative Action, vol. 2: Lifeworld and System: A Critique of Functionalist Reason*. Boston, Mass.: Beacon Press.

Habermas, J. (1989) *The Transformation of the Public Sphere*. Cambridge, Mass.: The MIT Press.

Hacking, Ian (1986) 'Making up people', in T.C. Heller et al. (eds), *Reconstructing Individualism*. Stanford, Cal.: Stanford University Press.

Hacking, Ian (1990) *The Taming of Chance*. Cambridge: Cambridge University Press.

Hacking, I. (1991a) 'The making and molding of child abuse', *Critical Inquiry*, 17 (2): 253–88.

Hacking, I. (1991b) 'Two souls in one body', *Critical Inquiry*, 17 (Summer): 838–67.

Hacking, I. (1995) *Rewriting the Soul: Multiple Personality and the Sciences of Memory*. New Jersey: Princeton University Press.

Hall, S. (1991) 'The local and the global: globalization and ethnicities', in A.D. King (ed.), *Culture, Globalization and the World System*. London: Macmillan. pp. 19–30.

Hall, S. (1992) 'The question of cultural identity', in S. Hall, D. Held and T. McGrew (eds), *Modernity and Its Futures*. Cambridge: Polity Press.

Halloran, J.D. (1964) *The Effects of Mass Communication, with Special Reference to Television*. Leicester: Leicester University Press.

Halloran, J.D. (1981) 'The context of mass communication research', in E. McAnnany, T. Schnitmann and N.Z. Janus (eds), *Communication and Social Structure: Critical Studies in Mass Media Research*. New York: Praeger. pp. 21–57.

Halloran, J.D. (1983) 'A case for critical eclecticism in ferment in the field', *Journal of Communication*, 33 (3): 270–8.

Halloran, J.D. (1987) 'The international research experience', in N. Jayaweera and S. Amunugama (eds), *Rethinking Development Communication*. Singapore: AMIC. p. 135.

Halloran, J.D. (1990) *A Quarter of a Century of Prix Jeunesse Research*. Munich: Prix Jeunesse. pp. 117–26.

Halloran, J.D. (1991) 'Mass communication research: UK obstacles to progress', *Intermedia*, 19 (4&5): 22.

Halloran, J.D. (1993) 'What we urgently require is a globalization of moral responsibility', *Intermedia*, 21 (2): 4–7.

Halloran, J.D. (1994a) 'Development in communication and democracy: the contribution of research', in Edward A. Comor (ed.), *The Global Political Economy of Communication*. New York: St Martin's Press. pp. 165–85.

Halloran, J.D. (1994b) 'Making the news', in R. Winsbury and S. Fazal (eds), *Vision and Hindsight*. London: John Libbey. pp. 153–9.

Halloran, J.D. (1995) 'Media research as social science', Unit 2, MA in Mass

Communications, Centre for Mass Communication Research, University of Leicester, Leicester.

Hamelink, C.J. (1983) *Cultural Autonomy in Global Communications*. New York: Longman.

Hamelink, C.J. (1994a) *The Politics of World Communication*. London: Sage.

Hamelink, C.J. (1994b) *Trends in World Communication*. Penang, Malaysia: South bound, Third World Network.

Hannerz, U. (1991) 'Scenarios for peripheral cultures', in A.D. King (ed.), *Culture, Globalization and the World System*. London: Macmillan.

Harnett, J. (1992) 'Japan leads the way', *Financial Times International Telecommunications Survey*, 15 October: 7.

Harrison, L.E. (1992) *Who Prospers? How Cultural Values Shape Economic and Political Success*. New York: Basic Books.

Harrison, P. (1993) *Inside the Third World*. Harmondsworth: Penguin.

Harvey, D. (1989) *The Condition of Postmodernity*. Oxford: Basil Blackwell.

Hedebro, G. (1982) *Communication and Social Change in Developing Nations: A Critical View*. Ames, Ia: Iowa State University Press.

Heilbroner, R.L. (1962) *The Making of Economic Society*. Englewood Cliffs, NJ: Prentice Hall.

Held, D. (1991) 'Democracy and the global system', in D. Held (ed.), *Political Theory Today*. Cambridge: Polity Press. pp. 197–235.

Heller, T.C., et al. (eds) (1986) *Reconstructing Individualism*. Stanford, Cal.: Stanford University Press.

Hennion, A. and Meadel, C. (1993) 'In the laboratories of desire: advertising as an intermediary between products and consumers' (trans. Liz Libbrecht), *Reseaux: The French Journal of Communication*, 1 (2) (Autumn) 1993: pp. 169–92. (192)

Hepworth, Mark (1989) *Geography of the Information Economy*. London: Belhaven Press.

Hills, Jill (1986) *Deregulation Telecoms, Competition and Control in the United States, Japan and Britain*. London: Frances Pinter.

Hills, Jill (1994) 'Public choice theory and the World Bank: privatization as ideology', Political Economy Section, IAMCR, Seoul, Korea, July 1994.

Hills, Jill, with Papathanassopoulos, Stylianos (1991) *The Democracy Gap*. New York: Greenwood Press.

Hills, J.S. (1986) 'Agencies and my new media buy systems', *New York Times* (International Section), 22 December.

Hobday, Michael (1990) *Telecommunication in Developing Countries: The Challenge from Brazil*. London: Routledge.

Hobson, J.A. (1902) *Imperialism: A Study*. London: Nisbet.

Hollander, P. (1981) *Political Pilgrims: Travels of Western Intellectuals to the Soviet Union, China and Cuba*. New York: Harper & Row.

Hoskins, C. and Mirus, R. (1988) 'Reason for the US dominance of the international trade in television programmes', *Media, Culture and Society*, 10 (4): 499–515.

Hudson, H. (1990) *Communication Satellites. Their Development and Impact*. London: Collier Macmillan.

Human Development Report (1992) New York: UNHDR.

Huntington, S.P. (1993a) 'The clash of civilizations?', *Foreign Affairs*, 73 (3) (Summer): 22–49.

Huntington, S.P. (1993b) 'The clash of civilizations: a response', *Foreign Affairs*, 73 (4): 2–14.

Ignatieff, M. (1993) *Blood and Belonging: Journeys into the New Nationalism*. London: Random House.

IMF (1988) *Privatization and Public Enterprises*, Occasional Paper, no. 56. Washington DC.

INTELSAT Annual Report (1988) Washington DC: INTELSAT

International Telecommunication Annual Report (1994)

International Telecommunications (1994). New Initiatives to Foster Telecommunications Development in the LDC's. Geneva: ITU.

Jameson, F. (1991) *Postmodernism or the Cultural Logic of Late Capitalism*. London: Verso.

Janus, N. (1984) 'Advertising and the creation of global markets: the role of the new communication technologies', in V. Mosco and J. Wasco (eds), *The Critical Communication Review Vol. 2: Changing Patterns of Communication Control*. Norwood, NJ: Ablex. pp. 57–70.

Johnson, P. (1988) *Intellectuals*. New York: Harper & Row.

Johnson, R. (1986) 'What is cultural studies anyway?', *Social Text*, 16 (Winter): 38–80.

Johnston, Carla Brooks (1995) *Winning the Global TV News Game*. Boston, Mass.: Focal Press.

Juergensmeyer, Mark (1993) *The New Cold War? Religious Nationalism Confronts the Secular State*. Berkeley, Cal.: University of California Press.

Jussawalla, M., et al. (1986) *Information Technology and Global Interdependence*. New York: Greenwood.

Kaku, M. (1994) *Hyperspace: A Scientific Odyssey Through Parallel Universes, Time Warps, and the Tenth Dimension*. New York: Oxford University Press.

Kaplan, R.D. (1994) 'The coming anarchy: how scarcity, crime, overpopulation, tribalism, and disease are rapidly destroying the social fabric of our planet', *Atlantic Monthly*, 273 (2) (February): 44–76.

Keegan, Victor (1996) 'Highway robbery by the super-rich', *The Guardian*, 22 July: 2–3.

Keeley, L. (1995) *War Before Civilization: The Myth of the Peaceful Savage*. New York: Oxford University Press.

Kennedy, Paul (1993) *Preparing for the Twenty-first Century*. New York: Random House.

Kenworthy, L.S. (1996) *Catching Up with a Changing World*. Pennsylvania: World Affairs Materials.

Keohane, Robert O. and Nye, Joseph S. (1989) *Power and Independence* (2nd ed.). Glencoe, IL: Scott Foresman.

King, A.D. (ed.) (1991) *Cultural Globalization and the World System*. London: Macmillan.

Kirby, M.D. (1993) 'Information. Good government and social responsibility', in *TIDE 2000. Improving Quality of Life in Asia with Information Technology and Telecommunications*. Amsterdam: TIDE 2000. pp. 261–73.

Kissinger, Henry (1994) *Diplomacy*. New York: Simon and Schuster.

Kivikuru, Ullamaija and Varis, Tapio (eds) (1986) *Approaches to International Communication*, No. 35. Helsinki: UNESCO.

Kraft, S. (1991) 'Who slams the door on research?', *American Demographics*, 13 (9): 14.

Krasner, S. (ed.) (1983) *International Regimes*. Cornell, NY: Cornell University Press.

Kuhn, T.S. (1970) *The Structure of Scientific Revolutions* (2nd edn). Chicago: University of Chicago Press.

Langdale, J. (1991) 'Telecommunications and international transactions in information services', in S. Brunn and T. Leinbach (eds), *Collapsing Space and Time*. London: Harper Collins. pp. 193–214.

Larrain, J. (1994) *Ideology and Cultural Identity*. Cambridge: Polity Press.

Larson, Eric (1994) *The Naked Consumer: How Our Private Lives Become Public Commodities*. Harmondsworth: Penguin.

Lash, S. and Urry, J. (1987) *The End of Organized Capitalism*. Madison, Wis.: University of Wisconsin Press.

Lash, S. and Urry, J. (1994) *Economies of Signs and Space*. London: Sage.

Lasswell, Harold (1926) *Propaganda Technique in the World War*. Cambridge, Mass.: The MIT Press.

Lazarsfeld, P.F. (1941) 'Remarks on administrative and critical communications research', *Studies in Philosophy and Social Science*, 9 (1): 2–16.

Lazarsfeld, P.F. and Stanton, F. (1949) *Communication Research 1948–9*. New York: Harper & Row.

Lee, A.J. (1976) *The Origin of the Popular Press in England, 1855–1914*. London: Croom Helm.

Lee, Philip (ed.) (1985) *Communication for All: New World Information and Communication Order*. Maryknoll, NY: Orbis Book.

Lee, Yie-Chien (1993) 'DBS issues in the Asia–Pacific', Unpublished paper.

Lenin, V.I. (1917) *Imperialism: The Last Stage of Capitalism*. Moscow.

Lerner, D. (1964) *The Passing of Traditional Society: Modernizing the Middle East*. New York: Free Press.

Levitt, Theodore (1983a) *The Marketing Imagination*. New York: The Free Press.

Lewin, Leonard (ed.) (1984) *Telecommunications: An Interdisciplinary Text*. Mass.: Artech House.

Lippmann, Walter (1922) *Public Opinion*. New York: Harcourt Brace Jovanovich.

Lippmann, Walter (1925) *The Phantom of Public*. New York: Harcourt Brace Jovanovich.

Lipset, S. (1963) *The First New Nation: The US in Historical and Comparative Perspective*. Cambridge: Cambridge University Press.

Lull, J. (1995) *Media, Communication, Culture: A Global Approach*. Cambridge: Polity Press.

Lyotard, J.F. and Thébaud, J.-F. (1985) *Just Gaming*. Manchester: Manchester University Press.

MacBride, Sean, et al. (1980) *Many Voices, One World: Communication and Society Today and Tomorrow*. Paris: UNESCO.

Mahoney, E. (1992) 'The ITU: increasing marginality in the telecommunications market' Unpublished paper, Centre for Mass Communication Research, University of Leicester, Leicester.

Maitland, D. (1985) *The Missing Link*. Geneva: International Telecommunications Union.

Maitland, Donald (1994) 'Foreign News Links: Focus on Developing Economies', *Plenary Presentations, Pacific Telecommunications Council's Sixteenth Annual Conference*, 16–20 January.

Mandel, Ernest (1980) *Late Capitalism*. London: Verso.

Mann, M. (1986) *The Sources of Social Power*, Vol. 1. Cambridge: Cambridge University Press.

Martin, B. (1993) *In the Public Interest? Privatization and Public Sector Reform*. London: Zed Books.

Martin-Barbero, J. (1993) *Communication, Culture and Hegemony*. London: Sage.

Marty, Martin and Appleby, Scott (eds) (1991) *Fundamentalism Observed*. Chicago: Chicago University Press.

Marty, Martin and Appleby, Scott (eds) (1992) *Fundamentalism and State*. Chicago: Chicago University Press.

Marty, Martin and Appleby, Scott (eds) (1993) *Fundamentalism and Society*. Chicago: Chicago University Press.

Masmoudi, M. (1979) 'The new world information order', *Journal of Communication*, 29 (2) (Spring): 172–98.

Massey, D. (1994) *Space, Place and Gender*. Cambridge: Polity Press.

Masuda, Yoneji (1981) *The Information Society: As Post-Industrial Society*. Washington, DC: World Future Society.

Mattelart, Armand (1983) *Transnationals and Third World: The Struggle for Culture*. South Hadley, Mass.: Bergin and Garvey.

Mattelart, Armand, Delcourt, X. and Mattelart, M. (1983) *International Image Markets: In Search of an Alternative Perspective* (trans. David Buxton). London: Comedia Series, No. 21.

Mazlish, Bruce (1993) *The Fourth Discontinuity*. New Haven, Conn.: Yale University Press.

Mcanany, G. Emile (ed.) (1980) *Communications in the Rural Third World*. New York: Praeger.

McGrew, T. (1992) 'A Global Society?' in S. Hall, D. Held and T. McGrew (eds), *Modernity and its Futures*. Cambridge: Polity Press.

McGuigan, J. (1992) *Cultural Populism*. London: Routledge.

McPhail, Thomas (1993) 'Television as an extension of the nation state: CNNI and the Americanization of broadcasting', paper presented at the Annual Conference of the French Association of American Studies, 21–23 May.

McQuail, D. (1994) *Mass Communication Theory*. London: Sage.

Mediamark Research, Inc. (1992) 'You may know their labels, but do you know *them?*, *American Demographics*, 14 (6): 8.

Melkote, S.R. (1991) *Communication for Development in the Third World: Theory and Practice.* Newbury Park, Cal.: Sage.

Middle East Broadcast Satellite (1994) October, 9 (9).

Moemeka, A.A. (ed.) (1994) *Communicating for Development: A New Pan-disciplinary Perspective.* Albany, NY: SUNY Press.

Mohammadi, A.S. (1991) 'The global and the local in international communication', in J. Curren and M. Gurewitch (eds), *Mass Media and Culture.* London: Edward Arnold. pp. 118–36.

Morgenthau, Hans J. (1985) *Politics Among Nations: The Struggle for Power and Peace* (6th edn), New York: McGraw Hill.

Morley, D. and Robins, K. (1989) 'Spaces of identity: communications, technologies and the reconfiguration of Europe', *Screen*, 30 (4): 10–34.

Mosco, Vincent (1996) *The Political Economy of Communication.* London: Sage.

Mosco, V. and Wasco, J. (eds) (1984) *The Critical Communication Review Vol. 2: Changing Patterns of Communication Control.* Norwood, NJ: Ablex.

Mosher, S.W. (1983) *Broken Earth: The Rural Chinese.* New York: The Free Press.

Mosher, S.W. (1990) *China Misperceived: American Illusions and Chinese Reality.* New York: Basic Books.

Mosley, P., Harringan, J. and Toye, J. (1991) *Aid and Power: The World Bank and Policy Based Lending*, Vols 1 and 2. London: Routledge.

Mowlana, H. and Wilson, L.J. (1990) *The Passing of Modernity: Communication and the Transformation of Society.* New York: Longman.

Negrine, R. (ed.) (1985) *Cable Television and the Future of Broadcasting.* London: Croom Helm.

Negrine, R. (1987) 'The new information technologies: is there an "alternative strategy"?', *Capital and Class*, No. 31: 59–78.

Negrine, R. and Papathanassopoulos, S. (1990) *The Internationalization of Television.* London: Pinter.

Negus, Keith (1992) *Producing Pop.* London: Edward Arnold.

Newcomb, H. (ed.) (1987) *Television: The Critical View*, 4th edn. Oxford: Oxford University Press.

Noam, E. (1991) *Telecommunications in Europe.* Oxford: Oxford University Press.

Nordenstreng, Karl (1995) 'The NWICO Debate', Unit 20, MA in Mass Communication Research, Centre for Mass Communication Research, University of Leicester, Leicester.

Nye, J.S. Jr (1990) *Bound to Lead: The Changing Nature of American Power.* New York: Basic Books.

Oliveira, O.S. (1991) *Genocido Cultural.* Sao Paulo: Edicoes Paulinas.

Organization for Economic Co-operation and Development (1992) *Country Report: Mexico.* Paris: OECD. pp. 92–5.

PA Consultancy (1987) *Evolution of the United Kingdom Communications Infrastructure*, Phase 1 discussion paper, September.

Pai, Sunny (1993) 'The Cable News Network', unpublished paper.

Paisley, W. (1984) 'Communication in the communication sciences', in B. Dervin and M.J. Voigt (eds), *Progress in the Communication Sciences*, vol. 5. Norwood, NJ: Ablex. pp. 1–43.

Pal, A. (1994) 'Coups and earthquakes: the influence of violence on TV network and *New York Times*' coverage of changes in government around the world, 1985–1990', unpublished MA thesis, University of North Carolina at Chapel Hill, NC.

Payer, C. (1982) *The World Bank: A Critical Analysis.* New York: Monthly Review Press.

Pendakur, Manjunath (1991) 'A political economy of television', in G. Sussman and J. Lent (eds), *Transnational Corporations: Wiring the Third World.* London: Sage. pp. 234–62.

Pfaff, W. (1993) *The Wrath of Nations: Civilizations and the Furies of Nationalism.* New York: Simon & Schuster.

Phillips, K. (1990) *The Politics of Rich and Poor.* New York: Random House.

Pool, I. de Sola (1979) 'Direct broadcast satellites and the integrity of national cultures', in K. Nordenstreng and H. Schiller (eds), *National Sovereignty and International Communications*. Norwood, NJ: Ablex.

Popper, K.R. (1971) *The Open Society and its Enemies, Vol. II: The High Tide of Prophecy: Hegel, Marx, and the Aftermath*. Princeton, NJ: Princeton University Press.

Porat, M. (1977) *The Information Economy*. Washington, DC: US Office of Telecommunication.

Rabinovitch, D. (1994) 'The First Picture Show', *The Guardian*, 24 December: 9–13.

Rama, A. (1982) 'Transculturacion narrativea en America Latina', *Siglo XXI*. Mexico.

Ramcharan, B. (1989) 'Universality of Human Rights in a Pluralistic World', in proceedings to the colloquy organized by the Council of Europe in co-operation with the International Institute of Human Rights, Strasbourg.

Ras-Work, T. (1992) 'Is global development feasible?', *New Breeze*, 4 (2) (July): 28–9.

REIS (1978) *Revista Española de Investigaciones Sociológicas*, 3: 229–63.

REOP (1976) *Revista Española de Opinión Pública*, 45: 266–92.

Ricks, David, Fu, Marilyn and Arpan, Jeffrey (1974) *International Business Blunders*. Columbus, Oh.: Grid Inc.

Righter, R. (1978) *Whose News? Politics, the Press and the Third World*. I.P.I.

Riggs, F.W. (1994) 'Development', in G. Sartori (ed.), *Social Science Concepts: A Systematic Analysis*. Thousand Oaks, CA: Sage.

Ritzer, George (1993) *The McDonaldization of Society*. London: Pine Forge Press.

Roach, C. (1987) 'The US position on the new world information and communication order', *Journal of Communication*, 37 (4) (Autumn): 36–51.

Robertson, R. (1992) *Globalization: Social Theory and Global Culture*. London: Sage.

Robins, K. (1983) *Capital and Cable*. London: Greater London Council.

Robins, K. (1989) 'Global Times', *Marxism Today*, (21 December).

Robins, K. (1991) 'Tradition and translation: national culture in its global context', in J. Corner and S. Harvey (eds), *Enterprise and Heritage*. London: Routledge. pp. 21–44.

Robins, K. and Webster, F. (1989) *The Technical Fix*. London: Macmillan.

Rogers, E.M. (ed.) (1976) *Communication and Development: Critical Perspectives*. Beverly Hills, Cal.: Sage.

Rosaldo, R. (1989) *Culture and Truth: The Remaking of Social Analysis*. Boston, Mass.: Beacon Press.

Rosenblum, M. (1979) *Coups and Earthquakes: Reporting the World for America*. New York: Harper & Row.

Rowe, C. and Koetler, F. (1992) *Collage City*. Cambridge, MA: MIT Press.

Said, E.W. (1979) *Orientalism*. London: Routledge.

Said, E.W. (1993) *Culture and Imperialism*. London: Chatto & Windus.

Sale, Kirkpatrick (1991) *The Conquest of Paradise: Christopher Columbus and the Columbian Legacy*. New York: Penguin Books.

Samarajiva, R. (1985) 'The murky beginnings of the communication and development field: Voice of America and "The passing of traditional society"', paper presented at the ICA (International Communication Association) Conference, Hawaii, May 1985.

Schiller, D. (1982) *Telematics and Government*. Norwood, NJ: Ablex.

Schiller, H.I. (1970) *Mass Communication and American Empire*. Boston, MA: Beacon Press.

Schiller, H.I. (1973) *The Mind Managers*. Boston, Mass.: Beacon Press.

Schiller, H.I. (1976) *Communication and Cultural Domination*. New York: M.E. Sharp.

Schiller, H.I. (1985) 'Electronic information flows: new basis for global domination?', in P. Drummond and Paterson (eds), *Television in Transition*, London: BFI Publishing. pp. 11–20.

Schiller, H.I. (1989) *Culture Inc.* New York: Oxford University Press.

Schiller, H.I. (1996) *Information Inequality: The Deepening Social Crisis in America*. New York: Routledge.

Schiller, H. and Nordenstreng, K. (1979) *National Sovereignty and International Communication: A Reader*. New Jersey: Ablex.

Schlesinger, P. (1991) *Media, State and Nation.* London: Sage.

Schlesinger, P. (1994) 'Europe's contradictory communicative space', in *Daedalus, Journal of the American Academy of Arts and Science*, 123 (2).

Schramm, Wilbur and Lerner, Daniel (eds) (1976) *Communication and Change: The Last Ten Years–and the Next.* Honolulu: East West Center Book.

Schwartz, J. and Edmonson, B. (1991) 'Privacy fears affect consumer behavior', *American Demographics*, 13 (2): 10–11.

Screen Digest (1992) 'Transferment scene in world television', February, pp. 33–40.

Sepstrup, P. (1991) *The Transnationalization of Television in Western Europe.* London: John Libbey.

Shapiro, J. Michael (1993) *Reading Adam Smith: Desire, History, and Value.* Newbury Park, Cal.: Sage.

Shamoon, Stella (1985) 'Marketing global brands', *World Press Review*, 52 (January).

Sheridan, Alan (1979) *The Birth of the Prison.* New York: Vintage Books.

Silj, A. (1988) *East of Dallas: The European Challenge to American Television.* London: BFI Publishing.

Simpson, Christopher (1994) *Science of Coercion: Communication Research & Psychological Warfare, 1945–1960.* New York: Oxford University Press.

Sinclair, J. (1992) 'The decentering of globalization: Televisa-ion and Globo-ization', in E. Jacka (ed.), *Continental Shift: Globalization and Culture.* Double Bay, NSW: Local Consumption Publication. pp. 99–116.

Singer, Max and Wildavsky, Aaron (1993) *The Real World Order: Zones of Peace/Zones of Turmoil.* Chatham, NJ: Chatham House Publishers Inc.

Sklair, L. (1991) *Sociology of the Global System.* Hemel Hempstead: Harvester Wheatsheaf.

Slack, J.D. (1984) *Communication Technologies and Society.* Norwood, NJ: Ablex.

So, Alvin (1990) *Social Change and Development: Modernization, Dependency and World System Theories.* Newbury Park, Cal.: Sage.

Soja, Edward W. (1989) *Postmodern Geography: The Reassertion of Space in Critical Social Theories.* Newbury Park, Cal.: Sage.

Sorush (1993) 'Access to 129 channels in Sourush', *Weekly Magazine of VVIR*, no. 652. Tehran: WIR.

Sowell, T. (1994) *Race and Culture: A World View.* New York: Basic Books.

Spero, J. (1986) 'The information revolution and financial services: the New North–South issue', in J. Meherru et al. (eds) *Information Technology and Global Independence.* New York: Greenwood.

Staple, G. (ed.) (1992) *Telegeography. Global Telecommunications, Traffic Statistics and Commentary.* London: IIC.

Stecklow, Steve (1993) 'Cyberspace clash: computer users battle high-tech marketers over soul of Internet', *The Wall Street Journal*, 16 September: A 1.

Steinfield, Charles, Bauer, M. Johannes and Caby, Laurence (eds) (1994) *Telecommunications in Transition: Policies, Services and Technologies in the European Community.* London: Sage.

Stern, D. (1986) 'The World Bank's role in fostering telecommunications development', paper delivered at the Telecommunications for Development, Exploring New Strategies: An International Forum. New York, 28 October 1986.

Stevenson, L.R. (1988) *Communication Development and the Third World.* White Plain, NY: Longman.

Stevenson, R.L. (1993) 'Communication and development: lessons from and for Africa', in F. Eribo et al. (eds), *Window on Africa; Democratization and Media Exposure.* Greenville, NC: East Carolina University Press.

Strasser, S. (1989) *Satisfaction Guaranteed: The Making of the American Mass Market.* New York: Pantheon Books.

Sung, L. (1992) 'WARC-92: setting the agenda for the future', *Telecommunications Policy* 16 (8), pp. 624–34.

Sussman, G. (1991) 'Telecommunication for transnational integration: the World Bank in the

Philippines', in G. Sussman and J.A. Lent (eds), *Transnational Communications*. London: Sage. 41–65.

Sussman, G. and Lent, J.A. (eds) (1991a) *Transnational Communications*. London: Sage.

Sussman, G. and Lent, J.A. (1991b) 'Introduction: critical perspectives on communication and Third World development', in G. Sussman and J.A. Lent (eds), *Transnational Communications*. London: Sage. pp. 1–27.

Tarjanne, P. (1992) 'Telecom: bridge to the 21st century', in *Transnational Data and Communications Report*, 15 (4): 42–5.

Tarjanne, Pekka (1994) 'The missing link: still missing', *Plenary Presentations, Pacific Telecommunications Council's Sixteenth Annual Conference*, 16–20 January.

Tawney, R.H. (1984) *Religion and the Rise of Capitalism: A Historical Study*. New York: Penguin Books.

Taylor, P. (1993) 'New generation in wings', *Financial Times, Telecommunications in Business Survey*, 16 June: 11.

Tehranian, Katharine (1995) *Modernity, Space and Power: The American City in Discourse and Practice*. Cresskill, NJ: Hampton Press.

Tehranian, Katharine and Tehranian, Majid (eds) (1992) *Restructuring for World Peace: On the Threshold of the 21st Century*. Cresskill, NJ: Hampton Press.

Tehranian, Majid (1982) 'International communication: a dialogue of the deaf?', *Political Communication and Persuasion*, 2: (2).

Tehranian, Majid (1989) 'History finished? It is just begun', *The Honolulu Advertiser*, 7 October.

Tehranian, M. (1990) *Technologies of Power: Information Machines and Democratic Prospects*. Norwood, NJ: Ablex.

Tehranian, Majid (1992) 'Khomeini's Doctrine of Legitimacy', in A.J. Parel and R.C. Keith (eds), *Comparative Political Philosophy*. New Delhi: Sage.

Tehranian, Majid (1993a) 'Ethnic discourse and the New World Disorder', in Colleen Roach (ed.), *Communication and Culture in War and Peace*. Newbury Park, Cal.: Sage.

Tehranian, Majid (1993b) 'Fundamentalist impact on education and the media: an overview', in M. Marty and S. Appleby (eds), *Fundamentalism and Society*. Chicago, IL: University of Chicago Press.

Thomas, A., et al. (1995) *Third World Atlas* 2nd edn. Buckingham: Open University Press.

Thompson, J.B. and Held, D. (eds), (1982) *Habermas: Critical Debates*. Cambridge, Mass.: The MIT Press.

Toffler, Alvin (1980) *Third Wave*. New York: Bantam Books.

Tomlinson, J. (1991) *Cultural Imperialism: A Critical Introduction*. London: Pinter.

Torrie, J. (ed.) (1984) *Banking on Poverty: The Global Impact*. New York: IMF and World Bank.

Toynbee, Arnold (1963) *A Study of History*. Vol. 8. New York: Oxford University Press.

Traber, M. and Nordenstreng, K. (1992) *Few Voices, Many Worlds: Towards a Media Reform Movement*. London: World Association for Christian Communication.

Trachtenberg, A. (1982) *The Incorporation of America: Culture and Society in the Gilded Age*. New York: Hill and Wang.

Tunstall, Jeremy (1977) *The Media Are American*. London: Constable.

UNESCO (1970) Cultural Rights as Human Rights. Paris: UNESCO.

UNESCO (1971) Proposals for an International Programme of Communication. Paris: UNESCO.

Unger, S.J. (1985) *Africa: The People and Politics of an Emerging Continent*. New York: Simon & Schuster.

United Nations Development Program (1996) *Human Development Report*.

Venus Report (1991) 'Venus Satellite Plan'. Tehran: Ministry of Post, Telegraph and Post.

Voloshinov, V.N. (1929/1986) *Marxism and the Philosophy of Language*, trans. by L. Matejka and I.R. Titunik. Cambridge, MA: Harvard University Press.

VVIR (Voice and Vision of Islamic Republic of Iran) (1994) Annual Report. Tehran: VVIR Publications.

Wallerstein, Immanuel (1974) *The Modern World System.* New York: Academic Books.

Wallerstein, I. (1990) 'Culture as the ideological battleground of the modern world system', in M. Featherstone (ed.), *Global Culture.* London: Sage. pp. 31–55.

Wallerstein, I. (1991) 'The national and the universal: can there be such a thing as world culture', in A.D. King (ed.), *Culture, Globalization and the World System.* London: Macmillan. pp. 91–106.

Waters, M. (1995) *Globalization.* London: Routledge.

Weber, M. (1958) *The Protestant Ethic and the Spirit of Capitalism,* trans. by Talcott Parsons. New York: Scriber.

Webster, F. and Robins, K. (1986) *Information Technology: A Luddite Analysis.* Norwood, NJ: Ablex.

Wells, C. (1987) *The UN, UNESCO and the Politics of Knowledge.* London: Macmillan.

Williams, Raymond (1961) *Culture and Society.* Harmondsworth: Penguin.

Williams, Raymond (1977) *Marxism and Literature.* Oxford: Oxford University Press.

Wilson, A. (1990) *Space Directory 1990–91.* London: Jane's Information Group.

Woodall, Pam (1994) 'A survey of the global economy', *The Economist,* 1 October.

Yudice, G., Franco, J. and Flores, J. (eds) (1992) *On Edge: The Crisis of Contemporary Latin American Culture.* Minneapolis: University of Minnesota Press.

Index

Note: Page numbers in **bold** refer to figures. Page numbers in *italic* refer to tables.